THE THREE WORLDS OF PAUL OF TARSUS

The world in which early Christianity developed consisted of a complex of distinct communities and cultural 'layers', which interacted with one another, sometimes co-operatively, and sometimes in confrontation.

The Three Worlds of Paul of Tarsus explores this world through the life of the apostle Paul, examining the three fundamental cultural 'layers': the native cultures; the common hellenistic culture which had been spread in the East as a result of the conquests of Alexander; and the culture of the political overlord, Rome. It considers how Paul, as a Jew, a Greek-speaker and a Roman citizen, participates in all of these 'layers'. The authors give an account of the places Paul visited, showing their historical, cultural and political differences, and discuss the varied categories, such as religion, philosophy and language, which contributed to the definition of an individual's identity.

The Three Worlds of Paul of Tarsus presents a colourful and lucid insight into the complexities of the early Christian world, arguing that the journeys of Paul are an example of the social, political and cultural heterogeneity of that world.

Richard Wallace is a lecturer in the Department of Classics at Keele University and the treasurer of the Classical Association.

Wynne Williams retired from teaching ancient history at Keele University in 1991. He is co-author, with Richard Wallace, of *The Acts of the Apostles: A Companion* (1993).

THE THREE WORLDS
OF PAUL OF TARSUS

Richard Wallace and Wynne Williams

London and New York

First published 1998
by Routledge
11 New Fetter Lane, London EC4P 4EE

Simultaneously published in the USA and Canada
by Routledge
29 West 35th Street, New York, NY 10001

Typeset in Garamond by Routledge
Printed and bound in Great Britain by Biddles Ltd, Guildford
and King's Lynn

British Library Cataloguing in Publication Data
A catalogue record for this book is available from the British
Library

Library of Congress Cataloguing in Publication Data
Wallace, Richard, 1941–
The three worlds of Paul of Tarsus / Richard Wallace and
Wynne Williams.
Includes bibliographical references and index.
1. Paul, the Apostle, Saint. 2. Rome–Social life and customs.
3. Rome–Religious life and customs. I. Williams, Wynne. II.
Title
BS2506.W32 1998
225.9'2–dc21   97–15856
CIP

ISBN 0–415–13591–5 (hbk)
ISBN 0–415–13592–3 (pbk)

CONTENTS

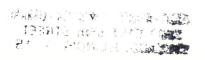

CONTENTS

CONTENTS

ILLUSTRATIONS

MAP

FIGURES

PREFACE

The main purpose of this book is to give readers who are interested in Paul of Tarsus some insight into the sort of world in which he moved. We do not aim to give an exhaustive bibliography on all the issues covered, but we direct readers who wish to explore particular topics more deeply to publications where such bibliographies may be found. Except where otherwise stated, biblical quotations are from the Revised Standard Version (RSV); where more recent editions of this version have, in the interests of using inclusive language, adopted translations which may not fully represent the meaning of the Greek or Hebrew originals, we have preferred to use the translations of older editions. All dates given are AD unless otherwise stated.

Richard Wallace wishes to thank his colleagues in the Department of Classics in the University of Keele for undertaking the extra work which made possible the leave during which this book was written, his colleagues in the Departamento de Historia Antigua in the University of Granada for their hospitality and help during a very productive stay among them, the British Academy for the financial support which made possible a three-week stay at the Fondation Hardt in Geneva, the staff of the Fondation Hardt for making his stay there so fruitful, and Swan Hellenic for facilitating much of the travel in the course of which the sites mentioned in this book were explored.

ABBREVIATIONS

The following abbreviations are used for epigraphic publications:

CIG   *Corpus Inscriptionum Graecarum*
CIL   *Corpus Inscriptionum Latinarum*
IG   *Inscriptiones Graecae*
IGRR   R. Cagnat, *Inscriptiones Graecae ad res Romanas pertinentes* (1906–27)
ILS   H. Dessau, *Inscriptiones Latinae Selectae*
OGIS   W. Dittenberger, *Orientis Graeci Inscriptiones Selectae*
SIG³   W. Dittenberger, *Sylloge Inscriptionum Graecarum*, third edn

Part 1

THE WORLD OF PAUL

1

INTRODUCTION: THE THREE WORLDS

If any other man thinks he has reason for confidence in the flesh, I have more: circumcised on the eighth day, of the people of Israel, of the tribe of Benjamin, a Hebrew born of Hebrews.

(Philippians 3, 4–5)

Paul replied, 'I am a Jew, from Tarsus in Cilicia, a citizen of no mean city.'

(Acts 21, 39)

Paul said, 'But I was born a [Roman] citizen.'

(Acts 22, 28)

This book is intended in part as background, and in part as a protest.

As background, it has the modest aim of setting out the contexts (historical, social, political and cultural) within which the activities of Paul of Tarsus and other figures in the earliest history of Christianity outside Palestine are to be seen. Christianity is, of course, a historical religion, in that its appearance at a particular time and in a particular place is not just incidental, but is intrinsic to the way it is to be understood. However we wish to approach it (historically, theologically or spiritually) it is relevant that it sprang from first-century Judaism, that it first developed as a separate, new religion within the hellenised communities of the eastern Mediterranean, and that the whole process took place within the Roman Empire.

The protest is against the oversimplification of these contexts. One of the reasons that the Roman Empire and the communities within it can seem so alien is that the modern Western way of looking at the world has inevitably been moulded (whatever the religious beliefs of the individual) by attitudes, perceptions and

3

presuppositions which ultimately derive from Christianity and/or Judaism. But when looking at the world from within a particular culture (as those of us who have been educated within the Western tradition naturally tend to do if we look at the Roman world when we are dealing with the history of Christianity) it is easy to think in terms of facile dichotomies, taking an 'us-and-them' attitude and regarding everything outside the group as an undifferentiated 'not-us'. So we see Christians (and Jews) set against 'pagans', or the church confronting the 'Roman state'. This approach has, of course, a long history in the ancient world itself. Notoriously, the Greeks divided the world into Greeks and 'barbarians' (that is, the undifferentiated mass of all those who had in common the fact that they were not Greeks). Jews responded by an exactly parallel distinction between Jews and Gentiles.

Things are, however, rarely as simple as they seem, and Paul of Tarsus is a good example of a man who identified himself, not through a simple dichotomy, but through a whole complex of them. In Romans 1, 14 he speaks of himself as 'under obligation both to Greeks and to barbarians'. Here, he speaks from within the Greek world, using the traditional 'Greek/barbarian' dichotomy. On the other hand, as a Jew he contrasts himself with the Gentiles, whom he again calls Greeks. Immediately after the passage cited above, he says (Romans 1, 16) that his message is given 'to the Jew first, and also to the Greek' (and the same contrast is repeated at Romans 2, 9 and 10; 1 Corinthians 1, 22–24 and 12, 13; Colossians 3, 11; Galatians 3, 28; see also Acts 11, 19–20 and 18, 4). For Paul, then, 'Greek' can be an exclusive (Greeks as opposed to the rest of the human race) or an inclusive (everybody but the Jews) term. The confusion of terminology in the milieu in which Christianity grew up is well illustrated by the woman who 'was a Greek, a Syrophoenician by birth' at Mark 7, 26 (the corresponding passage in Matthew 15, 22 calls her simply 'a Canaanite woman'). Other dichotomies Paul uses include slave and free (1 Corinthians 12, 13; Galatians 3, 28; Colossians 3, 11) and male and female (Galatians 3, 28).

In reality, an individual could identify himself or herself in many different ways, depending on what s/he wanted to say about him- or herself, and with what s/he was contrasting his/her identity. We wish to concentrate on three cultural 'layers' within Paul's world, the 'three worlds' of the title. Not everyone would, like Paul, move through all of them, but most would be affected by them all.

4

First there are what might be called the 'native' cultures of the region. Many parts of the eastern Mediterranean lands had been the seats of distinct and ancient civilisations, and elsewhere local traditions, languages and peoples had deep roots. These included the local Greek cultures of the ancient lands of the Hellenes. Though an internationalised and homogenised version of parts of that culture had been widely exported, local Greek traditions and dialects survived in the Greek heartland. Again, when Paul says that he is 'of the people of Israel, of the tribe of Benjamin, a Hebrew born of Hebrews' (Philippians 3, 5), and when he addresses the Jerusalem mob in Aramaic and claims that he was 'brought up in this city at the feet of Gamaliel, educated according to the strict manner of the law of our fathers' (Acts 22, 3), he is asserting his membership of another of those local 'native' cultures, that of the Jews of Palestine, and indeed he does seem to have family links in Jerusalem (at any rate his nephew turns up there: Acts 23, 16; see also his claim to have spent his life from his youth in Jerusalem in his speech to Agrippa at Acts 26, 4). It is not always easy to be sure which of these local cultures were still surviving, and which had succumbed to the hellenistic culture of the second 'layer' (for example, the incident in Acts 14, 11, when the people shout 'in Lycaonian' is one of the very few pieces of solid evidence we have for the survival, and continued use in popular speech, of one of the non-Greek languages of Anatolia; no doubt Paul and his companions passed through many regions where the local people spoke to one another in some local language, but the narrative nowhere else requires that it should be mentioned). In Syria and Palestine, however, the late Roman Empire saw the creation of a substantial literature in dialects of the local language, Aramaic, showing that, at any rate in some areas, it and the cultures whose vehicle it was remained current and vigorous when apparently overlaid by Greek.

The second layer is that of the 'Hellenes', speakers of Greek. In the fourth century BC, Alexander III of Macedon, ostensibly as the leader of the united Greek cities (which his father Philip had conquered), invaded the Persian Empire and replaced the Persian king. Alexander's empire was ephemeral. It did not survive his death, and the easternmost provinces were soon lost. The long-term result, however, was that most of the lands bordering the eastern Mediterranean came under the rule of dynasties descended from Alexander's generals and associates, whose language and culture was Greek. The Greek language (or a form of it) became the universal language of government, administration and international communication, aided by substantial Greek immigration to the east, the foundation of new Greek-style cities, and the desire of local élites to enhance their prestige by associating themselves with the new dominant Greek culture (nowadays usually called 'hellenistic'). The Jewish communities which from about the third century BC onwards spread throughout Egypt, Anatolia, Greece and beyond – the Jewish diaspora – also formed part of that 'layer' (and indeed some of these communities were the result of a deliberate policy of encouraging Jewish settlers on the part of the hellenistic kings). Generally they adopted the Greek language and, unlike the Jews of Palestine, inevitably had to make some sort of accommodation with the Gentile world within which they were living. Paul, a citizen of the hellenised city of Tarsus, clearly found himself at home in this world, and indeed it was the existence of this 'layer' which made his work possible at all. He wrote in hellenistic Greek, and needed no other language wherever he travelled. In most of the cities he visited, he found an established Jewish community. In some ways, because this was the culture through which he communicated, it is the hellenistic Paul who is most accessible to us.

The third and final 'layer' is that of the Romans, to which Paul belonged by virtue of his Roman citizenship. In some ways it is the least obtrusive of all. The popular picture of an aggressive Roman Empire conquering the world and ruling it with an iron hand is seriously misleading. Though the Romans were certainly an aggressive power, and uncomfortable neighbours to have, the precise motives for Roman imperial expansion remain a matter for controversy and speculation. It may have been driven by opportunism, private greed, fear, arrogance, the ambition of individuals, combinations of accidents, or some other motive, but there most certainly never was at Rome a central and consciously adopted master plan for world conquest. As the territories they ruled grew, they developed, initially by improvisation and *ad hoc* solutions to immediate problems, means of administering them. Certainly they expected to be obeyed, and their reaction to trouble when they had to deal with it was peremptory and memorable, but they expected the cities of the Empire largely to run their own affairs (within clear limits). For the ordinary man or woman in the street, an encounter with Roman power would be very unusual. Paul's life is a good example of this. He and his companions travelled throughout the East, apparently provoking trouble (which sometimes amounted to serious public disorder) in almost every city they visited. Yet he was brought for justice before a Roman governor only in Corinth and in Judaea (where his continued involvement with the Roman government was largely self-inflicted). Though the author of The Acts of the Apostles no doubt had his own reasons for depicting Roman authority as protecting the earliest Christians, there is no doubt at all that Roman rule brought stability and prosperity to the East, putting an end to a long period of disorder and warfare (some of it, admittedly, caused by the Romans themselves). The world in which Paul moved was recovering rapidly from the confusion and civil war which had been brought to an end by the emperor Augustus. The next century was to see the construction of the splendid public buildings which dominate the sites of the cities of the East as we see them today. It was not a crushed or defeated world, but one in the process of revival, and the rebirth of the hellenistic civilisation of the Greek East (which was the major cultural event of the second century) was already under way. As a Roman citizen by birth, and so a privileged member of that society, Paul was in a position to enjoy the benefits of Roman rule to the full.

SUGGESTIONS FOR FURTHER READING

(full details of these works can be found in the Bibliography):

Supplementing this work, Wallace and Williams, *The Acts of the Apostles: a Companion* looks at The Acts of the Apostles as a historical source.

W. A. Meeks' *The First Urban Christians* is a detailed discussion of the social background of early Christianity.

2

THE GEOGRAPHY OF PAUL'S WORLD

Apart from his final journey to Rome (and his stated intention in Romans 15, 24 to visit Spain) Paul's world (Fig. 2.1) is limited to the eastern Roman Empire (with the possible exception of his stay in Arabia, mentioned in Galatians 1, 17, which must refer to the kingdom of the Nabataeans, formally independent but actually within Rome's 'sphere of influence'). Within this region, and with a few exceptions, he stayed within reach of the sea. This was an area where travel by sea was particularly easy, as there were well-established ports with regular trade between them. The interior, however, was in most places cut off from the coastal fringe by mountain ranges and other physical barriers. There are few navigable rivers, and those which exist are navigable only within the coastal region (e.g. the Orontes as far as Antioch, the Cydnus as far as Tarsus). Though land connections with the interior did exist and were important (they explain the prominence of cities like Tarsus and Ephesos), the coastal region remained distinct and much more accessible than the interior. Paul usually remained in touch with the coast, hardly penetrating the interior at all. The main exceptions are his regular visits to Jerusalem, the journey to Damascus and Arabia early in his career before the pattern of his missionary activity had established itself, and his travels through the cities of southern Galatia which were initially (Acts 14) perhaps forced upon him by the necessity to escape from angry crowds, and which were later, at any rate in part, 'follow-up' visits to the churches established on the first visit (Acts 15, 36–16, 7; 18, 23).

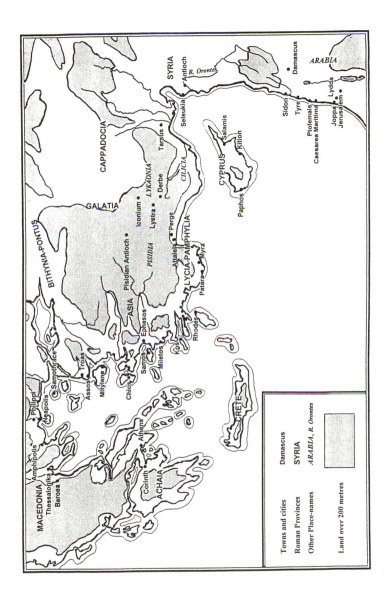

Figure 2.1 Paul's world

SYRIA AND PALESTINE

This is a region where the connection between geography and history is more clearly seen than perhaps in any other. It consists of a relatively narrow strip of land between the sea and the desert, divided into zones by mountain ranges which run from north to south, separating the fertile plains and in places presenting a formidable obstacle to travel inland from the coast. Paul normally traversed the region only on his visits to Jerusalem, a city which owed its importance not to its site – for it was not on an important route or in a place of strategic significance – but simply to the fact that King David chose it as his capital, presumably for political reasons, and that the building of the Temple there made it an important cult centre. At the beginning of his career he travelled on one of the inland routes, from Jerusalem north to Damascus, and thence to Arabia. Later, however, when he had become committed to the hellenistic world, he used the route along the coast.

Though the desert to the east of the region was certainly not impassable, and in fact the trade of some of the coastal cities depended on caravan routes running east (indeed in the more northerly sections of the region, 'steppe' would be a better term than 'desert', for it is habitable), what is historically important is that it is not passable by armies. As a result, any military campaign from or to Egypt has had to pass through Syria and Palestine, and thus control of this area has often been strategically important. It is one of those areas unfortunate enough to fall potentially within the natural sphere of activities of a number of regional 'great powers'. Whoever controlled Egypt, therefore, or Mesopotamia, or Anatolia, or the Mediterranean would inevitably take an interest in Syria and Palestine. Consequently the region has had an unenviably eventful history, and it became a battlefield between two of the dynasties which inherited Alexander's empire – the Ptolemies in the south and the Seleucids in the north – in the period immediately before the establishment of Roman rule. It is no coincidence that Armageddon, the great battle of Revelation (16, 16), is placed at a strategic pass through Mount Carmel near Megiddo (*Har Megiddo* = the mountain of Megiddo). Occasionally, however, when no major power was strong enough to control the area, a number of small 'buffer states' have been able to maintain themselves there. This was the situation as the Ptolemaic and Seleucid kingdoms weakened.

Despite the importance of sea-borne trade, particularly in

Phoenicia, the coast is poor in natural harbours. Nevertheless, because the cities of Syria and Palestine were the natural terminus for the trade routes from the East, a string of ports grew up along the coast, to carry on the trade. By Paul's time, however, ports like Tyre and Sidon, which had once been of international significance, had declined until they filled only a local rôle, serving the sort of coastal traffic which Paul himself used so often. The new, big, artificial harbours of Laodikea and Seleukia (the port of Antioch), and Caesarea, the creation of Herod, now handled most of the traffic. Caesarea was also important because it was an administrative centre, and because it was the natural port for Jewish visitors to Jerusalem (Rougé 1966: 127–9).

Syria and Palestine were 'frontier provinces', in the sense that they had borders with regions not under Roman control. It is remarkable that this frontier is never alluded to during Paul's activities (though on at least one occasion he passes out of the Roman empire: Galatians 1, 17). Recent work (and especially Isaac 1992) has established that the Roman frontier was not the defensive line fortified against the threat of foreign aggression which we might imagine. There is no evidence that the nomadic tribes of the desert gave serious trouble before the fourth century (Isaac 1992: 69–77), and in her relations with the Parthian Empire Rome was usually the aggressor, a fact which is reflected in the disposition of her main body of troops in Syria. Elsewhere the Romans were defending not frontiers, but routes, such as the important road leading down from the valley of the Orontes south through Gerasa, Philadelphia and Petra. The threat to such routes, which were important for supplying the army as well as for trade, came not so much from foreign raiders as from what Roman sources represent as internal bandits or brigands. In some mountainous areas banditry was endemic (Isaac 1992: 78–83), probably as the result not of individuals taking up crime as a career, but of imperfect Roman control in these difficult regions. Much of the military presence in difficult provinces seems to have been directed at internal disorder rather than threats from the outside.

ASIA MINOR

Asia Minor falls into two quite distinct geographical regions. The interior is a dry plateau, much of which is bleak and inhospitable, hot in summer and bitterly cold in winter. Grain can be grown in some areas – and there are places of considerable fertility – but the crop is precarious, and always liable to be reduced by drought. Much of the region was given over to stock-rearing, and such prosperity as there was came from its excellent wool, the basis of the wealth of the interior (Mitchell 1993: I, 143–7).

Along the southern and western coasts, separated from the interior by high mountains, was the coastal plain, one of the most fertile and prosperous regions of the ancient world. The author of the probably fifth-century BC Hippocratic treatise *On Airs, Waters, and Places* says of it:

> I assert that Asia is very different from Europe in the nature of everything that grows there, both the produce of the earth and the people; for in Asia everything grows much better and much bigger; the land is gentler than our land and the temperament of the people milder and more easy-going . . . Bravery, hardiness, the capacity for hard work, and spirit could not occur in such circumstances, whether among natives or immigrants, but pleasure must rule.
>
> (*On Airs, Waters, and Places* 12)

This passage, of course, reflects the view of Asia (by which the writer probably means the western coast of Asia Minor) from impoverished Greece, but the general picture of fertility and prosperity remained an accurate one throughout antiquity, and this region contained some of the most famous and flourishing cities of the Roman world. The strip of fertile land along the coast is in some places quite narrow, but broadens out considerably elsewhere.

To begin with Paul's home region of Cilicia, the most easterly part, where Tarsus is situated (called 'Smooth Cilicia' in antiquity), is a broad and fertile plain, with good connections both to Antioch and the East, and to the interior. Moving west we come to what the ancients called 'Rough Cilicia', a poor and rugged land where the mountains come down right to the sea. Next, in the region around Perge, Pamphylia, we again find a prosperous and fertile plain, watered by three rivers. Lycia, the next region as we travel west, is, like Rough Cilicia, mountainous terrain. Going further west and turning north up the western coast the pattern repeats itself, with a narrow coastal plain widening out into the valleys of the great rivers (such as the Cayster, the Maeander and the Hermus) which can be extremely fertile and which supported numbers of great cities. Though the fertility of these areas made them naturally prosperous, the access to the interior given by the river valleys made cities like Perge, Tarsus, Miletos and Ephesos the natural outlets for the products of the interior, which brought them considerable wealth. Thus in antiquity Miletos was famous for its woollen cloth, and this relationship between the coast and the stock-rearing interior survives today in an attenuated form in the leather jackets and woollen carpets sold to tourists in the coastal resorts. Like Palestine and Syria, the coastal strip of Asia Minor could be regarded as a natural part of the area controlled by more than one power, in this case the interior and the Aegean. During the hellenistic period it was frequently the case that the cities on the coast were not under the control of whoever held the interior. The resulting confusion made possible the creation of small independent states like Pergamon.

In contrast to Syria and Palestine, both the south and west coasts of Asia Minor are well supplied with excellent natural harbours. On the south coast, only Tarsus – at a conjunction of routes, and with access both to Antioch and (through the Cilician Gates) to the Anatolian plateau – was of more than regional significance. The ports on the west were more important, especially those which, like Smyrna, Miletos and Ephesos, were near river valleys giving access to the interior. The perennial problem of these western ports, however, was silt brought down by the rivers, which explains why today the sites of both Ephesos and Miletos are some way from the sea (Rougé 1966: 129–30).

MACEDONIA AND GREECE

Greece itself, the original home of the Hellenes, was a poor country broken up by mountain ranges, with occasional fertile plains – some of which did well enough to generate a surplus for export (corn from Thessaly, olive oil from Attica: Alcock 1993: 80). It was not a good country for travelling by land, and Paul sensibly bypassed most of it. Macedonia, to the north, was a different proposition. It had always been more fertile than its neighbours to the south, but in Paul's day its importance was enhanced first by its mineral wealth, especially in gold and silver – Philippi began its existence as a mining town – and also by the Via Egnatia, the great road which the Romans had built in the mid-second century BC linking Epidamnus on the Adriatic with Thessalonika. So in this region Paul encountered a series of flourishing cities (Philippi, Thessalonika, Beroea) doing well under Roman rule.

The principal ports in the region were Thessalonika, the port of Macedon, on the Via Egnatia (an excellent port, with access to the Danube region through the valley of the river Vardar), and Corinth, the main port for Greece. The port of Athens, the Piraeus, had declined along with Athens herself and was no longer on the main shipping routes, though no doubt it still served tourists and students. The satirist Lucian, in the next century, represents the arrival there of a big merchant ship, driven off course by a storm, as a major event attracting crowds of sightseers (*The Ship* 1–9; Rougé 1966: 131–2).

SUGGESTIONS FOR FURTHER READING

(full details of these works can be found in the Bibliography):

Although ostensibly concerned only with the sixteenth century, Fernand Braudel's *The Mediterranean and the Mediterranean World in the Age of Philip II* can be recommended as a vivid account of the physical environment of the Mediterranean lands.

As a general reference work, the third edition of the *Oxford Classical Dictionary* (edited by S. Hornblower and A. Spawforth) contains a wealth of reliable and up-to-date information on the Greek and Roman worlds.

3

TRAVELLING THE WORLD

ANCIENT TRAVELLERS

To a modern reader, used to the relative convenience of twentieth-century travel, Paul's incessant journeyings through Palestine, Syria, Anatolia, Greece and, ultimately, to Italy, as reported in The Acts of the Apostles, seem quite remarkable. Yet the truly remarkable thing about them is that they are not remarkable at all; indeed he seems to live within a circle of people continually on the move (Meeks 1983: 16–19). Among Paul's associates, Barnabas comes originally from Cyprus but turns up first in Jerusalem (Acts 5, 36), then goes to Antioch (Acts 11, 22) and Tarsus (Acts 11, 25) before accompanying Paul on his first journey, while Apollos, who comes from Alexandria, is found first in Ephesos (Acts 18, 24), and then in Corinth (Acts 19, 1). When persecution drives the disciples from Jerusalem, they scatter to Phoenicia, Cyprus and Antioch (Acts 11, 19) and it turns out that some of them come from Cyprus and Cyrene (Acts 11, 20). These and other journeys, like those of Paul, go quite unremarked, and seem to have been undertaken and completed without special arrangements, as a matter of routine. This fact was the indispensable condition not only for the creation but also for the maintenance of the Christian church. Indeed, in the next generation travelling 'apostles' seem to have been so common as to be almost a nuisance, and churches had to be advised how to deal with them:

> Let every apostle who comes to you be received as if he were the Lord, but he should not stay more than one day, or (if necessary) two. If he stays three days, he is a false prophet. When he leaves, the apostle should take nothing but bread to

keep him going to his next lodgings. If he asks for money he is a false prophet.

(Didache 11, 4–6)

Apart from those travelling specifically for religious purposes, we find a large number of individuals in Acts and in Paul's letters who are clearly travelling widely for business and other purposes, and whose mobility – and resultant network of connections – was an important factor in facilitating the spread of Christianity. So Aquila and Priscilla, tentmakers (like Paul) from Pontus on the Black Sea, had moved to Rome (whence they were expelled), are then found in Corinth (Acts 18, 2–3) and subsequently in Ephesos (Acts 18, 19); the purple-seller Lydia, who meets Paul in Philippi, was originally from Thyateira in Asia Minor. The exchanges of greetings in Paul's letters (see especially the long list in Romans 16, 1–16, and compare also 'those who come from Italy' at Hebrews 13, 24) are evidence of the maintenance of links from city to city – as is also the facility with which letters could be sent – presumably by regular travel. The transmission of letters was entirely a matter of private arrangements between individuals. Though there was an imperial post, it was exclusively for the use of the emperor's staff, and it was not available to the general public. To send a letter to another city, it was necessary to find someone who was going there and would be willing to take it.

Apart from trade and commerce, there were many other motives which set people travelling long distances. Jews, of course, would wish to travel to Jerusalem for religious reasons. Though the list of the homelands of those present at Pentecost has its odd features (Wallace and Williams 1993: 34–5), there is no doubt that the picture it gives of large numbers of Jews from all over the world being present in the city is broadly accurate; similarly, Jews from Asia are present in Jerusalem during Paul's last visit there (Acts 21, 27). But it was not only Jews who travelled for religious reasons. Major shrines like the temple of Artemis at Ephesos attracted visitors from all over the world (which is why the silver-smiths of Ephesos are represented as being indignant at the activities of Paul: Acts 19, 24–27), as did oracles like that at Klaros (see p. 100). Pilgrimages were by no means a Christian invention and when, after the establishment of Christianity as the religion favoured by the emperors in the fourth century, visits to Christian holy sites became a common expression of piety, a

16

mature travel industry was already in existence ready to cater for such travellers.

The shrines of Asklepios at Pergamon, Kos, Epidauros and elsewhere fell into a special category: sick people would go to them in the hope of being cured by the god (André and Baslez 1993: 270–2). Indeed, travel itself was recommended by doctors as a cure (Casson 1974: 130–4). The physician Celsus (roughly contemporary with Paul) advises those suffering from *phthisis* (presumably tuberculosis) to try 'a long sea voyage, a change of air . . . ; the journey from Italy to Alexandria is most suitable' (*On Medicine* 3, 22, 8), but if the patient is not strong enough to face such a long journey 'it is better to be rocked on a journey which is shorter; if something prevents a sea voyage, the body should somehow be moved about in a litter' (*On Medicine* 3, 22, 9).

Travel simply for pleasure, what we would call tourism, was surprisingly well established. As early as the fifth century BC the historian Herodotos was travelling the world simply to satisfy his curiosity, and in the fourth century Xenophon tells us of a Spartan who was a lover of travel (*philapodēmos*: *Hellenica* 4, 3, 2). Subsequently a series of regular tourist circuits developed, which continued to attract travellers throughout antiquity (as the very large number of tourist graffiti of all periods to be found on ancient monuments in Egypt bears witness). Such tourist excursions would often be combined with official business (André and Baslez 1993: 71–3, 105–9). Thus when the Roman general Aemilius Paullus had settled the affairs of Greece after his victory at the battle of Pydna in 168 BC, according to Livy (45, 27–8) he travelled round Greece to see the famous sites, including Delphi, the oracle of Zeus Trophonios, the Euripos, the famous straits between Euboea and the mainland, Aulis, from where the Greek fleet sailed to the Trojan War, Athens, Corinth, Sicyon, Argos, Epidauros, Sparta and Olympia where, according to Plutarch, he admired Pheidias' statue of Zeus (*Aemilius Paullus* 28, 2). This mixture of shrines, places famous from mythology, history or literature, works of art and natural curiosities is a fair representation of the sort of thing the ancient tourist hoped to see. On arrival at a famous site he would be shown round by a guide, a *monstrator* (Lucan, *Pharsalia* 9, 961–79; Seneca, *To Marcia On Consolation* 25, 2); these guides may be the ultimate source of a depressingly high proportion of the information on famous sites reported to us in ancient authors. Guide-books too were available, such as the one to Greece produced by Pausanias in the second century AD. Cities seem to have cultivated tourism, and taken care to lay on spectacles likely to be attractive to visitors. Sparta, for example, developed aspects of her traditional educational system into contests of great brutality between young men, in which deaths were not uncommon, and which appealed to tourists with a taste for sadism (Cartledge and Spawforth 1989: 205–10).

If we add to this the enormous number of officials, magistrates and local representatives travelling to and from Rome to carry petitions, to conduct business and to take up posts, athletes doing the rounds of the great games (André and Baslez 1993: 216–20 and p. 105), itinerant performers like actors and rhetoricians, young men intending to spend some time in intellectual centres such as Athens (Acts 17, 21) and many others, we get a picture of a society where travel over long distances was no great thing but a mundane part of normal life. That, unfortunately, is the problem. Ancient writers will usually tell us in great and vivid detail about unusual things, but take it for granted that we know all about the ordinary and commonplace. As a result, the account of Paul's journeys in Acts is one of the best sources we have for travelling conditions in antiquity. Apart from that we are reduced to using the comic account of a land journey through Italy given by the poet Horace (*Satires* 1, 5), episodes in novels and other works of fiction, and incidental references elsewhere, supplemented by archaeological evidence.

TRAVEL BY LAND

The famous Roman roads, though intended primarily for military purposes, did indeed to some extent facilitate movement and trade overland (especially as the forts which lay on them were significant markets for goods). Nevertheless, land travel was always slow, dangerous and uncomfortable, and travel by water remained by far the preferred option throughout antiquity. The only firm evidence we have on comparative freight costs comes from an edict issued at the beginning of the fourth century AD by the emperor Diocletian, which attempted to fix prices for a wide range of goods and services. The interpretation of the details of the edict is controversial (and we cannot assume that the situation had not changed since the first century), but one plausible calculation (Rickman 1980: 14) is that a land journey of 300–400 miles would double the price of wheat, whereas sea transport from Alexandria to Rome (about 1,700 miles) would increase the cost by only 16 per cent (transport from Syria to

Spain was more expensive, increasing the cost by 26 per cent). In fact, the advantage of water over land remained until the invention of the railway – before 1815 it cost as much to carry goods thirty miles inland in the USA as it did to bring them across the Atlantic (McPherson 1990: 11). The only positive advantages of land travel (apart from the fact that where no waterways were available there was no choice) was freedom from the real danger of shipwreck and relative predictability. Although sea transport was in general quicker, it did depend on the winds and good sailing conditions. Also, it was possible (though never desirable) to travel by land during the winter months when sailing was suspended. The greater expense of land transport for goods would, of course, not have the same importance when it was people who were being transported, but it is a reflection of the general inconvenience and slowness of land travel. Horace took about two weeks to travel some 275 miles from Rome to Brundisium (though one section of the journey, through the marshes south of Rome, was by boat). It would naturally make a difference if the traveller could afford to ride or carry his baggage on animals. When Paul is escorted from Jerusalem to Caesarea, he is accompanied by a mixed force of cavalry and infantry, and provided with a mount (Acts 23, 23–4). Presumably this is for speed rather than comfort; the infantry are left behind as soon as the party reaches the coastal plain where the cavalry can make good time (Acts 23, 32). Elsewhere we have no information as to how he travelled. The most natural assumption is that he walked. The really rich and powerful would, of course, travel in a litter carried by bearers, which would be no quicker – but considerably more comfortable – than walking.

Usually, then, Paul travelled by land only when there was no choice, up to Jerusalem, for example, or from Jerusalem to Damascus, or when he struck inland from Perge (Acts 13, 14–14, 25). He chose to take the Via Egnatia through Philippi – presumably to take in the inland towns of Macedonia – but after Beroea decided to skip the rest of northern Greece and took ship to Athens (Acts 17, 14–15). When travelling to Rome, he went by land from Puteoli (Acts 28, 13–16) because it was the nearest good port to Rome. Broadly speaking, he travelled by land only when he positively wished to visit inland places, or when there was no alternative. One possible exception is the journey from Troas to Assos, which Paul made by land, but the others made by sea (Acts 20, 13–14). Presumably there was a reason for this, but we are not told what it was. In the case of his final journey to Rome, it is possible that the original intention of the centurion escorting Paul was to travel by ship up to Troas, make the crossing from there to Neapolis, and then travel across to the Adriatic by land. This seems to have been the route taken by a later prisoner of the Romans, Ignatius the bishop of Antioch, who was taken from there under escort to be martyred in Rome in 108. On the journey, he wrote a series of letters to various churches, and these are the source of our information. Although travel conditions are not foremost in his mind as he writes, it looks most probable that he travelled along the coast of Asia Minor by land. At any rate, the only sea trip he mentions is the crossing from Troas to Neapolis (*Letter to Polycarp* 8, 1). The number of churches he visited, and the fact that they provided him with escorts, fits more easily with a land journey, though some short sea journeys from port to port need not be ruled out. Paul's escort thus had a real choice to make when deciding how to travel. It would have been relatively easy to pick up coastal traffic to take them to Troas, but the end of the sailing season was coming, and the centurion cannot have expected to be able to sail all the way (Rougé 1960: 194–8). He must have thought that his luck was in when he found an Alexandrian ship at Myra which was still on the way to Rome so late in the year, offering him the opportunity to make the rest of the journey in one easy voyage. He was, of course, mistaken.

TRAVEL BY SEA

With a very few exceptions (such as the ships carrying passengers between Brundisium and Cassiopa or Dyrrachium: *Digest* 14, 1, 12), those wishing to travel by sea had to take passage on a ship carrying goods. Even the emperor Vespasian's son, Titus, in a hurry to get back to Rome to see his father, used a merchant ship (Suetonius, *Titus* 5), and a letter from the emperor Hadrian in 129 asks the archons and *boulē* (magistrates and council) of Ephesos to admit Lucius Erastus to the Council on the grounds that:

> He says he frequently sails the sea . . . and always conveys the governors of the province [i.e. Asia]; and he has now twice voyaged with myself, first when I was carried from Rhodes to Ephesos, and now when I have come to you from Eleusis.
>
> (*SIG*[3] 838, lines 6–11)

Pliny the Younger summed up the advantages and disadvantages of sea and land travel when he announced his attention to travel from Ephesos to his province, Bithynia, partly on coastal ships (*orariis navibus*) and partly by land transport (*vehiculis*) on the grounds that heat made the land unbearable, but the winds were unfavourable for sailing (*Letters* 10, 15). As things turned out, his judgement was quite accurate: the heat on land made him ill, and the unfavourable winds held him up (*Letters* 10, 17A). It is on 'coastal ships' like this that Paul did most of his travelling. They hugged the coast not just because ancient sailors generally, when they had a choice, preferred not to get out of sight of the land, but also because they wished to put in to port frequently to load and unload cargo up and down the coast. So from Philippi (Acts 20, 6) Paul's party sails to Troas, where they stay for seven days, either while the ship completes its business or while they find a new ship; then they go by way of Assos (20, 14), Mitylene and Samos to Miletos (20, 14) where there is a stay of undisclosed length. From Miletos they sail to Kos, Rhodes and Patara (21, 1), where they change ship, and then on to Tyre, where there is a stay of seven days while the ship unloads its cargo (21, 2–4) before taking them on to Ptolemais. Similarly, on the first leg of the journey to Rome, they take a ship travelling to 'the ports along the coast of Asia' (Acts 27, 2: presumably the captain intends to call in at a selection of them), and they appear to have a protracted stay at Sidon (Paul is allowed to visit friends: Acts 27, 3), no doubt while some kind of business is transacted. This is a normal pattern for travel. For example, the poet Ovid, who was (he claimed) sent into exile to a city on the Black Sea, wrote an elaborately poetic account of his journey there in which they move from port to port in the same way as Paul (*Tristia* 1, 10), and Philo describes Flaccus' journey to exile in Andros from Cenchreae by way of Athens, Helene, Kia, Kythnos and a number of other unnamed islands (*Against Flaccus* 155–6).

This pattern of 'tramping from port to port' (Rickman 1980: 125), picking up whatever cargoes and passengers offered themselves while the sailing season (from March to November) lasted, remained the usual one throughout antiquity and the middle ages. The corn supply of Rome, however, was a special case, for which special arrangements had to be made, and Paul makes the last stages of his journey to Rome in ships which were involved in this trade, in this case transporting Egyptian corn from Alexandria. The city of Rome had grown to an enormous size, and was totally dependent on food imports for the survival of its population. Perhaps more than half of the total Egyptian grain production was sent to Rome (Garnsey 1988: 231), in a substantial fleet which, though consisting of privately owned ships, was encouraged and regulated by the state. The ships were very large – when the emperor Claudius was trying to promote the building of corn ships, the lower limit to qualify for the incentives on offer was a ship with a capacity of about 68 tons. Most were bigger, and the standard size of ship may have had a capacity of about 340 tons (Rickman 1980: 123). In a work called *The Ship*, the second-century writer Lucian purports to give a description of a monstrous Alexandrian grain ship, the *Isis*, allegedly driven by storms into the harbour of Athens at Piraeus (cf. p. 14). From his description it has been calculated that it could carry a cargo well in excess of 1,000 tons, but Lucian was a rhetorician, and even if we do not go along with the view that the whole description is an invention – 'a literary construct' (Houston 1987: 444–50) – considerable allowance must be made for rhetorical exaggeration. Nevertheless, there is no doubt that some of these ships could be very large indeed.

In view of the jettisoning of the cargo from Paul's ship (Acts 27, 18 and 38) it would be interesting to know how the corn was stored, and so what steps would be necessary to get rid of it. Unfortunately the evidence is hard to interpret. It would have been absolutely essential to keep the corn dry; otherwise, if it got wet, not only would it spoil, but it would also swell, with disastrous consequences for the safety of the ship. It would, then, have to be stored high in the hold, well clear of the bilges, and protected by waterproof hatches. Steps would also have to be taken to ensure that the cargo did not shift and destabilise the ship. Storing the grain in sacks would make it easy to stack it in such a way as to minimise the likelihood of its shifting, and to make it relatively simple to jettison the cargo in emergencies. However, although the corn was brought on to the ship in sacks, such evidence as there is suggests that the sacks were emptied into the hold, which may have been divided into compartments, solving the problem of shifting, but making jettisoning the cargo a formidable task (Rickman 1980: 132–4; Casson 1986: 200). In view of this, it is difficult to be certain exactly what was going on in Paul's ship before she ran aground.

Though merchant ships might carry a few oars for manoeuvring in harbour, they were normally driven by a single square sail borne on a single mast in the centre of the ship. Smaller sails fore and aft could be added, but they were of secondary importance. It might be supplemented by a topsail – we know from a description by Seneca of the arrival of the Alexandrian grain ships at Puteoli that these ships did normally carry such a sail (*Moral Epistles* 77, 2). They were designed to be sailed with a following wind (or as near to it as possible). Ships of this kind could tack to some degree, but not easily or conveniently (Casson 1986: 239–43, 273–8). This led to some difficulties for the Alexandrian grain fleet, and helps explain the route taken by Paul. From Puteoli to Alexandria, the ships would be sailing with the prevailing winds, and would make very good time indeed. Pliny the Elder (*Natural History* 19, 3) reports one crossing which took only nine days, but two or three weeks would have been more normal. Philo (*Against Flaccus* 26) has the emperor Gaius advising Herod Agrippa I to take one of these ships back to Alexandria, and travel from there to Palestine, rather than take the slow route through Brundisium, because they were 'very fast merchant ships, with skilled captains who drive them as a charioteer drives his team, and provide a straight passage on the direct route'. Passengers would have been especially welcome on this route, providing at least some income on a voyage when the ship would usually have little or no cargo. Coming back, however, they would be going against the prevailing winds. Since they could not sail into, or nearly into, the wind, they would have either to go west along the coast of North Africa (running the danger of falling foul of the notorious shallows in the Gulf of Sirte) and then strike north, or to go north first up to the south-west tip of Anatolia, and then turn west along the coast of Crete to Sicily (where they would have to face the dangers of the Straits of Messina). The ship which Paul boards was taking the second of these routes, and was sailing late in the season (Acts 27, 9), perhaps because the captain made good time in his first run that year, and was trying to get another run in the same year before the sailing season ended (which would of course considerably increase his profit). The captain of the ship which they find overwintering in Malta (Acts 28, 11) will have made the same calculation, but had better luck in finding a safe harbour when the weather turned (Casson 1986: 297–9; Rickman 1980: 130–2).

Acts reports that the ship Paul took from Myra was carrying 276 persons (Acts 27, 37). This is by no means an incredible number. Josephus (*Life* 15) says that there were six hundred people on board his ship which sank on the way to Puteoli (in his case there were only eighty survivors). Of these, the crew would form only a small percentage – the small ship in which Synesius sailed from Alexandria to Cyrene in the early fifth century had, he says in a letter to his brother, thirteen crew to fifty passengers, but some of them seem to have been rowers (Synesius, *Letters* 5). There was, however, no separate passenger accommodation. Especially favoured (or rich and powerful) passengers might be allowed to use the captain's cabin, the *diaeta* (Petronius, *Satyricon* 115), but normally they would have to make the best arrangements they could on the deck, depending on their circumstances. So in Achilles Tatius' novel *Leucippe and Clitophon*, the narrator tells of a young man 'camping out' (*paraskēnōn*) beside him on the deck (2, 33, 1), but on a later voyage the protagonists have a private cabin (*idia kalubē*) built for them on the deck (5, 15, 3). On Synesius' short voyage, women were separated from men by a curtain, but there is no evidence of such a practice earlier.

Passengers cannot have been an unmixed blessing for the crew of a ship. Unsolicited bad advice from ignorant landlubbers must have been a regular irritation. Paul himself urges the captain not to move on from a harbour which was unsuitable to find one in which it was possible to overwinter (Acts 27, 9–12), and stirs up trouble when the crew take the ship's boat to lay out more anchors (Acts 27, 30–2; Wallace and Williams 1993: 129). Fear of being abandoned by the crew in a storm may, however, have been quite common, for a scene in Achilles Tatius' novel has a violent disturbance breaking out when the crew attempt to take to the boat (*Leucippe and Clitophon* 3, 3, 1–5). Synesius and his fellow travellers shout out in protest when their ship first seems to be heading straight for the rocks and then abruptly swings round and heads far out into the open sea, having completely misunderstood a tacking manoeuvre, though the ship's captain, Amarantus, does his best to explain politely: *Toiouton ephē to technē nautillesthai*, 'that is the proper way to manage a ship' (*Letters* 5; Casson 1974: 159–62). Even the hypochondriac rhetorician Aelius Aristides (second century AD) feels able to advise his ship's officers about whether the weather is suitable for sailing (48, *The Sacred Tales* 2, 67); despite his protestations at their incompetence they get him to Smyrna quite safely. The presence of soldiers on the ship seems not to have been helpful. Paul's escort supports his ill-advised intervention (Acts 27, 31–2); a group of soldiers on Synesius' ship prepare to kill themselves during bad weather rather than face drowning. Many of the passengers will have been merchants carrying their merchandise with them. A considerable body of law had built up over who had to stand the loss if such merchandise had to be abandoned to lighten the ship in a storm (*Digest* 14, 2; Rougé 1966: 365–6; André and Baslez 1993: 443–4). It is possible that the fact that the cargo in Paul's ship was jettisoned in two stages (Acts 27, 18 and 38) may be related to this complication.

ORGANISING TRAVEL

Since arrivals and departures were dependent on the vagaries of the weather and the whims of the captain (so that there could be no such thing as a schedule or a timetable), there was no choice when taking passage on a ship but to go down to the port and find out which ships were there, where they intended to sail next, and when. Responsibility for taking on passengers and negotiating the fare with them seems to have been taken not by the master but by another member of the crew (*Digest* 14, 1, 1–5), who may have been called the *naustologos* (Casson 1986: 320; Rougé 1966: 364). It would then be necessary for passengers to wait until summoned by a public announcement (Philostratus, *Life of Apollonius* 15) or by a personal call from one of the crew (Petronius, *Satyricon* 99). Passengers seem to have been responsible for providing their own food. Thus in Achilles Tatius' *Leucippe and Clitophon*, the narrator and his companion pool their resources with another passenger and dine together (2, 33, 1). Responsibility for the provision of water is less easy to determine. There is some evidence of large water tanks in ships (Casson 1986: 177–8). Plutarch (*Greek Questions* 54) tells the story of a ship's master called Dexicreon who was advised by the goddess Aphrodite to load his ship with nothing but water. They were becalmed during the voyage, and Dexicreon made his fortune by selling water to rich passengers. If charging for water was a normal practice, then passengers might well wish to bring their own supply with them, which could be readily replenished at the frequent ports of call; the goddess' advice to Dexicreon to set sail as quickly as possible suggests that given time the passengers might have provided their own water supply, and so reduced Dexicreon's profit.

Readers of the gospels, remembering the birth narrative of Luke (2, 7) and the parable of the Good Samaritan (Luke 10, 34–5), will need no introduction to the ancient inn. It is hard to get a balanced picture of the sort of service they provided. It may be that many of them were clean, decent establishments run by honest people offering good food and accommodation at reasonable prices. Such inns, however, do not make good stories or interesting reading, and as a result the picture we get of the ancient inn is a very bleak one. During Horace's trip to Brundisium (*Satire* 5) he encounters mean innkeepers at Appii Forum (4; this is the same place at which Paul meets 'the brethren' from Rome: Acts 28, 15), and at Beneventum the innkeeper almost sets the house on fire (71–6). Inns were reputed to be dangerous places where anything might happen (Apuleius, *Metamorphoses* 1, 17), and to be infested with vermin: Pliny (*Natural History* 9, 154) compares the small sea creatures which prey on fish to the 'creatures found in inns during the summer, which bother us with a quick jump or those which usually hide in the hair'; the apocryphal *Acts of John* (60–1) narrates an incident where the saint is bothered by bed-bugs in an inn where he is sleeping, and banishes them from the room (they obey, and next morning are found standing outside the door waiting for the saint's permission to return).

Whether or not this is an accurate picture, there is no doubt that for preference a traveller would stay in a private house, if he could contrive to be invited to one. So Apuleius' hero travels to Hypata in Thessaly with an introduction from his friend Demeas to one Milo, in whose house he is invited to stay (*Metamorphoses* 1, 22–3); while there he meets a relative and friend of his mother, who also offers him an invitation (2, 3). Paul follows the same pattern. At Philippi he stays at Lydia's house (Acts 16, 15), at Thessalonika probably at Jason's house (Acts 17, 5) and in Corinth with Aquila and Priscilla (Acts 18, 3). He stays with unnamed fellow Christians in Tyre and Ptolemais (Acts 21, 2–3 and 7), with Philip in Caesarea (Acts 21, 8) and with Mnason in Jerusalem (Acts 21, 16). Networks of contacts like this would make travel a very much easier and more comfortable experience (André and Baslez 1993: 449–54; Casson 1974: 197–218). It is likely that travelling Jews turning up at the local synagogue might hope to find offers of hospitality; at any rate, Jewish congregations seem quite accustomed to the arrival of strangers (e.g. Acts 13, 15). This tradition of hospitality to visitors was one of the reasons why travelling preachers could become such a burden to Christian communities later on:

> If he who comes is a traveller, help him as much as you can.
> But he must not stay more than two days, or three if necessary.

If he wishes to settle among you, he must work, if he has a trade, and so eat. If he has no trade, make whatever provision for him you can, so that no Christian should be idle among you. If he is not willing to do so, he is making a trade of Christ. Beware of such men.

(*Didache* 12)

Paul's final journey as a prisoner to Rome is in a different category from his other travels, for he is in the charge of a centurion who is on official business. They must still, like any private traveller, take their chance with whatever merchant vessels happen to be in port, but the centurion would not have to bargain with the ship's *naustologos* for their passage. Travellers on official business were supplied with passes, *diplomata*, which gave them authority to require civilians to help them on their journey (this is the situation envisaged in the saying of Jesus in Matthew 5, 41: 'If anyone forces you to go one mile, go with him two miles'). The system was, in fact, a kind of informal (and random) taxation, and as such was capable of abuse (see Pliny, *Letters* 10, 45 and 46; when Pliny gives a *diploma* to his wife he is careful to tell the emperor about it: 10, 120 and 121; see also Williams 1990: 105–6). The demands of holders of *diplomata* could be very peremptory. The philosopher Epiktetos, perhaps a little younger than Paul, says:

You should, as far as you can, as long as you may, treat your body like a loaded donkey. If it is commandeered, and a soldier takes hold of it, let it go, do not resist or complain. Otherwise you will be beaten up, and still lose your donkey.

(Epiktetos, *Discourses* 4, 1, 79)

However, in Apuleius' *Metamorphoses* (9, 39–40), when a soldier tries to requisition an ass from a gardener, it is the soldier who is beaten up; the gardener is subsequently arrested and, presumably, executed (42). Paul's centurion will have been able to demand the supply of whatever he wanted in the way of transport and accommodation.

THE HAZARDS OF TRAVEL

Three times I have been shipwrecked; a night and a day I have been adrift at sea; on frequent journeys, in danger from rivers, danger from robbers, . . . danger in the wilderness, danger at sea, . . . in toil and hardship, through many a

27

sleepless night, in hunger and thirst, often without food, in cold and exposure.

(2 Corinthians 11, 25–7)

Paul's list of tribulations has one surprising omission. Anyone reading ancient fiction would get the impression that piracy was ubiquitous. The pirate raid is a common device for separating lovers in the novel; in Roman comedy (surviving examples of which date from the second century BC) the unsuitable girl-friend of a young man of good family will turn out to be the long-lost daughter of a neighbour, kidnapped in infancy by pirates. And yet Paul, in a list of misfortunes in which he is clearly sparing us nothing, does not think that pirates are worth mentioning. The fact is that the suppression of pirates was one of the successes of the Roman Empire. From the middle of the second century BC piracy had grown to be a serious problem. In part, this was the fault of Rome herself. Her interventions, particularly against the Seleucid Empire, had destabilised the eastern Mediterranean lands, and this, together with her checking of the naval power of Rhodes, made possible the conditions in which piracy could flourish (pirates need not only freedom of the seas, but also good land bases). The result was that by the first century BC the pirates were a major force; they controlled the seas to the extent of threatening Rome's corn supply, and were raiding Italy itself. The turning point came when in 67 BC the Roman general Pompeius was given a commission to deal with the problem. In a carefully planned campaign his fleets swept through the Mediterranean, while simultaneously the pirates' land bases in Crete and Cilicia were brought under control. It was some time before the problem was completely solved, but eventually the extension of Roman power over the coastline and the islands put an end to serious piracy (Casson 1991: 177–83; André and Baslez 1993: 444–7).

Robbers on land are a different matter. The suppression of brigands was a recurring concern for Roman magistrates, and we have already seen (p. 11) that Roman sources tend to classify imperfectly pacified provincials as bandits. No doubt they did succeed in checking robbery on the large scale – there is some evidence that in the period in which Paul was travelling brigandage had been substantially reduced, at any rate in Asia Minor (Robert 1937: 96) – but in many regions it was endemic and could not practically be controlled, despite the maintenance by the cities of local police forces (Robert 1937: 98–110). Such a region was Cilicia (see Tacitus, *Annals* 12, 55 for an outbreak of serious brigandage among the hill tribes there in Claudius' reign), and Paul's encounter with robbers is as likely to have occurred here as anywhere. Low-grade muggings, however, were possible everywhere, and danger on that scale is simply taken for granted in every period. For example, the parable of the Good Samaritan (Luke 10, 25–37) takes it as unremarkable that a brutal robbery should take place on the relatively short (about fifteen miles) and well-travelled road from Jerusalem to Jericho (Shaw 1984).

Shipwrecks feature in ancient fiction almost as often as pirates, raising the possibility that when they are found in history or biography they too may be no more than literary devices. It is certainly the case that the narrative in Acts owes a great deal to literature, and that many of the elements depicted there have their counterparts in the novel. The development of underwater archaeology, however, has made us much more aware of the reality of this kind of hazard (Hopkins 1980: 105–6). Though the author of Acts squeezes all the drama out of it that he can, there is no reason to doubt that Paul really was shipwrecked. Overloading with cargo and sailing at unsuitable times of year, not to speak of simple human error, will have accounted for many wrecks but, despite appearances, the Mediterranean is a dangerous sea, and one which at certain times of year is liable to sudden, dangerous storms. There is nothing in the account of Acts which should make us doubt it.

SUGGESTIONS FOR FURTHER READING

(full details of these works can be found in the Bibliography):

L. Casson's *Travel in the Ancient World* gives a good general account of the subject. His *The Ancient Mariners* is a clear and non-technical study of ships and shipping.

Part 2

PEOPLES, CULTURES AND LANGUAGES

4

THE NATIVE CULTURES

As we have explained in the first chapter, in the geographical area through which Paul travelled three 'layers' of language and culture can be distinguished in the first century AD. First (in the area east of the Aegean coast) there are what Greeks and Romans would have termed 'barbarian' peoples, and nineteenth-century Europeans 'natives', 'barbarians' who made noises which sounded like 'rhubarb-rhubarb' to Greeks who could not (and did not want to) understand them. The term (and the classification) was taken over from the Greeks by the Romans, though the Greeks unquestionably included the Romans in the category 'barbarian' so long as it was safe to do so. Then there were those who used the Greek language and led the distinctive 'Hellenic' way of life. Finally there were the visiting representatives of Imperial Rome, as well as a small body of emigrants from Italy, who (at least for official purposes) used Latin. Paul, as the quotations at the beginning of this book show, belonged in some measure to all three layers: as a Jew he belonged to the 'barbarian' culture which had most fiercely resisted assimilation into the Greek way of life (see pp. 68–9 on the events of the 170s and 160s BC in Jerusalem); as a citizen of the hellenised city of Tarsus he belonged to the Greek world; and as a holder of citizen status by birth he belonged to the Roman world.

GREECE AND MACEDONIA

In the Greek peninsula, the islands of the Aegean, and along the eastern coasts of the Aegean (with outposts along the north and south coasts of Asia Minor and in Cyprus) the 'native' culture was of course the Hellenic/Greek culture, a version of which was exported to the regions further east. To the north of the Greek peninsula the kingdom of Macedon (which comprised only part of the Roman province of Macedonia), the home of the conquerors Philip and Alexander (see p. 42), had down to their time been regarded as only half Greek. The status of the Macedonian language remains controversial; it may well have been a dialect of Greek, but one which other Greeks found peculiarly impenetrable. The ruling dynasty had successfully claimed to be authentically Hellenic, but the way of life of the people was regarded by the Greeks who lived to the south as 'barbarian'. After Alexander, however, hellenisation proceeded rapidly and was probably complete by the first century.

ASIA MINOR

In the interior of Asia Minor a number of 'native' languages continued in use, at least in rural areas, down to the first century and later. In Acts 14, 11 there occurs one of the rare references to one of these languages being spoken in a town (see p. 5). At Lystra 'the crowds, seeing what Paul had done, raised their voices, crying out *in Lycaonian* (*Lykaonisti*) "the gods have come among us in the likeness of men"'. The absence of any such reference elsewhere in the accounts of Paul's journeys in Asia Minor need not mean that Lystra was unique or even unusual in this respect. In the Lystra episode the narrative requires it to be made clear that Paul and Barnabas did not at first understand that they were being hailed as gods. The inscriptions of this period which survive from Lystra give no clue that the native language was still in use: all are in Greek or Latin.

In the areas west of the Euphrates the following linguistic/ethnic names are recorded in classical sources: Mysian, Lydian, Carian, Phrygian, Pisidian, Pamphylian, Lycaonian, Cilician, Cappadocian, Paphlagonian and Bithynian. The geographer Strabo, writing at the end of the first century BC or the beginning of the first century AD, knows of the survival of Carian (at Kaunos: *Geography* 14, 2, 3, 652), Lydian, Solymian and Pisidian (13, 4, 17, 631); his claim that '*most* of them [i.e. the peoples of north-west Asia Minor] have lost their dialects and their names' (12, 4, 6, 565) implies that some at least had retained them in his day. In the northern part of the central plateau three Celtic tribes – the Trocmi, the Tectosages and the Tolistobogii – had settled after being shipped across from Europe to serve as mercenaries by a king of Bithynia in 278/7 BC. Since all Celtic-speakers were known as *Galatai* by the Greeks, the country in which these tribes lived came to be known as Galatia, and their language as Galatian. St Jerome records that it was still in use in the late fourth century. This reference is in his commentary on Paul's epistle to the Galatians. Like other Christian commentators of the fourth century he mistakenly assumed that in this epistle Paul was addressing Celtic (and presumably bilingual, see p. 46) converts. Those areas which lay closest to the ancient Greek cities along the west coast of Asia Minor and which had been exposed to Greek influence for the longest time must have been the ones where the vernacular languages died out earliest: Mysia, Lydia, Caria and Lycia. In Phrygia on the other hand, which lay immediately to the east, inscriptions reveal a revival of the native language as late as the third century, and in late antiquity Christian writers (who, unlike the writers of the classical period, sometimes take an interest in those untouched by 'official' culture) reveal speakers of the native languages continuing to survive in central and eastern Asia Minor (see Mitchell 1993: I, 172–5). It seems likely, then, that except in the most thoroughly hellenised regions, local languages continued to coexist with Greek over much of Asia Minor, and a high proportion of the population would have been effectively bilingual.

SYRIA AND PALESTINE

Twentieth-century historians refer to the 'Fertile Crescent' of land with one tip at the head of the Persian Gulf and the other on the Mediterranean coast between Egypt and Judaea. The inner curve is formed by the edge of desert or steppe and the outer by the east coast of the Mediterranean and the Amanus, Taurus and Zagros mountain ranges. From 539 to 331 BC the whole area had formed part of the Persian Empire. Ever since the third millennium BC, related languages of the group known as Semitic had been in use in the Fertile Crescent – Hebrew in Palestine, Phoenician along the Mediterranean coast to the north of Palestine, Aramaic in the interior of Syria, Akkadian in Babylonia and Assyria. By the Persian period Aramaic had become the main spoken language throughout most of the region, and indeed was used by the Persian imperial government as an official language of administration beyond the Fertile Crescent. (Examples of such official documents are reproduced in the Book of Ezra; cf. the Aramaic papyri produced by a colony of Jewish soldiers established on the southern frontier of the Persian Empire in Egypt.)

By the early first century the Fertile Crescent had been divided between the Roman and Parthian Empires, with the frontier at the great western bend of the Euphrates before it turns to run south-east through the desert towards Babylonia. The kings of Commagene with their capital at Samosata to the north-west of the bend were vassals of Rome, whereas the kings of Osrhoene with their capital at Edessa across the river to the south-east were vassals of the Parthian Great King. The foundation of Greek cities by the Seleucid kings had introduced a powerful rival to Aramaic as a *lingua franca*. The evidence for its continued use (or rather for the use of different dialects or branches of Aramaic) in speech or in writing varies from region to region. In what had been Babylonia and Assyria it is usually assumed (although there is very little direct evidence) that Aramaic continued as the main vernacular, with Greek being confined to such cities as Seleukia-on-the-Tigris, Parthian to the royal court and government and Akkadian almost extinct, even as a 'dead' language (Millar 1993: 498–500). There were large Jewish diaspora communities in these areas, which sent contributions to the Temple at Jerusalem and went on pilgrimages there. Herod had also settled a body of Babylonian Jews in the north-east territories of his kingdom. Since the Babylonian Talmud was composed (considerably later) in Aramaic, Babylonian Jews presumably used it in the first century, albeit reading the scriptures in Hebrew. When Josephus reports (*War* 1, 3, 6) that he had composed an earlier version of his *Jewish War* (the surviving version is in Greek) in his native or ancestral tongue and sent it to 'the barbarians up-country' – defined as 'Parthians and Babylonians, and the most distant of the Arabs, and our kindred beyond the Euphrates, and Adiabenians' – this tongue must have been Aramaic, and he assumed that it would be understood by Jews and Gentiles living in the western part of the Parthian Empire. In the most westerly part of the area beyond the Euphrates, Osrhoene, the local branch of Aramaic was to be developed for the writing of literary works (mainly Christian) in the form known as Syriac from the second century onwards, by which time Osrhoene had passed under Roman rule (Millar 1993: 125). In the most easterly part of the Roman Empire in the first century, the city of Palmyra south of the Euphrates, the local variety of Aramaic was used in public and private inscriptions alongside Greek and, alone of the peoples of the Empire, Palmyrenes carried this practice with them beyond their homeland (Millar 1993: 328–9), even to the most distant north-west corner of the empire: below a Latin epitaph found at South

Shields in the north of England is inscribed a brief addition in Palmyrene.

At the southern end of the Fertile Crescent Aramaic was the main language of everyday life of the Jews of Galilee, Judaea and neighbouring territories, as well as of the Samaritans (Schürer 1973–87: III (1), 177–80); it was also used for works of literature (e.g. the *Genesis Apokryphon* from Qumran etc.). To the south and the west of the Jewish heartland lay the territories of the Nabataean kings who had their capital at Petra, extending round from the Negev to the southern Hauran. A large number of inscriptions, as well as a number of texts on parchment or papyrus, reveal that the subjects of the Nabataean kings used a dialect of Aramaic close to that used by the Palestinian Jews (Millar 1993: 401ff.).

For the region north of Galilee and the Hauran and west of Palmyra and the Euphrates bend (including Damascus), which formed the bulk of the Roman province of Syria and, until the annexation of Judaea in AD 6, the only part of the Fertile Crescent under direct Roman rule, there are no inscriptions in any Semitic language surviving from the Roman period; even temples and shrines in rural areas and high up in mountains are built in the Greco-Roman style and contain inscriptions in Greek (Millar 1993: chs 7–9). Only Semitic personal names (transliterated into Greek or Latin) reveal the ancestry of some of the persons who paid for the buildings and put up the inscriptions. It is, however, notoriously impossible to prove a negative. While those who could afford to pay for inscriptions preferred to advertise their hellenism even if they were descended from native Semitic-speakers, that need not mean that the poorer people, especially outside the great cities like Antioch founded by the Macedonian kings, did not continue to use their ancestral language in their everyday life. A high degree of bilingualism seems more probable than a complete extinction of spoken Aramaic and exclusive use of Greek.

Two other Semitic languages had been in use in earlier centuries in the western part of the Fertile Crescent – Phoenician and Hebrew. The Phoenician cities along the coast north of Palestine had long had close links with the Greek world, and by the time of Paul had undergone three centuries of hellenisation. Some knowledge of the Phoenician language survived: there is *one* securely dated bilingual Greek/Phoenician inscription (from 25/24 BC) and some of the coins of Sidon and of Tyre continued to carry legends in Phoenician, whereas other coin types have legends in Greek. But as

Millar points out, 'not a single connected sentence is attested as having been generated in Phoenician' after 25/24 BC (Millar 1993: 293). On the other hand, the long-held assumption that Hebrew was by Paul's day a dead language, neither spoken nor used for secular writing, but studied only to enable devout Jews to read the scriptures, is now discredited (see p. 137). Studies of the language used to write the Mishnah around AD 200 suggest that this form of Hebrew was the product of the evolution of a spoken vernacular, while documents of the early second century discovered in southern Judaea show that Hebrew was used to write letters and legal documents (Millar 1993: 373–4, cf. 545–52), though the question of the extent to which Hebrew was used as a living language, and who used it, remains a controversial one.

Aramaic, Hebrew and Phoenician all form part of the same group of Semitic languages, North-West Semitic (Sáenz-Badillos 1993: 29–44), and it is natural to ask to what extent they were mutually comprehensible. It may be better to describe the group as a 'dialect continuum' (Sáenz-Badillos 1993: 36) with Phoenician at one extreme, Aramaic at the other and Hebrew somewhere in the middle, rather than as a set of discrete languages. In other words, the boundaries between the different languages may not have been very clear. This is shown by the different ways in which Jews treated Aramaic and Greek versions of their scriptures. Whatever view we take of the survival of Hebrew, it is clear that a large number of Jews used Aramaic as their normal language. To serve their needs, the books of the Bible were translated into Aramaic. These translations were called Targums, and a number of them survive (Schürer 1973–87: I, 99–105). Though their dating is controversial, it is generally agreed that the process of producing them had begun well before the first century. Unlike the Greek translation of the Bible, however (see pp. 48–51), the Targums were not used as simple substitutes for the Hebrew text. Some of them have an element of commentary and exegesis alongside the translation. In synagogue services the Targum was read alongside the Hebrew text, rather than as a substitute for it (Fraade 1992: 256–62), the assumption being that although the congregation would need some help with the Hebrew, they could at least keep in touch with it to some extent. This lack of clear boundaries between Hebrew and its neighbours may help to explain the remarkable lack of 'linguistic nationalism' among the Jews (see pp. 136–7).

Another long-held assumption was that a form of a fourth Semitic language, Arabic, was the spoken language of the subjects of the Nabataean kings, and that the form of Aramaic used on inscriptions was only an 'official language'. One reason for this belief was that Greek writers always described the Nabataeans as 'Arabs', and indeed when Rome annexed the kingdom in AD 106 the new imperial province was named Arabia. Moreover, it was claimed that the Aramaic used by the Nabataeans showed the clear influence of Arabic. However, the word 'Arab' appears to be used to characterise a way of life – the nomadic life of the inhabitants of the steppe and desert – rather than to identify the speakers of a language. Indeed, as Millar points out (Millar 1993: 402–3), 'we have no more than scattered items of evidence before the late seventh century for the Arabic language'; the earliest is in fact two lines included in an inscription in Nabataean letters of the early second century. In any case, the very extensive use of Nabataean Aramaic in widespread graffiti makes it clear that it was much more than an 'official language' (Millar 1993: 402–3).

It would be a mistake to suppose that speakers of Semitic languages, or even speakers of different branches of Aramaic, felt any sense of common identity at this period or that their local cultures and religious practices displayed any common 'Semitic' or 'Aramaic' characteristics. It is the achievement of Professor Millar's recent book (1993) to reveal the absence of any evidence for such hypotheses. What unites the authors of the Nabataean inscriptions is the expression of devotion to the reigning king (e.g. 'Rabbel the king, king of the Nabataeans who has given life and deliverance to his people': Millar (1993): 404), while those of Palmyra reveal loyalty to the city of Palmyra with its Greek institutions, to its local deities and to the Roman emperors. As for the Jews, whether they were Aramaic-speakers or Greek-speakers, what mattered was the distinction between Jews and Gentiles (and for Samaritans the distinction between worshipping the God of Israel on Mount Gerizim and Mount Zion). The Jews (and the Samaritans) differed from the other subject peoples of Rome in the Near East in the *exclusive* claim made on their loyalty by their God and by the possession of a large body of sacred writings in their own language which preserved their own account of their nation's history. This made their relationship with their Roman overlords more uneasy than that of any other people which had been part of the Empire for so long; the two revolts of AD 66–70 and 132–5, which tied down a large section of the Roman army, were without parallel elsewhere.

SUGGESTIONS FOR FURTHER READING

(full details of these works can be found in the Bibliography):

On Greece under Roman rule, S. E. Alcock's *Graecia Capta* gives a detailed and comprehensive account.

For Asia Minor S. Mitchell's *Anatolia* can be recommended, though it is less comprehensive than its title suggests.

F. G. B. Millar's *The Roman Near East* is a full and authoritative description of the effects of Roman rule on Syria and Palestine.

For comparative material on Egypt, two books by N. Lewis, *Greeks in Ptolemaic Egypt* and *Life in Egypt under Roman Rule*, are both readable and full of information.

5

HELLENISATION IN THE NEAR EAST

The verb *hellenizein* in classical Greek meant 'to speak (correct) Greek' or 'to translate into Greek'; from a late usage 'to make (the barbarian) Greek' the verb 'hellenise' and the noun 'hellenisation' have been coined in modern European languages to refer to the adoption by non-Greeks of the Greek way of life as well as the language. The three centuries from *c.* 330 to 30 BC, between Alexander's overthrow of the Persian Empire and the final consolidation of Roman rule in the Near East, are conventionally described as 'the Hellenistic Age', i.e. the age during which large-scale hellenisation took place. Greek language and culture (especially art forms) had exerted great attraction over some of the Greeks' immediate neighbours long before 330 BC. The most striking case is that of the Carian and Lycian peoples in the south-west of Asia Minor. Mausolus, a native Carian dynast who ruled his own country as a vassal of the Persians in the middle of the fourth century BC, was commemorated by an immense tomb, the original Mausoleum (Hornblower 1982: 223–74), which was regarded as one of the masterpieces of Greek architecture and sculpture (Boardman 1994: 39–48). The growing intrusion of Greek forms into a native tradition of tomb building and sculptural decoration during the late fifth and fourth centuries BC is revealed by the Xanthian Marbles, which were removed from the Lycian city of Xanthos to the British Museum in the nineteenth century. After the events of 334–330 BC the geographical scope and the intensity of hellenisation increased enormously. These immense social and cultural changes were in large part the result of military and political events. It is, however, important to remember that the Greek culture which was imposed on the Near East following Alexander's conquests was one which was already proving popular, and perhaps even fashionable, among the ruling élites in regions beyond the political control of the Greek cities.

HISTORICAL OUTLINE

This process of expansion was made possible when the long-established and rather weak kingdom of Macedon was transformed into a major military power by Philip II. He had by 338 BC reduced the Greek cities of mainland Greece to the condition of satellites, and in 337 BC despatched an army to invade the territories of the Persian Empire in Asia Minor. This was a natural target for any ambitious and powerful ruler, since the Persian territories were rich (offering the prospect of enormous booty) and the empire had been showing signs of weakness; it had the additional advantage that such an invasion could be represented in propaganda to the Greek world as an act of piety and just vengeance for the Persian invasions at the beginning of the fifth century. Philip's assassination in 336 prevented him from going to Asia himself, but his plan was taken up in 334 by his son Alexander III (336–323 BC). What Alexander aimed to achieve was a 'hostile take-over' of the whole Persian Empire as a going concern. He would have known from Herodotos' *History* that the founder of that empire, Cyrus I, had built it up by defeating the rulers, and annexing the territories, of three large empires, the Median, the Lydian and the Babylonian. Alexander's task would be more straightforward since he had only a single target, Dareios III of Persia (336–330) and his armies. They were defeated in two great battles, Issos (333) and Gaugamela (331), and the discredited Dareios was murdered by some of his own satraps, or provincial governors, in 330. Alexander then presented himself as Dareios' legitimate heir, pursued and punished his assassins, married one of his daughters, and even made eighty of his own senior officers marry Iranian noblewomen. But the full development of his plans for his existing conquests and for further campaigns were cut short by his death at the age of thirty-three in 323 BC.

That event also put paid to any prospect of the survival of a unified Macedonian Empire lasting as long as the Persian Empire had. Alexander had left no competent adult heir; a mentally defective half-brother and a posthumous son were recognised as joint kings by the Macedonian army but were murdered in the course of power-struggles between Alexander's Macedonian generals. Those who tried to keep the united empire going or tried to reassemble

Alexander's legacy under their own rule were defeated by coalitions of jealous rivals. In 305–4 five of these generals took the title 'king'; apart from the one who happened to control the Macedonian homeland they were not kings of any existing state or nation, but kings of whatever territory they could grab by force. Twenty-five more years of warfare left the greater part of Alexander's empire divided between dynasties descended from three of his generals: Macedon itself and parts of Greece were ruled by descendants of Antigonos; the Ptolemies (all of Ptolemy I's male successors bore his name) had their main base in Egypt, but also controlled Cyrenaica, Cyprus, Palestine, southern Syria and coastal areas in Asia Minor; the descendants of Seleukos had the most extensive territories, the truncated torso of the old Persian Empire stretching from western Asia Minor through northern Syria to Iran.

The Ptolemies and the Seleucids were not the kings *of* Egypt or *of* Syria in the modern sense, but Macedonian dynasts ruling *in* these lands. The native population remained as much conquered and exploited subjects as if they were still living in a unified Macedonian or in a Persian Empire. The dynasties could not rely on any enthusiasm or loyalty from their native subjects; after Ptolemy IV had been obliged to have native Egyptians trained to fight in the Macedonian style to defeat an invasion by the Seleucid king Antiochos III in 217, the sequel was twenty years of native risings and guerrilla warfare in southern Egypt. It is, then, important to realise that the hellenistic kingdoms in no way resembled modern 'nation-states'. They had no national identity or cultural unity. The only thing the parts of these kingdoms had in common was the fact that they were all under the control of a particular military adventurer or his family. An individual would have loyalty to his city (or perhaps his region); he might be invited to show loyalty to the dynasty; but there was no 'state' which had a claim on his loyalty.

CULTURAL HELLENISATION

It must be stressed that the dynasties remained Macedonian by descent and Greek in culture to the end. After Alexander's death all his officers (except Seleukos) repudiated their Iranian wives and married Macedonian noblewomen. The kings of the various dynasties married wives from other dynasties or, in the case of many of the Ptolemies, their own sisters. Although the Ptolemies maintained the native Egyptian cults and received from the native priesthood the honours once paid to the Pharaohs (as recorded on the famous Rosetta Stone), the last ruler of the dynasty, Kleopatra VII (51–30 BC), is alleged to have been the first to have had any knowledge of the Egyptian language (Plutarch, *Antony* 27). Their courts and the senior administrators and generals who served them were also overwhelmingly Macedonian or Greek by ancestry and culture. Dynasties of such soldier-administrators served the same royal family in successive generations, but leading Greeks with political or military experience who were exiled from their native cities after losing out in civil wars also sought employment from the kings. Eminent intellectuals and artists were attracted by the lavish patronage of the royal courts where, among other things, they provided royal children with the best education money could buy. At Alexandria in the third century both the poet Kallimachos and the polymath Eratosthenes (most famous for his remarkably accurate calculation of the circumference of the Earth) acted as tutors to the young Ptolemies (Fraser 1972: I, 308–33).

At a far lower social level than that of the royal courts, Greek immigrants and their descendants clung fiercely to their ethnic and cultural identity. This is best attested for Egypt where the preservation of papyrus archives provides evidence for the lives of fairly humble people not available for other parts of the hellenistic world. One example is that of the papers of two brothers, Ptolemaios and Apollonios, sons of a Macedonian soldier named Glaukias, who lived within the precinct of the great Egyptian temple-complex, the Serapeion, west of Memphis, in the middle of the second century BC. They earned a living by dealing in second-hand clothes and selling porridge. In this Egyptian environment and in comparative poverty the brothers asserted their Macedonian identity (their father Glaukias had been a 'Macedonian of the *epigonē*', a term whose significance is completely obscure) and tried to keep up their acquaintance with classical Greek literature. They had excerpts from Greek plays and poems and Apollonios who, unlike his brother, had advanced beyond printing to joined-up writing, copied out sixteen lines of Euripides' tragedy *Telephos*, whose hero was a Greek king ruling far from home among the barbarians; at the bottom of this he wrote 'Apollonios the Macedonian . . . the Macedonian, I say' (Lewis 1986: ch. 5; Thompson 1988: ch. 7). The vocabulary of the Greek of the papyri also illustrates the way in which the speakers of Greek kept their culture distinct from that of the Egyptians; one papyrologist has written that 'except for place-names, measures, etc. no native Egyptian word made its way in one thousand years into the Greek that was used in Egypt' (Lewis 1986: 154–5). It seems natural to compare these Greeks, insisting on their Greekness in an alien environment, with the Jewish diaspora. It was, however, a relatively isolated phenomenon, in this case dependent on the very unusual conditions in Egypt. Elsewhere, the wide spread of the hellenistic *polis* provided a context in which a thoroughly Greek life could be lived. In Egypt this did not happen, and away from Alexandria and those areas (like the Fayoum) which were heavily populated by Greek settlers, the life of the local community, including their language and their religious traditions, remained wholly alien. There was a strong resistance among Greeks to assimilating themselves with 'barbarians'.

On the other hand, among the native subjects of the Macedonian dynasties there must have been widespread zeal (or at any rate perceived necessity) for learning Greek and adopting Greek ways. Although there is no evidence of any great enthusiasm for the Greek way of life among the mass of the population (and some for actual hostility, see Green 1990: ch. 19), there were obviously practical reasons for the ambitious to acquire a degree of hellenisation. For one thing, to deal successfully with the new rulers, to win favours from them, it would be a great advantage to be able to talk directly to them and not appear uncivilised and offensively barbarian in their eyes. That rulers could experience and express cultural and racial prejudice against subjects whose way of life seemed alien is shown by the words of the Roman emperor Caracalla (AD 211–17) during a visit to Alexandria: 'the true Egyptians can easily be perceived . . . to have alien accents, appearance, and dress; furthermore, in their way of life customs which are the very opposite of civilised behaviour show them to be Egyptian rustics' (Hunt and Edgar 1932–4: II, no. 215). In the second place, the prestige conferred by Alexander's sudden and overwhelming military success must have inspired imitation of the way of life of the victors, just as similar Western victories did in non-Western parts of the world in the nineteenth century. Then there is the ever-powerful tug of fashion, the desire to 'keep up with the Joneses next door'. Something of this kind is expressed in the words put into the mouths of the Jewish hellenisers of the early second century BC by the author of 1 Maccabees (1, 11, RSV): 'Let us go and make a covenant with the Gentiles round about us, for since we separated from them many evils are come upon us.' Finally, the intrinsic attractiveness of classical Greek art, literature and philosophy should not be discounted. There was after all one native aristocracy which never experienced Macedonian or Greek conquest, but themselves directed successful campaigns of conquest in the hellenistic world – that of Rome. Yet in the second and first centuries BC a passion for things Greek became the prevailing fashion among the Roman ruling class. 'Captive Greece took captive her savage conqueror' (Horace, *Epistles* 2, 1, 156).

Hellenisation affected people both as individuals and as members of communities. As individuals the simplest and most public step they could take to display their aspirations was to adopt Greek names and/or give their children Greek names. The 'or' option is illustrated by a list of benefactors of the Galatian Federation inscribed on the Temple of Augustus at Ankara early in the first century AD: men with Celtic names such as Gaizodiastes and Albiorix, himself the son of Ateporix, had given their sons the Greek names of Amyntas and Aristokles (*OGIS* II, no. 533, lines 24, 27, 64). The New Testament reveals a world where Jews were known by Hebrew/Aramaic, Greek or Latin names, or by different combinations. So Saul of Tarsus uses a Latin form, Paul, of his Hebrew name, Saul, which is sometimes given to us in a transliteration of the Hebrew form (*Saoul*, e.g. Acts 9, 5) but more often in a hellenised form equipped with standard Greek case-endings (*Saulos*, e.g. Acts 9, 1). Simon Peter has a curiously complex set of names: his original name, which is given as Simon (Mark 3, 16), is the closest Greek equivalent to the Hebrew Symeon; to that was added another name, usually given in its Greek form Petros (= 'rock'), presumably a translation of the Aramaic Kephas, which is how Paul usually refers to him (e.g. Galatians 1, 18). In the papyri from Egypt one finds families descended from mixed marriages (usually native wife and immigrant Greek husband) whose members had two sets of names, Greek and Egyptian. The standard formula in Greek was *A hos kai B* , 'A who is also B' (Lewis 1986: 4, 95, 102).

Perhaps the most startling case of the adoption of Greek names, given the exclusiveness of Judaism, is that of the high priests at Jerusalem. Onias III, deposed in 175 BC by King Antiochos IV, has his Hebrew name (? = Honi) transliterated, but the brother who displaced him and launched a hellenising reform bore the name of a hero of Greek legend, Jason, chosen presumably because it shared two consonants with his original name Jeshua (= Joshua; more usually transliterated in Greek and Latin as Jesus, see Josephus,

Ant. 12, 239); so did the man who got Antiochos to put him in
Jason's place, Menelaos; his successor, who was called Alkimos
(Greek = 'brave, stout'), is said also to have had a Hebrew name,
Joachim (Josephus, *Ant.* 12, 286). The next high priests were the
brothers of the leader of the resistance to hellenism, Judas
Maccabaeus, who like him had Hebrew names, Jonathan and
Simon. But Simon's grandsons, who combined the high priesthood
with the kingship, had Greek names, Aristobulos and Alexander, in
addition to the Hebrew names Judah and Jonathan. That the great-
nephews of Judas Maccabaeus should adopt Greek names is a sign of
the attractiveness of hellenism. The papyri make it possible to see
what happened to the Jewish immigrants in Egypt and their
descendants. Although names such as Simon, Joseph and Samuel
remained in use, Greek names also became popular, especially royal
ones such as Alexander and Ptolemy (compare the vogue for the
name Albert in later nineteenth-century Britain). In the Semitic
languages theophoric names (i.e. those which included the names of
a god or goddess) were common, and these were often translated
into Greek (e.g. Apollodoros, Athenodoros, Isidoros = gifts of
Apollo, Athena, Isis). Strict Jews, with their horror of foreign gods,
preferred to use the abstract Greek root for god, *theos* – hence
Theodoros, Dositheos, etc. But the papyri show that in due course
even Jews were prepared to give their children names such as
Isidoros (Tcherikover *et al.* 1957–64: I, 27–8).

The next and the most essential step was to learn how to speak,
and if possible to read, the Greek language. The immigration of
Greeks into the territories of the old Persian Empire as mercenaries
and settlers (Greeks who themselves were notoriously reluctant to
learn 'barbarian' tongues) provided the source of knowledge. The
spread of monoglot Greek-speakers has been illuminated by discoveries in modern Afghanistan, a region where Alexander had forcibly
settled the mercenaries of Dareios III in new Greek cities: two
inscriptions carry Greek versions of the expositions of Buddhist
teaching by the Maurya emperor Asoka, ruler of the greater part of
the Indian peninsula in the third century BC (translations of these
documents are to be found in Burstein 1985: no. 50).

How someone with no knowledge of Greek could acquire the
language is not entirely clear. Once hellenisation was fully established, presumably there would be widespread bilingualism, at any
rate in major urban centres, and a knowledge of Greek would
simply be picked up along with the local language. The process of

intermarriage would also eventually produce a group of people fluent both in Greek and in the local language. In the early stages of the progress of hellenisation, no doubt crude 'market Greek' for practical purposes could be learned fairly easily by trial and error, but we have no knowledge of how one could go about learning the language seriously as a beginner. The Greeks themselves had no interest in learning foreign languages (not even, with a couple of exceptions, Latin), and so Greek sources do not tell us how language was taught to beginners. Later, of course, Romans did learn Greek. Well-off families had their children taught the language by the simple expedient of having them brought up by Greek-speaking slaves (Marrou 1956: 262), and indeed Quintilian warned (*Inst. Or.* 1, 1, 12–18) that if they concentrated on Greek too exclusively and too early in their lives they might end up speaking Latin like foreigners. Families of more modest means had their children taught Greek at school. St Augustine clearly had unhappy memories of the process, and tells us: 'The difficulty of learning a foreign language tainted as if with bile the sweetness of Greek literature; for I knew none of the words and was constantly and violently forced to learn them with cruel threats and punishments' (*Confessions* 1, 14). Some textbooks for teaching Latin to Greeks survive, consisting mostly of vocabulary lists, useful phrases in both languages, and little dialogues with parallel texts in Greek and Latin. Some translation exercises also survive on papyrus (Marrou 1956: 263–4). Methods, then, seem to have been fairly crude and were applied, as was usual in ancient education, with considerable brutality – which did not, however, prevent people complaining that discipline was not what it used to be: 'These days the boys just play around at school' (Petronius, *Sat.* 4, 1). Teaching methods are unlikely to have been more sophisticated in the newly hellenised east.

The spread of the Greek language among people who were not of Greek ancestry is illustrated by one of the fundamental features of Paul's world, the existence and the widespread use in the Jewish diaspora of a Greek translation of the Hebrew scriptures, the so-called Septuagint. This title, 'Seventy', (*septuaginta* = 'seventy' in Latin) derives from a legend written up by a Jewish author passing himself off as a Greek courtier of Ptolemy II (Aristeas); he describes how seventy-two Jewish elders were summoned to Alexandria by the king and in seventy-two days produced a translation of the five books of Moses. Although the details are clearly fictitious it is probable that the translation of the Pentateuch was produced in Alexandria in the middle of the third century BC (Fraser 1972: II, 960–1; Bickerman 1980: II, 355–8; Schürer 1973–87: III (1), 474ff.). Although only the Pentateuch, or the books of Moses, was universally regarded as authoritative by all Jews, a number of other works (the 'Prophets' and the 'Writings') came to be associated with it, and to acquire a similar (though secondary) degree of authority and sanctity. By the time of Josephus (*Against Apion* 1, 8, 38–41), twenty-two canonical books (very likely those regarded as canonical today) had already been identified; the position was formalised at the end of the first century AD (Schürer 1973–87: II, 316–21). The existence of the Greek translation of the Pentateuch must have inspired others to translate these books of the Hebrew scriptures (as well as other Hebrew works) during the later third and second centuries BC. One can be dated precisely: a preface to the Greek version of Ecclesiasticus records that the translation was produced in Egypt after 117 BC by Jesus ben-Eleazer, the grandson of the author Jesus ben-Sira (Eissfeldt 1965: 597; Schürer 1973–87: III (1), 477). (The Hebrew original was lost until fragments covering about two-thirds were discovered in Cairo a century ago; it is a work which in the end was not included in the Jewish canon.)

Though subsequently the Septuagint translation came to be regarded as the standard (and authoritative) all-purpose Greek version not only for diaspora Judaism but also for the Christian church, we have no information on the translators' primary goal. Was their version intended for liturgical use (i.e. for reading in the synagogue, though the practice of systematic readings from the scriptures at synagogue services seems to have developed rather later than the accepted date for the translation of the Pentateuch (Bickerman 1988: 102)), for private study as a 'crib' to the Hebrew text, or for educational purposes? In the absence of such information it is not possible to assess how well the translators succeeded in their aim. The translations of the books of the Bible are clearly by different hands, and there is little consistency either in practice or in quality. As is natural when handling a sacred text, the translators err on the side of literalness, sometimes at the cost of comprehensibility in Greek. The meaning of some Greek words is expanded so that they can act as 'labels' for Hebrew words. So, the Greek word *doxa* (= opinion, fame, glory) is used to translate various Hebrew expressions conveying the presence of God conferring an outward magnificence, or a perceptible effulgence, a usage which would be quite incomprehensible to any Greek-speaker who was not a Jew (e.g. Exodus 16, 10; cf. also Acts 22, 11). Hebrew idioms are sometimes translated literally with phrases which make little sense in Greek. One of the best examples of this is found at Numbers 9, 10, where the Hebrew expression for 'anyone', *'ish 'ish* (= 'man man'), is translated literally into Greek as *anthrōpos anthrōpos*, a phrase as bizarre in Greek as its equivalent is in English. More commonly, the Hebrew interjection *hinne* is regularly translated by the Greek imperative *idou*, and sentences often begin with the Greek *kai egeneto* ('and it came to pass') which is simply a translation of a common Hebrew phrase used more or less as a conjunction. These and other instances of Hebrew linguistic practices influencing the Greek of the Septuagint (though the precise position of the borderline between 'Hebraisms' and the influence of, for instance, colloquial Greek remains a matter of controversy) give it a characteristic flavour which affects not only other Jewish writers but also the writers of the New Testament and later Christian works, who adopted its usages as a way of conveying in their writings a sense of sanctity and authority. A similar influence can be observed in English religious literature, which used to adopt the literal translations of the same idioms in the Authorised Version of the Bible as an appropriate way of signalling piety, seriousness and religious dignity.

More interesting from the point of view of hellenisation and the interaction between Greek and non-Greek communities are those passages where the translators depart from the obvious meaning of the Hebrew in order to adapt their texts to the new hellenistic world. In some cases it is simply a question of political expediency (or prudence). For example, the Hebrew word *melek* ('king') is usually translated by its normal Greek equivalent *basileus*, which was also the title of the Ptolemies as rulers of Egypt. There are, however, some passages in the Bible which are highly critical of the notion of foreign kings (e.g. Deuteronomy 17, 15: 'One from among your brethren you shall set as king over you; you may not put a foreigner over you'), or which might be interpreted as unflattering comments on the regime under which the Jews were living in Egypt (e.g. Deuteronomy 28, 36–7: 'The Lord will bring you, and your king whom you set over you, to a nation that neither you nor your fathers have known; and there you shall serve other gods, of wood and stone. And you shall become a horror, a proverb, and a byword, among all the peoples where the Lord will lead you away').

In these cases the translators play safe and use the neutral word *archōn* ('ruler') to translate *melek* (and indeed in the second case they take the further precaution of translating as a plural, 'rulers'). Another example of this kind of caution, or tact, is found at Leviticus 11, 5 and Deuteronomy 14, 7, where the hare is listed among unclean animals. The usual Greek word for hare is *lagōs*. Unfortunately Lagos was the name of the father of the first King Ptolemy, so the translators use instead the rare poetic word *dasypous* (literally = 'hairy-foot'). Sometimes phrases which look obscure or grotesque when rendered literally into Greek are interpreted rather than translated. So the phrase 'circumcise therefore the foreskin of your heart' (Deuteronomy 10, 16) becomes instead 'circumcise your hardheartedness'. Some translators tried to avoid expressions which seem to imply an anthropomorphic view of God. So 'the hand of the Lord' (Joshua 4, 24) becomes 'the power of the Lord'. In addition to these presumably deliberate changes, the use of Greek legal and governmental terms in translating Hebrew words places the translation firmly in the hellenistic world. (Schürer 1973–87: III (1), 478–9; Bickerman 1988: 106–16; Bickerman 1976: I, 167–200; Orlinsky 1989: 548–51).

The dependence of the diaspora communities (outside the Aramaic-speaking areas) on the Septuagint indicates that the vast majority of the Jews of the Roman Empire outside Palestine were monoglot Greek-speakers by the first century. Even very learned and devout Jews may not have been able to read the original Hebrew; it is remarkable that modern scholars cannot agree whether Philo of Alexandria (died after AD 41), who produced a very large body of scriptural interpretation in Greek, actually knew any Hebrew at all (Schürer 1973–87: III (1), 479; III (2), 873–4).

It should be emphasised that although there were Jews whose espousal of hellenism went so far as to compromise their Jewishness, this was by no means inevitable, and that there were many Jews, Greek-speaking and living in a hellenistic environment, who were nevertheless fully Jewish. Paul of Tarsus is a good example of such an individual. He was a citizen of a Greek city – indeed, a centre of Greek culture – Tarsus. He moves with confidence in the Greek world; nowhere in Acts or in his letters is there any suggestion that he looks out of place or 'foreign'. He not only writes Greek, he writes in a style which is fluent, powerful and accomplished. If anything, it is his Palestinian credentials which need to be asserted: he addresses the Jerusalem crowd in (presumably) Aramaic (Acts

21, 40), and assures them that he is a pious Jew both by upbringing ('... brought up in this city at the feet of Gamaliel, educated according to the strict manner of the law of our fathers': Acts 22, 3) and by family background ('I am a Pharisee, a son of Pharisees': Acts 23, 6). Though there is no reason to suppose that Paul could not read Hebrew well, when he quotes the Bible it is usually in the Septuagint version. The Hellenists of Acts (introduced and distinguished from the 'Hebrews' at 6, 1) are presumably people of the same kind. There is no suggestion that their Jewishness is in question. They will have been distinguished from the 'Hebrews' by the facts that their primary language was Greek rather than Hebrew or Aramaic, and that their Bible was the Septuagint. It is certainly the Hellenists who lead the way in spreading Christianity first in Palestine (Stephen, Acts 6, 8–10; Philip, Acts 8, 4–13) and later, after their dispersion as a result of persecution in Palestine, in the hellenistic world (Acts 11, 19). Having a foot in both the Palestinian and the hellenistic worlds, they played a crucial part in starting the transformation of Christianity from a Jewish sect to a world religion.

Learning to speak, and to read and write, everyday Greek in order to fit into the life of a Greek-speaking community such as Alexandria or to communicate with royal officials or to deal with traders was one thing; acquiring the skill to write and speak correct and polished 'classicising' Greek prose was another. For the everyday Greek which served as the *lingua franca* of the hellenistic world and the Greek of the Septuagint and the New Testament were very different in vocabulary and syntax from the Greek used in the formal writings and speeches of the highly educated.

By the fourth century BC Attic Greek (the dialect of Athens and its hinterland) was beginning, partly because of the prestige of Athenian writers, to be used as a sort of international Greek dialect. For instance, a decision of the league established by the Thebans following their victory in the battle of Mantinea in 362, recorded in an inscription set up in Argos (where the Doric dialect was spoken), was written in Attic Greek, though the Athenians were not in any sense leaders of the league, having been on the losing side at Mantinea (*IG* 4.556; Cartledge and Spawforth 1989: 8). Though local dialects of Greek undoubtedly survived, Attic Greek rapidly became the standard literary dialect. (There were some exceptions: Doric Greek, for example, was always used for pastoral poetry, and the mathematician Archimedes wrote his treatises in the same dialect).

Inevitably, as hellenisation spread into regions where Greek had not traditionally been spoken, it was Attic Greek which was used and taught. The Greek of the hellenistic world, however, developed in ways which made it significantly different from classical Attic; it is usually called *koinē* Greek, a modern term derived from the Greek *koinē dialektos*, 'common language'. *Koinē* Greek added to its Attic base influences from a number of other Greek dialects, and indeed from non-Greek languages. Forms peculiar to Attic were lost, and there was a general process of simplification. Athematic verbs ('*–mi*' verbs) lost ground to thematic verbs ('*–ō*' verbs); weak aorist endings tended to replace strong aorists; anomalous forms were eliminated in favour of more regular forms; diminutives tended to be favoured. The optative mood, a distinctive feature of classical Greek, becomes less and less popular – in the books of the New Testament, only Luke and Acts use it with any frequency, with twenty-eight occurrences (of which eleven are the present optative of the verb 'to be', *eiē*); Paul has thirty-one, but fourteen of them are in the set phrase *mē genoito*, 'may it not be', and all of them are third-person except the first-person *onaimēn* in the carefully composed letter to Philemon (Philemon 20).

The principal documents surviving in *koinē* are the Septuagint translation of the Old Testament, the New Testament and other early Christian writings, a few literary texts (e.g. the works of Epiktetos), and a vast body of papyrus letters and other writings which survive from Egypt. Given the wide currency of the language, it is remarkably consistent, but inevitably there are variations. The language of the Septuagint, for example, is strongly influenced by the speech patterns of the Hebrew which it is translating. These in turn colour the Greek of the New Testament and other Christian writings, which may also be influenced by the Aramaic which the earliest Christians probably spoke. Clearly a semi-literate Egyptian writing a note to his family uses a less formal (and often less grammatical) style than a philosopher like Epiktetos. In the New Testament itself, there are distinct variations: Luke and Acts are in a careful Greek which uses a wide vocabulary; Paul's letters are vigorous and sometimes quite elegant; Revelation is written in a Greek so eccentric that it has sometimes been speculated that the author had a very imperfect knowledge of the language. In the narrative of the healing of the paralytic in the synoptic gospels, when the sick man is lowered through the hole in the roof, in Mark (2, 4) his bed is a *krabbatos* (a word borrowed by *koinē* Greek from the Latin *grabbatus*), in Luke (5, 19) it is a *klinidion*, a characteristic hellenistic diminutive form, while Matthew, telling a similar story (9, 2), uses the classical form *klinē*. Some of these variations may be simply personal, dependent on the taste or capacity of the author, but it is also clear that writers of *koinē* could operate within a range of linguistic registers, which approached or diverged from the classical 'norm' depending on how stylish they wished to be. Thus in the second century AD Arrian, writing up the lectures of his teacher Epiktetos, puts them into a decent *koinē* which is quite close to the language of Paul, but the preface to the work, in which Arrian speaks in his own right, is, like the rest of his works, in an extreme Atticising style. Likewise, in Acts, when Paul makes his defence before Agrippa, he is made to speak in a formal style which uses Attic forms (for example, *isasi* 26, 4; *akribestatēn* 26, 5) not found elsewhere in Acts. (For more detailed accounts of *koinē* Greek see Browning 1969: 27–58 and Blass and Debrunner 1961: 1–6.)

Ironically, at about the same time that the New Testament was being written, a new literary movement was gathering strength which by the middle of the second century had revived the Attic Greek of the fourth and fifth centuries BC (as found in a handful of favoured authors), and established it as the only respectable medium for literary composition. Literary *koinē* ceased to exist, and the writings of early Christians came to be regarded, with contempt, as semi-literate. The implications of this both for the future development of Christian culture and for the survival of pagan literature (which was preserved in part for use as school textbooks, since Christian writings were not in a Greek style thought suitable for imitation by schoolboys) are considerable, but beyond the scope of this book. It is enough here to stress the point that, at the time they were written, the books of the New Testament were, despite the obvious influence of the Hebrew Bible, within the linguistic mainstream.

The difficulties involved in making the advance from the straightforward *koinē* to the sort of Atticising style which was necessary for more formal literary compositions are revealed in comments by another Jew who produced voluminous works in Greek, Flavius Josephus (born AD 37/8, died by 100). Josephus was born and brought up in an eminent priestly family in Jerusalem in the middle of the first century, not therefore in a Greek-speaking milieu. However, given his high status he may well have acquired a basic knowledge of Greek when a young man (thus Rajak 1983: ch. 2) although he was still conscious until late in life that his pronunciation was defective (*Ant.* 20, 263). After the Roman capture of Jerusalem in AD 70 he began his first work in Greek aimed at an educated Gentile public, the *Jewish War*, for which he had to 'make use of certain fellow-workers in respect of the Greek tongue'; presumably they had to weed out any unclassical or unidiomatic constructions (1, 50; Rajak 1983: App. 2) – compare similar acknowledgements in the prefaces to books in English written by exiled European scholars in recent decades. By the time he wrote *Antiquities of the Jews*, although he refers to hesitation and delay in presenting the subject 'in a foreign and strange language' (*Ant.* 1, 7), he emphasises his efforts to acquire some knowledge of Greek literature and poetry (*Ant.* 20, 283), the necessary basis for writing in a polished style, and makes no mention of 'fellow-workers'.

Josephus and Philo were following in a tradition reaching back to the third century BC in going beyond the mere translation of the Hebrew scriptures, and not only using more polished Greek but also recasting Jewish traditions in literary forms familiar to, indeed the only ones acceptable to, readers steeped in a knowledge of the Greek classics. So Philo wrote what we might now call a 'fictionalised biography' of Moses, in which he not only presents him as a hellenistic philosopher and law-giver, but also gives much of the credit for his education to Greeks (e.g. *On the Life of Moses* 1, 21: 'other [teachers] were invited from Greece with the promise of great rewards'; 1, 23: 'Greeks gave him his general education') though he can hardly have been unaware that the traditional dates for Moses placed him long before the beginnings of the development of Greek civilisation. Some Jews even had recourse to Greek verse. Fragments have been preserved of two narrative epics in hexameter verse in the tradition of Homer. One (by a different Philo) dealt with the Jewish Patriarchs while the other, on the history of Shechem, is by one Theodotos, who is held by some scholars to have been a Samaritan (Schürer 1973–87: III (1), 559–62). Substantial excerpts are preserved of a tragedy in the manner of Euripides, the *Exagōgē* of Ezekiel, dealing with events in the life of Moses (Jacobson 1983). Moses was also the main subject of a prose work entitled *About the Jews* by Artapanos, best characterised as a 'historical romance' (Schürer 1973–87: III (2), 521); in it Moses is identified with a figure of Greek legend, Mousaios, and is also claimed as the founder of Egyptian religious institutions. Could we be certain that such writings were intended by their authors to be read primarily by Jews (or Samaritans), it would suggest that the attractions of classical Greek literature were such that 'unclassical' Jewish scriptures, even in Greek translation, seemed rebarbative to educated diaspora Jews, and that to keep them loyal to their ancestral traditions those traditions needed to be recast in Hellenic literary genres. Perhaps we can see something of the kind happening with Josephus' retelling in *Antiquities of the Jews* of the Jewish history recounted in the Bible in a form closer to that of Greek historians, or Philo's hellenised biographies of Abraham, Joseph and Moses, and his writings on the Bible in a form reminiscent of a commentary on a philosophical text.

Given the spectacular way in which Greek culture permeated Rome, so that not only was all Latin literature strongly influenced by Greek literature, but many educated Romans also chose to write in Greek rather than Latin, one would expect to see a good number of non-Greeks in the East, where they were in much closer contact with Greek culture, acquiring proficiency in Greek literary forms. Unfortunately, firm evidence is hard to find and, though a good many literary figures came from non-Greek areas, it is usually impossible to decide for certain whether they are hellenised natives or the descendants of Greek incomers. For example, the city of Gadara in the Dekapolis seems to have had a flourishing Greek culture: in the third century BC Menippus the Cynic was very influential as an early writer of satire; Meleager (second to first centuries BC) was a famous writer of epigrams, about 130 of which are included in the *Greek Anthology*; Philodemus (first century BC) was an Epicurean poet and literary critic, who lived on the Bay of Naples and strongly influenced many Roman poets; Oenomaus (second century AD) was a Cynic philosopher and author of a number of works (which survive only in fragments). Of all these, however, only Meleager shows any sign of contact with the local, Semitic, culture of Gadara's hinterland:

> My nurse was Tyre, but my native land is Attic Gadara among the Syrians . . . . If I am a Syrian, what is surprising about it? We live in the same world, and that is our native land, stranger. The same Chaos brought forth all mortals.
>
> (*Greek Anthology* 7, 417)

Walk softly, stranger. For an old man, Meleager son of

Eucrates, lies among the righteous, sleeping the sleep we all
must sleep . . . . He was a son of Tyre, child of the gods, and of
the sacred land of Gadara. Lovely Meropian Kos cared for him
in old age. If you are a Syrian, *Salam!* If you are a Phoenician,
Naidios! If you are a Greek, *Chaire!*

(*Greek Anthology* 7, 419)

Yet even in Meleager's case we cannot be sure that he is not simply
making local references for the sake of a little exotic colour. The
same may be true of the second-century AD Lucian of Samosata and
Iamblichus, author of the fragmentary novel *Babyloniaca* (for references and discussion, see Swain 1996: 298–308), both of whom
claim non-Greek origins, since the biographical details they give are
manifestly fictionalised, while the novelist Heliodorus' claim to be
'a Phoenician from the city of Emesa' is no easier to interpret. In the
field of philosophy, it is often claimed that Zeno, the founder of the
Stoic school, was a Phoenician, but there seems to be no grounds for
this apart from his father's name, Mneseas (which was often used by
Phoenicians), the fact that he was born in Kition in Cyprus (a city
where there were a lot of Phoenicians), and a good deal of rather
wishful searching for alleged 'Semitic influences' in Stoicism. In any
case, given the long Greek presence in Cyprus, there is no reason to
suppose that Zeno was not Greek by culture. A more intriguing
case is that of Kleitomachos (second century BC), Karneades'
successor as the head of the school founded by Plato, the Academy
in Athens. According to Diogenes Laertius (*Lives of the Philosophers*
4, 66) he was a Carthaginian with the Punic name Hasdrubal who,
besides his activities in Athens, wrote philosophical works in his
native language as well as in Greek. Carthage, of course, never came
under Greek control, so that this report, if accurate, is a striking
testimony to the potent attractions of Greek culture at this period.
It remains true, however, that although it seems very probable that
a good number of hellenistic and later Greek authors may not have
come from a native Greek cultural background, they are hard to
identify with any certainty.

This side of hellenistic culture, its literary expression, is, of
course, something which we think of as being accessible largely
through books, and so the question naturally arises of what proportion of the population was literate, and how many of those who
were literate were able to obtain and use books.

Literacy is not a straightforward concept. The ability to recognise letters, and to spell out a word, is relatively easy to acquire, and may well have been reasonably widespread (percentages may have been in double figures), but this is not the same as being able to read books or communicate in writing. These skills require not just education but, more importantly, constant practice. Though members of the cultivated élite certainly possessed books (and occasionally substantial libraries), they formed a very small proportion of the population. The vast majority would have been faced with a written document only very rarely in their lives. They therefore could not have developed the sort of fluency necessary to participate in a fully literate culture. One of the problems in assessing the general level of literacy is that much of the evidence comes from Egypt, where bureaucracy seems to have been more fully developed than elsewhere in the hellenistic world, and where papyrus must have been comparatively cheap (and where there is the additional complication that an individual who appears to be illiterate in Greek may actually not have spoken the language at all, but may well have been literate in his native Egyptian). Furthermore, the reuse of papyrus documents (as mummy-wrapping, for example) means that the place where it is found is not necessarily the place where it was used as writing (so that the discovery of papyrus bearing literary texts in villages and small towns does not necessarily tell us that such texts were read in these places). It is noteworthy that virtually nothing which could be described as popular literature (in the sense of undemanding works for a less well-educated readership) has been found; almost all that survives are fragments of standard literary texts (Harris 1989: 126). There is also widespread evidence of the use of scribes and professional writers and readers by those incapable of writing or reading on their own. If this is truly a reflection of general inability to handle writing, then it looks as if there are implications not only for the spread and significance of hellenistic literary culture, but also for the development of Judaism and Christianity, religions which have sacred books at their heart.

Paul himself, however, should warn us that the situation is more complex than it seems. It is clear that he did not normally write his letters himself (Galatians 6, 11; 2 Thessalonians 3, 17; Philemon 19) but used amanuenses (one of whom, Tertius, reveals himself at Romans 16, 22). His comment on his handwriting ('See with what large letters I am writing to you with my own hand': Galatians 6, 11) should not be taken as evidence that he had difficulty with writing himself. Quintilian (*Inst. Or.* 1, 28–9) deplores the bad handwriting of the educated classes, and this is borne out by evidence from Egypt where documents in neat handwriting produced by professionals (perhaps slaves) have had a couple of lines added by their masters, in a barely legible scrawl (Harris 1989: 249). It was not only the illiterate who had others do their writing for them. The same is true of reading. In most cases, a document would not be read privately by an individual, but would be read aloud to him, even if he could read himself. Similarly, most literature was designed to be heard rather than read. Even the completely illiterate would be able to enjoy dramatic performances in the theatre or public displays by visiting rhetoricians. Illiteracy (or lack of fluency with the written word) would have been no barrier to participation, at least to some degree, in literary culture. Even manifestly illiterate Egyptians seemed to handle their paperwork with relative ease, by using relatives, friends and professionals (Harris 1989: 34–5). Though Paul could clearly both read and write, had he not been able to do so his activities would hardly have been affected, and in those churches which received his letters a single literate member would have been all that was needed to communicate them to the whole group.

Having said this, however, there can be little doubt that the ability to read and become familiar with the standard works of the classical authors was regarded as one of the defining characteristics of the élite class. It can therefore be taken for granted that all men of the highest social class were literate. The question is how far down the social scale literacy went, and here the provision of schools is crucially important. The very rich no doubt made their own arrangements for educating their children through private tutors, but the rest depended on some sort of school system (which means that out in the countryside, where no school was available, literacy may not have been an option for the majority). There is some evidence that the hellenistic period saw an expansion of public provision for education, either through private benefactions or civic initiatives (Harris 1989: 130–7). So at the beginning of the second century BC a citizen of Miletos called Eudemos gave a sum of money to provide four teachers for his city, and there are indications of similar donations elsewhere. At Teos in the late third century one Polythrous made generous provision not only for the education of all free boys in the city, but also for girls (three teachers). The account we have given so far treats literacy as an essentially male attribute, and this is probably realistic since there seem to have been many more literate men than women (Harris 1989: 136–7, 279–80). There is, however, evidence of the formal provision of education for girls elsewhere in the Greek world, and later in the Roman Empire (Harris 1989: 239–40). In aristocratic families, of course, women would almost certainly be literate, and might be highly educated (Harris 1989: 252–3). Thus Plutarch tells us that Cornelia, the wife of Pompeius, 'was well versed in literature, lyre-playing, and geometry, and she used to benefit from listening to philosophical treatises' (*Life of Pompey* 55, 1).

It has been argued (Harris 1989: 244–6) that the level of literacy may actually have declined under Roman rule, on the grounds that the only record from that period of a benefaction for the provision of education (for both boys and girls) is recorded in an inscription of the mid-second century found in Xanthos in Lycia, telling of a gift by a very prominent and wealthy man, Opramoas. Whether or not this is true, there is no reason to believe that literacy actually became more common under the Romans.

The availability of books for those who were literate was, by modern standards, very limited. Though there was a book trade (and bookshops began to become more common in the first century AD), it was very limited (Starr 1987: 219–20; Easterling 1985: 19–21) and a book might not necessarily be published as we understand the term in the sense of handing over a work to professionals for reproduction and distribution (that this could happen is shown by, for instance, Pliny, *Letters* 1, 2, 5 and 6). Normally, a work would first be read in a private recital to the author's friends, to whom he or she might subsequently send copies. From these further copies might be made, and it was in this way, by privately made copies, that a book would be disseminated. There were a very few public libraries, in which authors could (if they chose) deposit copies of their work, from which further copies might be taken. School-books were usually created by the teacher dictating the text to his pupils (Starr 1987: 213–16, 220). It seems, then, that the process by which works like Paul's letters were disseminated was much closer to the normal method of 'publication' for literary works than we might imagine. Presumably the letters were initially sent to the communities to which they were addressed, and read out there; those individuals who wanted copies would take them, and further copies would be spread to Christians elsewhere either on request or as gifts from friends who had them. This is almost exactly what would have happened with most literary works. We may presume that other Christian writings (like the gospels) were passed around in much the same way. The book trade would become involved only when it was a question of producing luxury editions (Easterling 1985: 21–2).

There is no reason to believe that Jews and Christians were more likely to be able to read or write effectively than people in general, with the exception that the existence of sacred texts which had to be expounded and interpreted made necessary the creation of new classes of literate experts (scribes, pharisees, bishops, readers). For the majority in both communities, however, the texts would be something they heard rather than read.

One change which is noticeable (or at any rate apparent) in the hellenistic period is the greater visibility of women (Pomeroy 1975: 120–1). It may be, of course, that no real change did take place, and what we see is simply the result of a wider range of evidence becoming available. A high proportion of the evidence for the classical period relates to Athens, where the position of women may have been particularly poor, and the prevailing ideology will have played down the rôle of women who may, by choice or by force of circumstances, have taken part in activities more public than conventional views thought respectable – in trade or commerce, for example; market-women are sometimes mentioned. Also, the dynastic politics of the hellenistic rulers threw up a series of prominent and powerful royal women (culminating in the famous Kleopatra VII) about whom we consequently know a great deal, but who were certainly not typical. Nevertheless, we find a number of inscriptions of the hellenistic period recording honours given to women apparently in their own right. Many relate to priesthoods and other religious activities – a field in which women had traditionally a significant rôle – but we find others rewarding, for example, female poets and benefactors. Some of these honours appear to confer something like citizen rights (*politeia*), and in a couple of cases we hear of what may be female magistrates (for references see Pomeroy 1975: 125–6). Though this may reveal a marked improvement in women's status, it may also reflect a tendency for civic offices to become honorific, together perhaps with an improvement in the status of all members of élite families in comparison with the population in general. There is, however, solid evidence that women were becoming more active in making financial decisions (Pomeroy 1975: 130). For example, about one-quarter of those listed in inscriptions at Delphi before 150 BC as freeing slaves are women. It is possible, then, that the extension of formal education to women noted above may be part of a pattern of modest but real improvement in their condition in at least some social classes. It has often been noted that in general women are conspicuous by their absence in Paul's world. Nonetheless, even here a few are named in their own right, independently of a husband or other male relative, like the purple-seller Lydia at Philippi (Acts 16, 14) and the mysterious Chloe, whose 'people' (1 Corinthians 1, 11) brought Paul the news of the quarrels in the church at Corinth. Perhaps such people had existed before, but it is in the hellenistic period that they first begin to become visible.

HELLENISTIC INSTITUTIONS

If we move from individuals to institutions, the one institution below the level of the fully fledged Greek city-state (*polis*) which all Greeks regarded as the most important symbol of the Hellenic way of life was the gymnasium, in which adolescent males were initiated into that way of life by undergoing athletic training. As we shall see (p. 105) running, boxing and wrestling competitions had been one of the main ways in which upper-class Greeks had sought to win glory in their communities. Greek emigrants in the Near East were anxious that their sons should receive the traditional athletic training; in the interior of Egypt, where the Ptolemies did not permit the creation of Greek *poleis* (except for one, Ptolemais), gymnasia founded by the immigrants multiplied, and those trained there must have come to form an unofficial élite – a status formally recognised by the Roman administration after 30 BC. Once again it is a Jewish writer who gives us the most detailed and vivid account of a gymnasium being founded by a non-Greek people (or at least its wealthy élite) anxious to become hellenised and show themselves civilised. In this case the evidence concerns not the diaspora but the priests at Jerusalem, and gives a unique picture of the process of (attempted) hellenisation from the viewpoint of those who disapproved of it. 1 Maccabees is very brief: 'So they built a gymnasium in Jerusalem, according to Gentile custom, and removed the marks of circumcision . . . ' (1, 14–15). 2 Maccabees (the epitomator of Jason of Cyrene) is, characteristically, more vivid:

For with alacrity he founded a gymnasium right under the

citadel, and he induced the noblest of the young men to wear the Greek hat. There was such an extreme of hellenisation and increase in the adoption of foreign ways because of the surpassing wickedness of Jason, who was ungodly and no high priest, that the priests were no longer intent upon their service at the altar. Despising the sanctuary and neglecting the sacrifices, they hastened to take part in the unlawful proceedings in the wrestling arena after the call to the discus, disdaining the honours prized by their fathers and putting the highest value upon Greek forms of prestige.

(2 Maccabees 4, 12–15)

Whether Jason and his associates secured King Antiochos' permission to turn Jerusalem into a fully fledged Greek *polis* is a debatable question; according to 2 Maccabees Jason sought the King's leave to establish a gymnasium and an ephebate (a body of adolescents undergoing athletic and military training) in it, and '*tous en Hierosolymois Antiocheis anagrapsai*' (2 Maccabees 4, 9). The RSV translation, 'to enrol the men of Jerusalem as citizens of Antioch', is baffling to the general reader – which Antioch? A more accurate version is probably 'to draw up a list of the Antiochenes at Jerusalem'. One plausible interpretation is that there was to be a new *polis* of the Greek type named Antioch after the king and distinguished from the many other Antiochs by the addition of 'in (or at) Jerusalem'. Not all the existing residents were to be full citizens, only those whom Jason and his associates thought fit to belong to their new 'civilised' state.

The other residents and the rural population of Judaea must have continued as an *ethnos* ('nation', 'tribe') under the authority of the high priests appointed by Antiochos. In the narratives of the events of the 160s it is with the high priests that the royal officers deal, and there are no references to the institutions of a *polis*, namely, archons, *boulē* and *ekklēsia* (see p. 111 below). Hence the other possible interpretation of the crucial phrase: the Antiochenes were to be 'a select club of progressive hellenisers', 'a Greek-style *politeuma* within the Jewish theocracy' (Green 1990: 509–10). In any case the ultimate success of the Jewish armed resistance to Antiochos' religious persecution put an end to 'Antiochenes in Jerusalem', whatever they may have been.

All over Western Asia from the west of Asia Minor as far east as Iran there were to be found by the first century BC numerous

Alexandrias, Antiochs, Seleukeias, Laodikeias, Stratonikeias, Apameias, and even an occasional Ptolemais or Berenike. Most of these cities, named in honour of kings or members of their families, were certainly equipped with the institutions of a Greek *polis*. What is debatable is how many were purely Greek foundations for settlers from the old Greek homeland and how many were native towns which had, with royal permission, adopted these institutions.

In the case of 'settler' *poleis* it is reasonable to assume that Greek exclusiveness would make it difficult for non-Greeks to get naturalised as citizens, though as resident aliens they might have access to some of the amenities, though probably not the ephebate and the gymnasium, if Green is right (Green 1990: 319). Yet the evidence of Paul's language is that diaspora Jews of the first century were acquainted with Greek athletics (see pp. 103–4; cf. Harris 1976). In some cases, however, like that of Cyrene, where it was by no means easy for a Jew to obtain citizenship (Applebaum 1979: 175–86), some Jews seem to have been prepared to make the compromises which would allow them to participate in the ephebate. A stele of the first century AD bearing an inscription listing ephebes includes several indubitably Jewish names (Applebaum 1979: 177) despite the fact that it is dedicated to the pagan gods Hermes and Herakles. There is also evidence of Jews in the gymnasium at Ptolemais in the first century BC (Applebaum 1979: 178)

The other great public spectacle in the *poleis* was drama. Ezekiel (see p. 55) shows that diaspora Jews were interested in it as a literary form; at the theatre of Miletos there was in the Roman period an area which was reserved for 'Jews who were also god-fearers', *topos Eioudeōn tōn kai Theosebeiōn* (see Schürer 1973–87: III (1), 167–8 for the problems, and for the suggestion that only Gentile god-fearers were concerned). Some non-Greek rulers acquired a taste for seeing Greek plays performed; one striking anecdote concerns the court of the Parthian king Orodes, where the severed head of the Roman general Crassus, defeated by a Parthian army, was delivered just in time to be used as a highly realistic stage prop in a performance of Euripides' *Bacchae* (Plutarch, *Crassus* 33, 1–4). A perhaps more reliable piece of evidence is a long inscription found in Athens in which King Ariarathes V of Cappadocia (163–130 BC) is honoured by the association of professional actors (*OGIS* I, no. 352).

One important difference between hellenism in its original homelands around the Aegean and hellenism in Western Asia is that in the latter case it was an almost wholly urban phenomenon. De Sainte Croix (1981: 9–19, 427–30) argued that the difference between *polis* (city-town) and *chōra* (countryside) was of enormous importance; in Asia the *poleis* were Greek-speaking islands in a sea of peasants who still used local vernaculars. Jesus' mission had been largely confined to the *chōra*, whereas Paul travelled from *polis* to *polis*, his only recorded trip into the countryside coming after the flight from Iconium to Lystra and Derbe, 'and to the surrounding country' (Acts 14, 6). Egypt, it should be noted, in this as in many other respects, was exceptional; in a sense Alexandria was the *polis* with the whole Delta and Nile Valley as its *chōra*, but Greek immigrants settled throughout the interior. By the first century in southern Syria and Palestine two chains of *poleis* extended from north to south. One ran along the coast: Berytos, Sidon, Tyre, Ptolemais (Acre), Caesarea (founded by Herod) and so on. The other was in the Rift Valley: Heliopolis, Chalkis and Cyrrhus in the Beqaa, and the 'Ten *Poleis*', or Dekapolis.

The hill country in between the coastal plain and the Jordan Valley, Galilee, Samaria, Judaea and Idumaea, had not been parcelled out into *polis* territories, apart from Sebaste, which was founded on the site of the town of Samaria by Herod and which, like Caesarea, was named in honour of Augustus (Greek *Sebastos*) but was administered directly by royal officials and later by the staff of the Roman Prefect. Jerusalem itself was an anomaly. It was a large town with a governing council and executive, but the executive officer was the high priest nominated for an indefinite period by the suzerain (king or Roman governor), not a body of archons elected and replaced annually. The Council (the 'Sanhedrin') which functioned as a religious court must also have seemed quite unlike a Greek *boulē*. Jerusalem cannot therefore really be categorised as a *polis*, with all Judaea as its territory; until the revolt of AD 66–70 the Jews of Judaea remained in Greek and Roman eyes an *ethnos*. The town's main *raison d'être* was to support the Temple and its elaborate cult. Such 'temple-states', in the sense of cities whose political and social life was dominated by the cult at a particular shrine, may not have been unusual in Syria and Asia Minor. For example, in the third century Elagabalus (218–22), a member of a prominent family from Emesa in the Orontes Valley, became emperor. The historian Herodian (5, 3, 3–6) tells us that he was a priest of the local god Elagabal, who was worshipped in the form of a black stone, and that he attempted to introduce the cult to Rome (to which we owe a description of its exotic practices). The interpretation of Herodian's account is not without its difficulties (Millar 1993: 300–9), but it is clear that this too was a city where the local ruling class was involved in, and devoted to, the cult of the local god. Similarly the cults of Jupiter at Heliopolis (modern Baalbek in Lebanon, see Millar 1993: 281–4; Hajjar 1990: 2458–508) and of Atargatis at Hierapolis in Syria (Millar 1993: 243–7) formed the centre of the local community and its identity.

Some of the 'cities' of the hellenistic age grew to a much greater size than even the largest of the *poleis* of classical Greece. These were the royal capitals of the Ptolemies and the Seleucids, Alexandria-next-to-Egypt, Antioch-on-the-Orontes and Seleukia-on-the-Tigris. This last was incorporated into the Parthian empire in the middle of the second century BC. Antioch and Alexandria continued to flourish as centres of Hellenic culture under Roman rule, and both –especially Alexandria – attracted large numbers of immigrants, including Jews. So did the one city of the Western world which outstripped them in population, Rome itself. A high proportion of these immigrants came from the eastern Mediterranean. Some came voluntarily, attracted by the vast wealth to be tapped at the capital of a conquering power, but the majority did not: vast numbers of prisoners of war were sold as slaves and shipped to Italy in the second and first centuries BC. Such slaves, if formally set free by a Roman owner, became Roman citizens (see pp. 140–1); as early as 131 BC a hostile crowd was attacked by Scipio Africanus the Younger as 'stepchildren of Italy' (Velleius Paterculus 2, 4, 4; Valerius Maximus 4, 2, 3; Plutarch, *Moralia* 201F; Pseudo-Victor *De Vir. Ill.* 58, 8). Many of these 'stepchildren' were Greek-speakers, and such did they and their descendants remain. For this reason Paul's letter to the early Christian community at Rome was written in Greek, and the early church at Rome remained mainly Greek for several generations. As late as the early third century, Hippolytus, living in Rome and composing a polemical work (the *Apostolic Tradition*) for a Roman readership, wrote in Greek. The earliest Latin Christian writer whose works are preserved is the North African Tertullian, who began to write at the end of the second century. Minucius Felix, who wrote the *Octavius* in Latin perhaps in the middle of the third century, may have been Roman, but is as likely to have been a North African imitator of Tertullian. The earliest undoubted examples of Christian Latin being written in Rome are the works of the sectary Novatian, who similarly wrote in the middle of the third century (Barnes 1971: 5–10, 192–4). The same was true of early churches further west, such as that at Lugdunum in Gaul – Lyons – whose bishop Irenaeus was still writing in Greek at the end of the second century; the account preserved by Eusebius of the martyrdoms there in 177 reveals a high proportion of Greek names among the martyrs, and specifically records that one of them, Sanctus, replied to his interrogators in Latin, leading us to assume that the others used Greek, the language of the account (Eusebius, *Ecclesiastical History* 5, 1, 20).

REACTIONS TO HELLENISATION

How much resentment of hellenism was there in the regions ruled by Alexander's successors, and how much active resistance? One needs to distinguish between rule and exploitation by alien rulers who happened to be Macedonian/Greek on the one hand, and the adoption of a Greek way of life on the other. There was much resentment of alien rule, and some active resistance, when that was possible, as in the case of the revolts of Upper Egypt at the end of the third century BC (see p. 43), though the Egyptians had been no more reconciled to the rule of the alien Persians than they were to the rule of the alien Macedonians/Greeks who replaced them. It is the papyrus evidence from Egypt which reveals the forms 'underground' resentment could take. Three papyrus texts preserve the Greek version of a work probably first written in Egyptian, known by modern scholars as *The Oracle of the Potter* (trans. Burstein 1985: no. 106). It takes the form of a prophecy wrapped up in obscure language ('apocalyptic') which purports to have been delivered to a native pharaoh in the distant past; it describes the wretched conditions of life of the native Egyptians but also predicts the downfall of the 'Girdlewearers' (i.e. the Greeks), the desertion of Alexandria and a new age of prosperity under a native pharaoh. A different form of consolation for subjection to alien rule was the exaggeration of the past achievements of the native kings. Herodotos, on his visit to Egypt in the middle of the fifth century BC, had been told of a great Egyptian conqueror named Sesostris (there had been three pharaohs named Senwosret) whose empire had covered the territories ruled by the Persians, as well as those of the Scythians who had defeated a Persian invasion. By around 300 BC the scale of Sesostris' conquests had been expanded to match that of Alexander's recent successes: the version recorded by Diodorus Siculus, who was probably using the account of Egypt produced by Hekataios of Abdera under Ptolemy I, has Sesostris' conquests extending as far as India (1, 53–5). A similar process of expansion affected the versions of their own past related by the Babylonians to Greek visitors (see Eddy 1961).

But of resistance to the adoption of the Greek way of life there is little evidence (with one notable exception). Unlike paying taxes to the kings, adopting a Greek way of life was purely voluntary and the hellenistic kings certainly did not actively propagate hellenism among the native population. Furthermore, it was generally the local élites, the natural leaders of any serious resistance movement, who took the lead in hellenisation, most notably the non-Greek dynasties in Bithynia, Pontus, Cappadocia and Commagene who succeeded in asserting political independence from the Macedonian rulers. There is one reported case of popular hostility to aspects of hellenisation: in the 170s BC some of the priestly aristocracy in Jerusalem opposed the building of a gymnasium and the practice of Greek athletics. However, the narratives of 1 and 2 Maccabees were not composed until after the subsequent events, which led to armed revolts by the Jews and which identified the hellenisers with a Seleucid king who had defiled the temple. In retrospect the actions of the hellenisers are fiercely denounced ('they joined with the Gentiles and sold themselves to do evil': 1 Maccabees 1, 15; 'they hastened to take part in the unlawful proceedings in the wrestling arena . . . disdaining the honours prized by their fathers': 2 Maccabees 4, 14–15), but there is no reference in either narrative to any public expression of hostility actually at the time. It was the use of Temple treasures to meet the financial demands of the king and his officers which led to the first demonstrations (2 Maccabees 4, 39–42). What provoked large-scale armed rebellion, led by Judas Maccabaeus, was Antiochos IV's institution in 167 BC of a cult of Olympian Zeus in the Temple at Jerusalem (2 Maccabees 6, 1–5, cf. 1 Maccabees 1, 54), his order that the population of Judaea must take part in pagan sacrifices, and his proscription of Jewish religious practices such as circumcision (1 Maccabees 1, 44–61; 2 Maccabees 6–10). Such an act of compulsory religious reform was unprecedented in Greek history, and Antiochos' motive is one of the great puzzles of hellenistic history. 1 Maccabees claimed that it was part of a policy to unify his empire, and one which was accepted in all other parts of it (1, 41–3), but there is no evidence from inscriptions or Greek sources to support this. Claims, based on some classical authors, that Antiochos was a megalomaniac who identified himself with the object of this cult can be discounted. E. J. Bickerman (Bickerman 1979) argued that it was the exclusiveness of Jewish religion which made the situation in Jerusalem different from that in any other part of the hellenistic world, that the innovations of the hellenisers had earned them the bitter hostility of devout traditional Jews, that the hellenisers feared that under one of Antiochos' successors the traditionalists might return to power and take revenge on them, and that therefore it was they who induced Antiochos to proscribe the traditional religion of the Jews. This brilliant and ingenious hypothesis has only one flaw, namely, the absence of any direct evidence which might confirm it. Speculation about Antiochos' motive will continue, but must be conducted in a void unless some unexpected piece of new evidence turns up. Whatever his original motive Antiochos was a highly pragmatic religious reformer: in 165, after initial successes by Judas' forces over royal troops, he granted toleration for Jews who wished to follow their traditional religion and offered an amnesty to the rebels. However, as the traditional cult in the Temple was not restored, the war went on. After another victory by Judas in 164 the Seleucid general referred his demands to the king, but he died before he could respond (November/December 164 BC). In December 164 Judas entered Jerusalem and purified the Temple; in 163 the Seleucid commander (in the name of the boy-king Antiochos V) accepted this change and made Alkimos high priest in place of Menelaos, who was executed. Judas continued fighting until his death in battle in 160, but it was a fight for national independence rather than religious freedom. Civil wars in the Seleucid kingdom enabled his brothers Jonathan and Simon to secure royal recognition as high priests, and eventually make Judaea *de facto* an independent state.

As in the case of Egypt, Jewish resistance to hellenisation found an expression in apocalyptic writing and in pseudo-history. The Book of Daniel (the final version of which can be dated to 167–164 BC) sets in the period of the Babylonian exile prophecies both of the tribulation to come under the Greek kings and also of a glorious triumph (Schürer 1973–87: III (1), 245–9; Ginsberg 1989: 504–23). And although Jewish writers could not credibly claim the kind of world conquests invented by imaginative Egyptians, both Daniel and Esther (Delcor 1989: 364–8) place Jews, quite unhistorically, in central rôles in allegedly momentous events in world history.

SUGGESTIONS FOR FURTHER READING

(full details of these works can be found in the Bibliography):

By far the best book on the hellenistic period is now P. Green's *From Alexander to Actium*, which can be strongly recommended.

For the encounter between the Jews and Greek culture we suggest E. J. Bickerman's *The Jews in the Greek Age*.

W. V. Harris' *Ancient Literacy* is a lively and well-documented discussion of all facets of the subject.

6

ROMAN RULE IN THE NEAR EAST

HISTORICAL OUTLINE

In the year 200 BC the descendants of Alexander's generals still divided much of his empire between them. In Greece and the Aegean Philip V of Macedon (221–179 BC) had been pursuing an aggressive policy of expansion for two decades. In Asia Antiochos III (223–187 BC), after being defeated in an attempt to wrest southern Syria and Palestine from Ptolemy IV in 217, had undertaken a lengthy eastern expedition to reassert his authority in eastern Iran and was about to crush the forces of the boy-king Ptolemy V (204–180 BC) and complete his occupation of Palestine. Ten years later the power of both Philip and Antiochos had been humbled by the arrival in the lands east of the Adriatic of a new empire from the west – Rome; just over thirty years later the sons of Philip and Antiochos had had to capitulate completely to Rome's demands, and it was Roman protection alone which had ensured the survival of the Ptolemies. In 202 Rome emerged completely victorious from the second of two long wars against the only other great power in the western Mediterranean, Carthage. That war had started badly for Rome when the Carthaginian general Hannibal invaded Italy and defeated Roman armies in three disastrous battles (218–16). It had cost Rome a great deal in manpower and resources to check Hannibal in Italy and eventually to invade North Africa and defeat him on his home ground. Yet instead of 'taking a breather' and contenting themselves with handling the problems they faced in the Po Valley and in Spain (from which Carthaginian forces had had to be evicted), the Romans sent an army east across the Adriatic in 200. True, they had a grudge against Philip V who had made an alliance with Hannibal and with whom they had been

71

at war – though not very actively – until 205. Yet this raises the question of the motives of Roman imperial expansion: in recent decades modern historians have argued about whether the main motive was a paranoiac fear of potential enemies on the part of the Roman ruling class, who therefore favoured 'pre-emptive strikes' against any power which could conceivably cause Rome trouble in the future, or simply greed for the profits of successful warfare on the part both of the individual politicians who also acted as generals and of ordinary Romans who served in the ranks of the legions.

The two motives are not exclusive. The collective wisdom of the Roman aristocracy as expressed by the Senate could determine what the potential dangers were against which preventative action needed to be taken at any particular time; if the 'offending' state refused to capitulate to Rome's demands, then an opportunity opened up to satisfy the desire of some individual political leaders for glory, and of all Romans for loot. But what there certainly was not was any sort of imperial 'master plan' for world conquest (see p. 6), and hence there was no clear conception of or policy on how to administer or exploit territories which came, formally or *de facto*, under Roman control.

The detailed story of the growth of Roman control over the countries round the eastern Mediterranean is too complicated to be recounted here. What is significant is that Rome was very slow to turn her military and diplomatic supremacy ('hegemony') into permanent occupation (and taxation) of territory. After Philip V's defeat in 197 he was required to evacuate all his possessions outside Macedonia proper. In 196 in a spectacular propaganda coup the Roman general Flamininus announced that all Greek cities – not only the ones Philip had surrendered – were to be free and self-governing; there were to be no Roman garrisons or tribute (but, as they would learn, the Greek cities would be expected to show 'gratitude' and 'respect' for the Roman 'liberator'). A 'cold war' with the Seleucid king Antiochos III ensued since he had claimed as his own, and occupied, some of Philip's possessions; it turned into a 'hot war' in 192–189. A Roman invasion of Asia Minor inflicted a decisive defeat on the Seleucid army, and Antiochos had not only to pay a huge war indemnity by instalments but also to surrender all his territory in Asia north-west of the Taurus Mountains. But the Roman army withdrew from Asia and the bulk of this territory (which was not organised in cities with a tradition of self-government) was handed over to a local dynasty to rule. This was the

Attalid dynasty which, from a base in Pergamon in north-west Asia Minor, had maintained a precarious independence of the Seleucids since 280. King Attalos I (241–197) had assiduously courted Roman favour and his son Eumenes II (197–160) reaped the reward.

In 171 the Senate decided that the new king of Macedonia, Philip's son Perseus, was being too successful and assertive, and forced a war on him. After the battle of Pydna in 168 Perseus and his family were deposed, but Rome still did not proceed to actual annexation. Instead, Macedonia was split up into four republics which were to be self-governing. (In Greek these were termed *merides*, 'divisions' of Macedonia, and one is referred to in Acts 16, 12, see Wallace and Williams 1993: 76–7). Roman diplomacy now made it plain that Rome was unwilling to let any king in the Near East exercise what, *in Rome's eyes*, was an unwarranted degree of independence. Such preventative diplomacy was the more necessary if Rome was to maintain hegemony without any permanent military presence east of the Adriatic. Antiochos IV (175–164; see pp. 68–9) had invaded and overrun Egypt and in the summer of 168 was besieging Ptolemy VI (who was actually his nephew) in Alexandria. A Roman ambassador, strengthened by the news of the fall of Macedonia, called on Antiochos to evacuate Egypt and drew a circle in the sand around the king, demanding his answer before he stepped out of the circle; Antiochos capitulated, and Rome never fought a second war with the Seleucids.

Rome was, of course, not without allies in the East. To those smaller states (like Pergamon) which had broken away from the Seleucids, and which were under threat from them, Roman expansion seemed to be an opportunity, and an alliance or 'understanding' with Rome an important card to play in the politics of the region. So Judas Maccabaeus, the leader of the Jewish insurgency against the Seleucids, made contact with the Romans on a number of occasions, and the expectation that Roman support would be a valuable asset in the war produced a remarkably rosy picture of the Roman Republic:

> Now Judas heard of the fame of the Romans, that they were very strong and well disposed toward all who made an alliance with them, that they pledged friendship to those who came to them, and that they were very strong. . . . Those whom they wish to help and make kings, they make kings, and those whom they wish they depose; and they have been greatly

exalted. Yet for all this not one of them has put on a crown or worn purple as a mark of pride, but they have built for themselves a senate chamber, and every day three hundred and twenty senators constantly deliberate concerning the people, to govern them well. They trust one man each year to rule over them and to control all their land; they all heed the one man, and there is no envy or jealousy among them.

(1 Maccabees 8, 1–2, 13–16)

No doubt distant Rome seemed less of a threat than their Seleucid neighbours. At any rate, in their initial contacts with Rome, the rulers of the Jewish state saw her as a potential ally rather than a danger.

Given that the Macedonian royal dynasty, the Antigonids, were Roman prisoners and that the Ptolemies owed their survival to Roman protection, all the successor states of Alexander's empire were after 168 clearly under Roman hegemony, and in a sense were included in a 'Roman Empire'. For the 'Roman Empire', down to the late first century BC, did not comprise one continuous block of territory under direct rule by Roman officials and marked off by clear boundaries from independent neighbours, whether 'barbarian' tribes or eastern dynastic states. Instead, in between and beyond those 'provinces' outside Italy which were governed by Roman proconsuls there were self-governing cities, tribes and kingdoms in various degrees of dependence on Roman power, degrees which varied according to how remote they were from the heart of that power. After 168 BC the hellenistic East beyond the Aegean was the main zone of what modern historians term the 'client kings' of Rome. These kings were aware that if they offended Rome they could be destroyed, as Perseus of Macedonia had been; some, like Ptolemy VI, owed their survival, and others, like Eumenes II, the extent of their dominions, to Rome. After 168, Eumenes II learned that even a king once favoured by Rome could lose that favour if he was suspected of being not quite loyal enough; the Senate showed its suspicion of Eumenes by a display of public favour to his younger brother and eventual heir, Attalos II (160–138), and to his neighbour and enemy, King Prusias II of Bithynia (182–149). Kings had therefore to be careful of causing suspicion in the minds of wary senators (an awful object lesson was the fate of Carthage, utterly destroyed in 146 despite every effort to appease the Romans, for the crime of becoming wealthy and prosperous); they had to provide troops to fight alongside Roman armies and, eventually, to maintain order in any troublesome regions Rome had put under their rule (Amyntas, king of Galatia, was killed by treachery in 25 BC during a campaign to subdue rebellious mountain tribes in the area of Pisidia and Lykaonia: Strabo 12, 569). They were sedulous in courting the Senate's favour and seeking tokens of Roman support (such as grants of Roman citizenship); their sons were sent to Rome to be educated so as to gain an insight into the Roman mentality and to establish useful contacts with the young aristocrats who would be the future leaders of Rome. This practice continued after Rome had acquired a single imperial family, with sons and grandsons of Herod the Great, for instance, being brought up alongside the descendants of Augustus and Agrippa.

Public support from the authorities at Rome was not only necessary to avoid suffering the fate of Perseus of Macedonia, it was also useful for warding off potential dangers at home. One such danger was from neighbouring kings who would also be intriguing for influence at Rome and might hope to get part of your territories transferred to themselves (as a result of Roman arbitration in a boundary dispute, for instance); conversely one might do the same oneself at a neighbour's expense. Then there was the danger of a challenge from a rival to the throne, usually a brother or a cousin; during the late second and early first centuries BC there were recurrent wars between quarrelling members of the Seleucid and Ptolemaic dynasties. Fear of such challenges was probably the motive behind what seems the most striking acknowledgement a king could make of his dependence on Rome, to draw up a will bequeathing his goods and his territories to the Roman People. An inscription from Cyrene records such a will drawn up in 155 BC by the younger brother of Ptolemy VI, who was ruler of Cyrene at the time; the brothers were bitter enemies, and the text stresses that a copy of the will has been sent to Rome, calls on the gods to punish those who have plotted against his life and kingship (presumably his brother Ptolemy VI), and appeals to the Romans for help in case of attack. The bequest was on condition that there were no successors (i.e. sons), and since the testator eventually took over Egypt as King Ptolemy VIII (145–116) and fathered sons to inherit, the will never took effect. Later, however, the wills of three other kings did take effect, and this led to the creation of three new Roman provinces (see p. 79).

By the later first century BC kings were no more than Roman

appointees, little different from the equivalent of provincial governors serving for life, with no guarantee that they could pass on their
kingdoms to their sons. They were chosen with scant regard for
hereditary claims, previous links with the territories they were to
rule or respect for the wishes of their future subjects. An
outstanding example is that of Herod the Great, the King Herod of
the birth narratives of Matthew 2, 1–19 and Luke 1, 5. At the time
of Rome's first intervention in Judaea in 63 BC the Jews had been
ruled for four generations by the Hasmonean dynasty, the family of
Judas Maccabaeus, who combined the dignities of king and of high
priest. A Roman army under Pompeius intervened in a civil war
between the partisans of the high priest John Hyrcanus II and those
of his brother Judah Aristoboulos. The Temple was taken by storm
from Aristoboulos' partisans, and Pompeius followed the example of
Antiochos IV in entering the Holy of Holies, which only the high
priest was permitted to enter, and then only on the Day of
Atonement. According to the Roman historian Livy, Pompeius
found only an empty room (Tacitus, *Histories* 5, 9; cf. *schol. in Lucan.*
2, 593), but various accounts, hostile to Judaism, circulated in the
Gentile world about what Antiochos had found there. Some of these
involved the worship of an ass, others a kidnapped Gentile who was
being fattened for sacrifice.

Pompeius left Hyrcanus II as Rome's vassal ruler in Judaea, but
only as high priest, not as king; henceforth, from the Roman point
of view, it was Rome's right to decide how Judaea should be
governed. Throughout these events Hyrcanus had been a figurehead
manipulated by his chief adviser (or Grand Vizier) Antipater, the
father of Herod. Antipater was by birth an Idumaean, one of a
Gentile people living to the south of Judaea which had been
forcibly converted to Judaism by the first John Hyrcanus (died 104
BC), grandfather of Hyrcanus II; hence the description of Herod as
'half-Jewish' by his enemies (Josephus, *Ant.* 14, 403). Antipater
realised that henceforth the only way to keep power was to stay on
the right side of those in authority in Rome (and, after civil war
broke out among the Romans in 49 BC, by swiftly changing to
support the winning side). After his murder in 43 BC his sons were
able to avenge him and take over his rôle until an unexpected challenge to Roman power when a Parthian army occupied Judaea and
installed Aristoboulos' son Antigonos as king and high priest (he
had his uncle Hyrcanus mutilated so as to disqualify him from the
office of high priest). Herod got away and came to Italy late in 40 to

seek support against Antigonos (who was the vassal of Rome's great enemy), and there was one male Hasmonean left who would serve as a replacement figurehead for Hyrcanus, his young grandson Aristoboulos, who also became Herod's brother-in-law. But Marcus Antonius and the future emperor Augustus, who were at that moment collaborating as effective joint rulers of Rome after their victory over Julius Caesar's assassins, decided that the time for relying on figureheads in Judaea was past. Disregarding any questions of hereditary right and the affection and loyalty of the Jews for the Hasmonean family, not to mention Herod's suspect status in the eyes of most Jews as an Idumaean 'half-Jew', they had the Senate designate Herod King of Judaea. From the Roman point of view he proved an excellent choice – in 37 BC he recaptured Jerusalem and restored order. But he had to be ruthless to secure his position: Aristoboulos, appointed high priest in 36/35, 'accidentally' drowned during a bathing party, and old Hyrcanus was simply murdered in 31/30. After Antonius' defeat by Augustus in 31 Herod conciliated Augustus; he was confirmed in power, and even had extra territories put under his rule.

What Augustus had given, Augustus could take away. As a mark of special favour Herod was granted the right to draw up a will arranging the succession to his dominions (there is no recorded parallel for such a grant, see Braund 1984: 139–43). When he died in 4 BC there were two wills in existence. The earlier made his youngest son Antipas his main heir, while the later made Antipas' elder brother Archelaus Herod's successor as king (this is the Archelaus of Matthew 2, 22), though Antipas and a half-brother Philip would inherit parts of Herod's dominions as tetrarchs under Archelaus' suzerainty. Luke's version of the parable of the talents (Luke 19, 11–15) must be puzzling for readers not familiar with Josephus' narrative of the events in 4 BC: 'A man of noble birth went to a far country to win kingship for himself . . . and his fellow-citizens hated him and sent an embassy after him saying, "We do not want this man to be king over us." And it came about that he returned after winning the kingship. . . '. The parable reflects precisely what happened after Herod's death. Archelaus did not venture simply to proclaim himself king, but hurried off to Rome, as did Antipas and other members of the family. The Roman governor of Syria allowed a deputation of Jews to go as well, who bitterly denounced Herod's rule at a public reception. Augustus confirmed the main provisions of Herod's last will but showed his doubts about Archelaus' competence by allowing him only the title of ethnarch, not king, and granting his brothers complete independence as tetrarchs (Antipas in Galilee and in Peraea, east of the Jordan, Philip in areas north-east of the Sea of Galilee). Ten years' experience of Archelaus' conduct as ruler confirmed Augustus' doubts; in AD 6 Archelaus was summoned to Rome and exiled to Gaul, while his dominions (Judaea and Samaria) were turned into a Roman province. Even this settlement was not permanent, for in AD 41 one of Herod's grandsons, Agrippa I, was made king over most of his grandfather's dominions by the new emperor Claudius, who had known him in Rome as a young man. Agrippa also happened to be in Rome when Claudius' nephew Gaius (37–41), more popularly known by his nickname Caligula, was assassinated and Claudius was proclaimed emperor by the Praetorian Guard; Agrippa gave valuable support to the new emperor. However, when Agrippa died suddenly in 44 the province was revived and the territories which were eventually given to his young son Agrippa II to rule lay north and east of the Jewish homeland.

The annexation of Judaea came at a fairly late stage in the process by which territories regarded as being under Roman hegemony and under 'indirect rule' by kings who were 'allies and friends of the Roman People' were turned into provinces of the Roman Empire under 'direct rule'. To understand what this process involved requires an analysis of the changing nature of a Roman 'province'. The word originally referred to the particular task allocated to each of the senior officials of the Roman Republic who were elected and replaced every year – the two consuls and the praetors (two from *c.* 242 BC; four from 227; six from 197; eight from 80). Two of the praetors always had the job of administering justice at Rome, one between citizens, the other between citizens and foreigners. The consuls, as the most senior annual officers, commanded Roman legions in the most important military operations going on in their year of office, and the description of each consular *provincia* (= job or task) was often simply a geographical area: Spain, Macedonia, etc. In some cases the Senate decided that a permanent Roman presence was required after the end of military operations: first in Sicily after Carthaginian forces had been driven out in the war of 264–241 BC, then in Sardinia, seized from Carthage in 238, and in Nearer (eastern) and Farther (southern) Spain, conquered from the Carthaginians in 218–202. Unless major military operations were in progress (as they often were in Spain in the second century BC) each of these provinces was governed by one of the annual praetors whose main civilian function was, as at Rome, acting as judge. The supervision of the collection of taxes levied by Rome in the new territorial provinces was the job (*provincia*) of a quaestor, one of a group of more junior officials elected every year.

The first territorial province to be organised east of the Adriatic was Macedonia, in 148 BC. The Macedonians had not remained content with the system of four self-governing republics, and had rebelled in support of a man who falsely claimed to be a son of King Perseus. After Rome defeated and disbanded the Achaean League in southern Greece, a number of Greek cities were put under the Roman governor's authority. The annexation of Macedonia can be viewed as the inevitable consequence, delayed by twenty years, of a decision to 'wind up' a client kingdom whose ruler had come to be seen as 'unsatisfactory' from a Roman point of view. In fact, all the provinces formed east of the Aegean can been seen as the consequence of 'winding up' client kingdoms. In three cases these decisions followed the deaths without legitimate heirs of kings whose wills made the Roman People their heir: Asia, formed after the death at an early age of King Attalos III in 133; Cyrene, whose king died in 96 but which was left alone until 74 (and had Crete attached to its governor's 'province' after Roman campaigns against pirates based in that island); and Bithynia, also in 74. To secure this new province Rome had to fight its second major war against King Mithridates VI of Pontus, and the western part of his dominions was added to the new province. The annexation of northern Syria in 64 was to fill a power vacuum – the last Seleucids had been expelled by Tigranes of Armenia, the son-in-law and ally of Mithridates, but he in turn had had to evacuate Syria to face a Roman offensive. Cyprus was annexed in 58 (and subsequently attached to the province of Cilicia) allegedly as the consequence of a fit of pique on the part of the Roman politician Publius Clodius Pulcher (Strabo 14, 6, 6). The story goes that the ruler of Cyprus, the younger brother of Ptolemy XII, failed to respond with satisfactory generosity when Clodius was captured by pirates and was trying to raise a ransom; when Clodius later became tribune he engineered the deposition of the king and the annexation of the island (Sherwin-White 1984: 268–70).

The same pattern continues under the rule of the first emperor. In 25 BC after King Amyntas had been killed (see p. 75) his domin-ions were annexed as the province of Galatia, which features so

prominently in the life of Paul. This province comprised much
more territory than the original regions settled by the immigrant
Celtic tribes (see pp. 34–5); in particular the mountainous zone
along the edge of the Anatolian plateau, where Amyntas met his
end, was included. These territories had earlier formed part of a
province of Cilicia. Amyntas had begun his career as the secretary of
the Celtic king Deiotarus, and was appointed king and given the
extra territory to run after the death of Deiotarus' grandson. This
appointment, like that of Herod some years earlier, showed that by
this date the Romans cared nothing for family or ethnic origin in
appointing kings, but sought only toughness and competence.
Augustus decided that Amyntas' sons were not capable of doing the
job their father had done and that Roman troops were needed to
crush the mountain tribesmen. This was done (so that fifty years
later Paul could travel without reported incident through these
same mountains: Acts 13, 14; 14, 24), and a chain of Roman citizen
colonies, including Antioch-next-to-Pisidia, Iconium and Lystra,
was planted along the northern edge of the mountains to keep
watch on the hillsmen. The annexation of Judaea was likewise the
result of Augustus' disappointment with the ineffective sons of a
highly effective father.

By the time of Paul's travels in the 40s and 50s the Empire east of
the Adriatic consisted of the following territorial provinces:
Macedonia; Achaea (split off from Macedonia in *c*. 27 BC); Crete
with Cyrene; Cyprus; Asia; Bithynia with Pontus; Galatia; Lycia
with Pamphylia (formed AD 43); Cappadocia (formed AD 17 when
an able but long-lived king had become senile); Syria (which
included the plain of eastern Cilicia, of which Tarsus was the most
important city); Judaea; and Egypt. Along the eastern fringe from
the Black Sea to the Gulf of Arabia there survived a number of client
kingdoms: eastern Pontus on the Black Sea coast; Armenia Minor
(ruled from 54 by one Aristoboulos, son of Herod of Chalcis, a son of
Herod the Great); Commagene (King Antiochos IV also ruled territories further west in southern Anatolia, including part of Lykaonia
but not Lystra and Derbe: Wallace and Williams 1993: 66); Emesa;
the kingdom of Agrippa II (see p. 78); and the kingdom of the
Nabataean Arabs, whose king, Aretas IV (died AD 40) is mentioned
by Paul in connection with his stay in Damascus (2 Corinthians 11,
32; see Wallace and Williams 1993: 50); the Nabataean kingdom
was the last of these client states to come under direct rule, being
annexed as the province of Arabia under Trajan in 106.

HOW ROME RULED

Even in the actual provinces the Roman official 'presence' would have been notable to anyone acquainted with modern bureaucracies by its absence. For the poor, especially the rural poor, the representatives of the Roman central government would be very remote, even shadowy, figures.

In provinces without a large garrison, where no serious fighting was to be expected (which includes all the provinces listed above except Syria – and even on the Syrian frontier with Parthia there was peace until AD 58) the governor's main function was to judge major civil and criminal cases. In the larger provinces at any rate this involved travelling on a circuit through a number of major cities which had been designated as the equivalent (until recent times) of assize towns in England and Wales. Litigants from neighbouring cities had to travel to their local 'assizes' (Latin *conventus*, Greek *agora dikēs*; whence the term *agoraioi* (sc. *hēmerai*) in Acts 19, 38 = 'assize days') to have their cases heard by the governor. We know that in the large, populous province of Asia there were thirteen such cities. In a few places royal palaces had come into Roman possession and served as the governor's residence; such was the *praetorium* of Herod at Caesarea in which Paul was held on Felix's orders (Acts 23, 35; for more details see Wallace and Williams 1993: 121), and it was probably the *praetorium* throughout which Paul's chains were manifest (Philippians 1, 13; Wallace and Williams 1993: 121). Elsewhere there was no equivalent of a 'Government House' of the kind found in British colonies; indeed there was no provincial 'capital' with a permanent headquarters for the governor. The local authorities in each city would have to provide him with suitable accommodation by requisitioning the house of some local grandee. When the future emperor Antoninus Pius visited Smyrna while governor of Asia he was billeted in the splendid home of the notoriously arrogant rhetorician Polemon, who was away from the city. Returning at night, Polemon kicked up such a fuss at being excluded from his own home that the governor had to move to another house (Philostratus, *Lives of the Sophists* 533-5 (Loeb edn pp. 111–13); when Polemon visited Rome after Pius had become emperor, he said, 'Give Polemon a lodging and don't let anyone throw him out of it').

Nor did governors have large staffs. On the official level, they had in some provinces a deputy (*legatus*) of senatorial rank, clerks of much lower status came out with them from Rome, drawn from fixed panels, while in provinces with military units, soldiers 'on secondment' served both as clerks and as guards and executioners (see the Passion narratives; cf. the centurion Julius, from the Augustan cohort, entrusted by Festus with the job of escorting Paul and other prisoners to Rome: Acts 27, 1). At an unofficial level governors, as Romans of the highest status, would have large domestic households of slaves (when the senior senator Pedanius Fuscus was murdered by one of his own slaves in AD 61, and an old custom that every slave living under his roof should be executed was enforced, four hundred slaves were involved: Tacitus, *Annals* 14, 42–5). They also invited a few personal friends to travel with them as their *comites* or 'companions': some were chosen for some special expertise; others perhaps as agreeable mess-mates, for it was not wise for governors to look to local residents for social companionship. In the early third century AD the emperor Septimius Severus warned governors of the danger of accepting too much hospitality from provincials and quoted an old proverb 'not every*thing* at every *time* nor from every*one*' (*Digest* 1, 16, 7, pr.).

There was a more numerous category of official agents of Rome who also remained in one province for much longer than governors and their entourages – the members of what Paul calls 'the household of Caesar' in Philippians (4, 22). Augustus and his successors owned vast properties throughout the provinces, as a result of confiscations during the civil wars. They also became responsible for the collection of taxes paid to Rome by the provincials of about half the provinces, those 'outer provinces' put under Augustus' direct control in 27 BC, where he appointed the governors. In these provinces the governor was called 'Augustus' deputy' (*legatus Augusti*) and usually served for a longer term than the single year to which the proconsuls who governed the other 'public' provinces were limited. Macedonia, Achaea, Crete with Cyprus, Asia, Bithynia with Pontus and Cyprus were governed by a proconsul; the Greek equivalent of the title is *anthypatos*, used in Acts 13, 7; 18, 12; 19, 38 of Cyprus, Achaea and Asia. All the other provinces east of the Adriatic were 'imperial' provinces. In every province Augustus appointed a procurator who handled Augustus' finances; in the public provinces this comprised the rents from imperial estates only, but in the imperial ones it included the tribute as well. These top men were usually of high status, recruited from the body known (for complex reasons of distant historical origins) as 'Roman knights/cavalrymen', next in status only to senators, but to assist them they had substantial staffs of clerks, accountants and so on. At Rome the emperor himself needed much larger numbers of such people and, whether at Rome or in the provinces, they were all regarded as part of 'Caesar's household' (*domus Caesaris* in Latin = *Kaisaros oikia* in Paul's Greek).

A Roman household included not only the resident relatives of the head of the household but also all his/her servants, all of whom would be slaves or 'freedmen', that is, former slaves of the head freed by him/her. In the Roman world chattel slaves were not used just as domestic and personal servants, in the way that they have been in a great many societies throughout history, but supplied the labour on the country estates of the rich, or were set up in business as urban craftsmen or traders by their owners (for the relevance of this to Paul's inherited status as a Roman citizen, see pp. 140–2 below). Small businesses which expanded beyond the capacity for labour of the owner and his relatives acquired slaves who lived under the owner's roof and laboured in the workshop – the household of Lydia, the 'dealer in purple' whom Paul converted at Philippi, must have been of this kind (Acts 16, 14–15), as probably was that of the *archisynagōgos* Crispus (Acts 18, 8) at Corinth. In a society where 'full-time employees' were mostly slaves it would be degrading for any freeborn person, especially those of any education or status, to become the hired servant of any other freeborn person. This 'taint of doing the washing up' (Crook 1967: 180) extended even to full-time employment by the state or local authorities – in cities of the eastern provinces town jailers, for example, were usually municipally owned slaves. The jailer at Philippi, who was baptised with all his people (Acts 16, 23, 33), may well have been a municipal slave. 'His people' and his 'household' (*oikos*: 16, 31) could well have included slaves, for slaves used in responsible positions were allowed to accumulate property, and that property could include slaves; when a slave accountant from Caesar's household died at Rome in the reign of Tiberius, a memorial was set up by no less than sixteen slave servants who had accompanied him from Lyon, including a physician and two cooks (*ILS*: 1514).

Thus the Roman aristocracy had had to acquire and train slaves to serve them as managers, accountants and secretaries. The great generals of the late Republic had used such men as their confidential agents in political and administrative, as well as private, business. Augustus simply extended this practice on a very large

scale. Under the rule of later members of Augustus' family, especially Claudius (41–54) and Nero (54–68), senior members of this
household, all freedmen, were in effect the chief ministers and
advisers of the emperors, exercising far more real power than most
senators. These men often flaunted their wealth and power to the
intense resentment of the traditional ruling nobility. Marcus
Antonius Pallas (whose services Claudius must have inherited from
his mother, to judge from Pallas' names) was even publicly
honoured by a resolution of the Senate in praise of his traditional
frugality and justice (Tacitus, *Annals* 12, 53; Pliny, *Letters* 7, 29, 2;
8, 6, 1). It must have been Pallas' influence which secured the
promotion of his brother Felix, another freedman, before whom
Paul appeared when Felix was governor of Judaea. Felix had reached
a post usually reserved for Roman *equites* (= knights/cavalrymen, see
pp. 82–3) of free birth, and he even married the daughters of client
kings: Drusilla, daughter of the king of Mauretania and grand-
daughter of Kleopatra VII, and another Drusilla, daughter of Herod
Agrippa I. But such cases of 'status dissonance' were mainly
confined to the first century; although Caesar's household continued
to supply the lower-level administrators, later emperors were careful
to avoid provoking the kind of anger voiced by the younger Pliny
by appointing only *equites* of free birth to the procuratorial service.

The governors of Judaea (from AD 6 to 41 and 44 to 66), like
those of Cappadocia (from 17 to 72), of Thrace (from 46 to *c*. 100)
and of Egypt (from 30 BC to AD 291), differed from those of other
provinces directly appointed by the emperor in three respects: (1)
rank – they were *equites* (or in the case of Felix imperial freedmen)
rather than senators; (2) title – *praefectus* (Egypt, and Judaea 6 to 41)
or *procurator* (Judaea 44 to 66) instead of *legatus Augusti*; (3) function
– they combined the judicial and military responsibilities exercised
elsewhere by the *legatus* with the financial ones exercised elsewhere
by the *procurator*. In part the reason for the exclusion of senators from
the governorship of Egypt was political caution. The importance of
the Egyptian corn supply for Rome, and the fact that through a
combination of geography and a tradition of centralised government
Egypt was easy to control and defend, made it imperative to keep
the province out of the hands of potential ambitious adventurers (for
the same reason senators could not even visit the province without
the emperor's express permission). All four provinces, however,
shared features which made a degree of experience of financial
administration desirable in the governors. All four had been king-

doms with highly centralised systems of bureaucratic administration which produced substantial revenue, and with very few cities with traditions of local self-government (Jones 1940: 75–84). The system of direct rule by a body of civil servants was maintained, and that was why there must have been a considerable number of clerks and accountants, members of Caesar's household (Philippians 4, 22), resident in 'Herod's *praetorium*' at Caesarea (Acts 23, 35) during Paul's two years under house arrest there (Acts 24, 27).

The exceptional character of these provinces helps to explain why the governors of the 'normal' provinces were able to carry out their duties with such a small staff. The Romans preferred the method of 'indirect rule' under which all the 'donkey-work' was placed on the shoulders of the local leaders of self-governing communities – and in the East that meant *poleis* of a Greek type. As a consequence Rome was more active in turning native towns into Greek *poleis* and creating *poleis* where none had existed before than the Macedonian kings had been. Within these *poleis* Romans preferred local rule to be in the hands of a hereditary élite of large landowners (much as it had been at Rome under the Republic). Augustus in some cases relied on individual 'bosses' and their families, but in general Rome preferred the collective leadership of all the important local families. In return for Roman support against disaffection among their own masses these local leaders were expected to co-operate with Rome in arranging for the collection of imperial tribute, the provision of potential conscripts for the army and the provision of transport and lodgings for imperial couriers and travellers on official business. Above all, they were expected to ensure tranquillity in their own communities, and especially to check the activities of urban mobs, since the Roman government did not devote resources of men and money to providing troops to act as riot police in the provinces of the interior. Cities where disorder did break out might be punished by the loss of rights and privileges – so the Clerk of the People at Ephesos had good reason to say, 'We are in danger of being called to account over this day's disturbance', in reference to the riot of the silversmiths (Acts 19, 40).

ROME AND GREEK CULTURE

It was not only as officials in provincial governments that upper-class Romans travelled from Italy to the Greek East. Ever since the later third century BC when the Roman élite began both to acquire immense wealth from successful warfare and to gain closer knowledge of the high culture of the Greek world, its members had spent more and more of the former on supplying themselves with examples of the latter. Greek paintings and statues were imported, often confiscated from defeated enemies, and Greek craftsmen were hired to produce copies or imitations of such works to decorate the houses and gardens of Roman grandees. Some intellectuals also came, poets and philosophers, to entertain their leisure hours (some of these were prisoners of war, sold as slaves). Cultivated Romans could be expected by the first century not just to be fluent in Greek but to be steeped in Greek literature of the 'classical' period (before *c.* 300 BC). Tourism was a natural result of such an education, but Roman visitors did not travel just as tourists; residence at Athens (or Rhodes) was a cross between a university course and a finishing school. Romans were coming to Athens to listen to philosophers as early as the second century BC. Cicero (*De Oratore* 3, 68) tells us that Metellus Numidicus, who was consul in 109 BC, had attended the lectures of the philosopher Carneades there as a young man, and at about the same time we hear of another Roman, T. Albucius, who attracted opprobrium by adopting Greek language and manners while studying at Athens (Cicero, *De Finibus* 1, 9). Later Cicero himself spent six months there in 79 BC, and we know from his letters that a number of his friends did the same. The poet Horace was there in 42 BC, and the poet Lucan, nephew of the proconsul Gallio whom Paul encounters in Corinth (Acts 18, 12) seems also to have spent some time there (Suetonius, *Vita Lucani*). This and other evidence suggests that a stay in Athens, or some other philosophical centre in the Greek East, was a common part of the education of a young upper-class Roman.

The most flamboyant of such visitors was the emperor Nero in AD 67; he conferred 'freedom on the Greeks' and planned a canal through the Isthmus of Corinth. All four of the ancient 'Panhellenic' athletic competitions were held out of sequence in the same year, to enable Nero to compete and, of course, to carry off the first prizes. On his return to Rome he even had a breach made in the ancient walls in order that he could exercise the rights of a victor in 'eiselastic games' and drive through them in triumph (see p. 105).

ROMAN COLONIES AND CULTURE IN THE EAST

Another category of Roman immigrant was the colonist settled permanently by the imperial government in a new community, a *colonia* of Roman citizens. Five of the places evangelised by Paul were the sites of 'colonies' of this kind: Antioch-next-to-Pisidia, Iconium, Lystra, Philippi and Corinth. It had been Roman practice during their conquest of Italy in the fourth and third centuries BC to use some of the land confiscated from their defeated enemies to provide farms for poor Romans to work as 'cultivators' (*coloni*). These new settlers were planted in organised communities with fortified urban centres and political institutions copied from those of Rome itself; these were known as *colonia(e)*, from *colonus* (= farmer-settler), and they were often sited at points of strategic importance where men with every incentive for loyalty to Rome could defend such 'bulwarks of empire' (*propugnacula imperii*) against revolt by the conquered. From the early second century it became necessary, in order to attract such settlers, to allow them to retain their full Roman citizenship. In the late second and first centuries BC colonies were founded in the provinces outside Italy, and came to be used as a means of rewarding men who had been discharged after long service in the legions. The first generation of such colonists were also well fitted to carry out the strategic function of Roman *coloniae*. The colonies at Pisidian Antioch, Iconium and Lystra belonged to a group of nine such colonies, planted in southern Anatolia under Augustus, whose main aim was certainly strategic, to act as watchdogs on the mountain tribes to their south. The colony at Antioch was founded soon after King Amyntas' death and the formation of the province of Galatia in 25 BC. Lystra was one of five settled around 6 BC after the victory of Augustus' general Sulpicius Quirinus (later to be governor of Syria in AD 6, cf. Luke 1, 2) over the people who had killed Amyntas, the Homonades, and Iconium may have been founded at the same time. Though the idea that such colonies had a primarily military function has recently been challenged (Isaac 1992: 311–32), on the grounds that they seem to have needed protection, rather than acting as a source of strength, and were rather ineffective in the face of serious challenges, they would at least serve as friendly bases, supply local militias and generally consolidate the Roman presence in the area. The colony at Corinth had been planned by Julius Caesar in 46 BC and its purpose was not strategic, but to provide an outlet for emigrants from the urban poor of Rome itself; the site, at a crossing of routes by land and sea, was an ideal one for a commercial centre and had lain empty since the Romans had destroyed the ancient Greek *polis* in 146 BC. Philippi was a kind of war memorial, founded at the site of a *polis* established by and named after Philip II of Macedon; nearby the armies of Caesar's assassins, Cassius and Brutus, had been defeated by the Caesarean armies of Antonius and the future Augustus.

Whether by Paul's day such communities remained 'Roman' and different in character from neighbouring Greek *poleis* in any significant cultural respect is very doubtful. Their chief elected officials retained their Latin titles, the most senior being *duoviri iure dicundo*, the 'two men for giving justice', and would be attended in public by Roman lictors carrying the bundles of rods which symbolised the judicial power of the *duoviri*. (Acts 16, 19–20 rendered the title of the *duoviri* at Philippi with the Greek word for 'generals', but accurately called the lictors 'rod-bearers', *rhabdouchoi*.) However, Greek was evidently the language for everyday life, and Latin had to be deliberately kept up for use in public pronouncements (Levick 1967: 130–62). If the colonists included in their public entertainments fights between gladiators and wild-beast hunts (*venationes*, shows in which wild animals – ranging from mundane bulls and bears to exotic beasts imported from all over the world – were fought and killed by specialised performers, *bestiarii*), practices which were distinctly Roman in origin and had not formed part of the traditional athletic festivals of the Greeks, that was a taste which soon came to be shared by the native Greeks.

The prevailing popular conception that games of this kind were somehow regarded as uncivilised or 'un-Greek' by the non-Roman inhabitants of the eastern provinces and rejected by them is based partly on wishful thinking and partly on moralistic clichés gathered from the writings of Greek philosophers and rhetoricians, though their moral contempt for these spectacles is usually based on no more than intellectual snobbery, and very often extends also to the thoroughly Greek institutions of athletics, boxing and wrestling (Epiktetos 2, 18, 22). In fact, these shows became extremely popular in the East. They were introduced originally by visiting Romans, such as Lucullus, who in the first century BC celebrated his victories with a gladiatorial show at Ephesos (Plutarch, *Lucullus* 23). In imitation of the Roman custom, the Seleucid king Antiochos IV Epiphanes put on a gladiatorial show (Livy 41, 20), and Herod gave a show involving gladiators and wild beasts in an amphitheatre quite close to Jerusalem, in honour of Augustus (Josephus, *Ant*. 15, 268–75). Amphitheatres, the structures most closely associated with Roman games, were built at, for example, Corinth, Antioch, Berytus and Caesarea, and theatres (often thought of as the most typically Greek buildings) were frequently modified to make them suitable for human or animal combats (as at Philippi, Thasos, Athens, Myra, Miletos, Ephesos and many other cities). Relief sculptures depicting the games are common all over the East (Robert 1971: 13–73, 239–66, 309–31). The dating of these structures is by no means easy to determine, but the popularity of the games in the East is well attested by the second century AD, and it seems reasonable to assume that the same was true in Paul's day. The spread of gladiatorial combats and wild-beast hunts is indeed one of the few cases where Roman culture had a significant effect on the Greek way of life. So the hellenised Celts whose nomenclature was discussed above (p. 46) were listed in the inscriptions on a temple wall at Ankara as having provided 'thirty pairs of gladiators and a hunt of bulls and wild beasts' or 'twice gave a fight of bulls and a beast hunt' (*OGIS* II, no. 533, ll. 5–8, 18–19). Similar inscriptions can be cited from many other eastern cities (see Robert 1971: 75–237).

A possible reference to the games is Paul's claim at 1 Corinthians 15, 32 that 'I fought with beasts at Ephesos'. This passage is often understood as a reference to the Roman habit of punishing criminals by making them appear in the amphitheatre to be killed by wild animals as one of the attractions at the games. It is, however, unclear whether this practice had spread to the East by the first century, though it certainly had by the middle of the second, when the demands of the mob in the amphitheatre at Smyrna that a lion should be loosed on the bishop Polycarp were refused by Philip the Asiarch on the grounds that the games had concluded; Polycarp was burnt instead (*Martyrdom of Polycarp* 12, 2–3). It is in any case unlikely, since fighting the beasts in this sense was an experience which the victim did not survive. It is much more likely that Paul is here metaphorically (since it is surely inconceivable that he ever took employment as a *bestiarius*) thinking of himself as one of the professionals who entertained the crowd by hunting and killing the beasts.

Another aspect of Roman culture which was adopted enthusiastically in the Greek East was the construction of hot baths on the

Roman model, often attached to the traditional Greek *gymnasia* and *palaistrai*, or wrestling grounds (Ward-Perkins 1981: 292–6; Farrington 1987: 50–9). These structures, often massive in scale, are found in virtually every city (indeed many cities had several of them) and provided not just facilities for hygiene and comfort but also social and cultural amenities. They became very important in the life of the cities, and the construction and adorning of them was one of the most significant ways in which the local gentry displayed their wealth and their beneficence.

However, gladiators, beast-hunts and baths apart, there is a most striking contrast between the impact of Roman rule on the western and eastern parts of their empire. In the West the first three centuries saw a process of Romanisation, of which the most enduring result is the domination of mainland Europe west of the Rhine by Romance languages derived from Latin; Latin must have replaced Celtic and other dialects as the main vernacular (as it did not in Britain, for Welsh and Cornish are Celtic, not Romance, languages). In the East the Greek language and Greek culture remained dominant, and the process of hellenisation continued, and was even promoted by Rome (see p. 85). The immense cultural chauvinism of the Greeks and the admiration of upper-class Romans for Greek culture (an admiration they did not display for the barbarian cultures of Europe unless, like Tacitus, they wanted to use the alleged primitive virtues of the Germans or Caledonians as a stick with which to beat the *mores* of contemporary Rome) accounted for this difference. Outside the Roman colonies there was only a very limited use of Latin, since visiting Roman officials would nearly all be able or willing to speak Greek. Occasionally Latin would be used to demonstrate Rome's authority, as when after the battle of Pydna in 168 BC the victorious general Aemilius Paullus summoned delegates from the Greek cities to Amphipolis and insisted on addressing them in Latin and having an interpreter translate his words (Livy 45, 29, 3), even though he was perfectly capable of delivering a speech in Greek (Livy 45, 8, 6). According to Plutarch (*Cato* 12, 4), Cato the Elder, admittedly a notorious opponent of all things Greek, also refused to address an Athenian audience in Greek, and insisted on making a speech to them in Latin. The same motive would account for putting up official pronouncements inscribed on stone in Latin. And, although the Greeks adopted some Roman building techniques, they remained impervious at the cultural level. Even those who rose high in the service of the Roman state and had therefore to learn and to use Latin for utilitarian purposes seem to have ignored the highly sophisticated literature which had been created in Latin by the first century (based, ironically, on Greek models). Even translation of Latin literature into Greek was very rare. Indeed, up to the time of Paul we know of only one case of a Latin literary work being translated into Greek, a prose translation of Virgil which was produced by Polybius, the freedman of Claudius. (For a full account of Greek translations of Latin classics see Swain 1991.)

There was, however, one enclave where the use of Latin was compulsory, and that was in the Roman legions. But Paul encountered no 'Roman' soldier outside Judaea (apart from those who sail with him from Judaea) and this reflects the historical situation. In the middle of the first century the only legions east of the Danube Valley were stationed outside Alexandria and in some towns of Syria. There were no permanent garrisons in Asia, Galatia, Macedonia, Achaea or Cyprus. The garrison of Judaea consisted of *auxilia*, that is, units recruited normally from non-Romans to fight in Rome's service. Therefore the 'Roman soldiers' of the Gospels and Acts were not Roman citizens, though the 'Italian cohort' to which the centurion Cornelius belonged (Acts 10, 1) may have been an exception – we know from inscriptions of two units with this title, and they consisted, unusually, of Roman citizens (Wallace and Williams 1993: 53). The unit stationed in Jerusalem, however, which Paul encountered in Acts 21, would certainly have consisted of non-citizens; even its commander, Claudius Lysias (Acts 21, 31; 22, 28; 23, 26), was not a Roman citizen by birth (Wallace and Williams 1993: 113–14).

SUGGESTIONS FOR FURTHER READING

(full details of these works can be found in the Bibliography):

For a historical outline of Roman involvement in the East, P. Green's *From Alexander to Actium* can again be recommended. A. N. Sherwin-White's *Roman Foreign Policy in the East* gives an interpretation of Roman policy in 133–70 BC, and W. Williams' *Pliny the Younger: Correspondence with Trajan from Bithynia* is suggested for an account of Roman methods of direct rule.

Relationships between Rome and her Greek subjects are discussed in S. Swain's *Hellenism and Empire*.

On aspects of citizenship and slavery, see J. F. Gardner, *Being a Roman Citizen*, J. A. Crook, *Law and Life of Rome* and K. Hopkins, *Conquerors and Slaves*.

Part 3

THE CITY, THE STATE
AND THE INDIVIDUAL

7

THE LIFE OF THE *POLIS*

WHAT WAS A *POLIS*?

Paul's Epistles (except for Romans, Philemon and the pastorals) were addressed to Christian congregations in Greek *poleis*, or Latin colonies which were probably thoroughly hellenised (p. 88); the narrative of Paul's missionary journeys in Acts 13–20 describes him moving to and fro between such *poleis*. What then was a *polis*? It was a political unit, a self-governing body of *politai* or 'citizens'; the official titles of the *poleis* referred to in English as Athens, Thebes, etc. were '*the* Athenians', '*the* Thebans' and so on. Each *polis* had a clearly demarcated territory, and usually one major urban centre (town) where its institutions of government were based and amenities such as theatres or gymnasia were to be found. In its Greek homeland in the 'classical' period (before 300 BC) a *polis* was not just a town, for the permanent residents of the surrounding countryside were just as important as those of the central town (see Osborne 1987). But outside that homeland in the hellenistic and Roman periods the territories which in law 'belonged' to the new hellenised '*poleis*' were farmed by peasants speaking their native languages and playing no part in the communal life of the *polis*. A gulf developed between the *polis* (town) and the *chōra* (countryside) (see p. 65 and de Sainte Croix 1975: 1–8; 1981: 9–19, 427–30; Meeks 1983: 9–16). This differentiation between town and country had even begun to affect the *poleis* of the Greek homeland by the Roman period (Osborne 1987: 193–4). Paul's mission is confined to the world of the *polis*.

In the *poleis* of the classical age, citizenship was largely determined by birth. In the *polis* for which we have the fullest information, Athens, full citizenship was mainly confined to the children of marriages between citizens, and naturalisation of foreigners was rare. Athens attracted numerous alien residents (*metoikoi*) who had legal but not political rights. This same general pattern prevailed in the cities of the Roman period, although we have little precise information about particular cases. It is probable that in Asia Minor and Syria the rural population did not have citizenship (Jones 1940: 160–2, 172–3). Paul's world as depicted in Acts is one in which traders and skilled craftsmen migrate readily from *polis* to *polis*. The descendants of such emigrants might live in a *polis* for several generations as 'resident aliens'; Roman jurists discussed the claims on a person of his place of residence (*domicilium*) and his place of ancestral origin (*origo*, i.e. where his ancestors had come from; the person concerned need not even have been born there). An interesting variation to this pattern is found in Tarsus, where there was a category of urban residents, 'the linen-workers', who were 'outside the constitution' (Dio of Prusa 34, 21).

THE *POLIS* AND ITS CITIZENS

The classical *polis* had generated intense communal loyalty and also fostered rivalry between *poleis*, which often led to warfare. Under the overlordship of kings or of Rome inter-city wars were no longer possible, but civic loyalty and pride still flourished and led to competition with neighbouring *poleis*, 'war pursued by other means'. The higher education of the ruling élites was almost exclusively literary and rhetorical. The works of literature they studied mostly dated from the 'classical' age, i.e. from before 300 BC. As a result the 'ideal world' of educated Greeks of the Roman Empire was that of the independent Greek *polis* of the fifth and fourth centuries BC. When Flavius Arrianus, himself to serve as consul and Roman governor of Cappadocia, deplored the literary inadequacies of histories of Alexander earlier than his own, it was to Xenophon's *Anabasis* and the verse panegyrics of the fifth-century tyrants of Sicily he compared them, not to histories of, say, Hannibal or Julius Caesar (Arrian, *Anabasis* 1, 12, 2–3). An important exercise for young men being trained as orators was to deliver an 'epideictic' oration, a 'display piece', in which the orator impersonated a historical figure at some crisis of his career and delivered the kind of speech he should have delivered (e.g. 'Demosthenes defends himself on a charge of cowardice in the presence of King Philip'). None of the recorded themes concern any event later than the suicide of Demosthenes in 322 BC (Bowie 1974: 170–3). In a sense it was as if nothing of any importance had happened to the Greeks since 322 BC.

Those cities which had played a glorious part in that history assiduously polished up their traditions, especially when, as often, they had suffered a decline in prosperity and glory. The far larger number (including all the cities with which Paul had any significant link except Athens and Ephesos – and Corinth, although there was no direct historical link between Greek and Roman Corinth), which had been 'barbarian' or had not existed in the classical age of Greece, sought to achieve respectability and to incorporate themselves into the world of Greek myth, legend and history. This could be done by fabricating foundation stories and associating local cults with the myths of the Olympian gods. For example, even Ephesos, a well-established old Greek settlement, had such a foundation legend: a group of settlers, led by one Androkles, had crossed the Aegean from Athens to Ionia at the instance of the oracle of Delphi (Rogers 1991: 144). It also had a great temple of the goddess Artemis, associated with a legend that Artemis and her twin Apollo had been born nearby, although the physical attributes of the cult statue were very different from those of the Artemis of Greek mythology (see pp. 197–8 and Wallace and Williams 1993: 103–4).

Many Greek *poleis* had been new settlements in foreign lands and preserved a historical record of the date of their foundation, of the identity of the city ('mother-city') from which the settlers had come and of the name of the leader of the migration, the 'founder' (*oikistēs*), who received semi-divine honours as a 'hero'. Another characteristic figure of the early history of a *polis* was the 'lawgiver' (*nomothetēs*) to whom eventually all the institutions of a *polis* would be attributed; in some cases he was a historical figure (Solon of Athens), in others legendary (Lykourgos of Sparta). When Greeks encountered 'barbarian' communities they enquired into their origins and interpreted what they were told to suit their preconceptions. Jerusalem, for example, came to be seen as very like a *polis*, with Moses as both its founder and lawgiver. Of course, the biblical narrative did depict Moses as the leader of an emigration from Egypt and the first five books in which the Law (= *Torah*) was embodied were indeed described as the Books of Moses (Genesis to Deuteronomy). But Greek accounts of Judaea distort Moses' rôle to fit him into the Greek model, especially that of the 'founder'; in Diodorus Siculus' account (40, 3) – written in the first century BC but based on a source of the late fourth century BC, Hekataios of

Abdera – Moses is said to have taken possession of an uninhabited country and to have founded, besides other cities, Jerusalem; in the biblical narrative, however, Moses is not permitted to enter the Promised Land, his successors have to fight an existing population and Jerusalem is captured by David only many generations later. In Diodorus Moses is also, as the lawgiver, made responsible for all the institutions of the Jews of the classical period: he (not Solomon) built the Temple; he divided them into twelve tribes (whereas the Hebrew tribes were held to be descended from and named after the sons of Jacob); he invested the high priest with supreme political authority and the Jews never had a king (a complete contradiction to the historical books of the Old Testament).

Though Jewish writers naturally felt a greater obligation to adhere to the biblical account, the desire to conform to a Greek model can be seen here too. So, in Philo's *On the Life of Moses*, Moses is a lawgiver (*nomothetēs*: 2, 1, 3) and is compared to other lawgivers (1, 1, 2). The details of his biography are filled in with Greek commonplaces, such as an exceptionally precocious childhood (1, 5, 21), a Greek education (1, 5, 23), a proper philosophical temperament (1, 6, 25–9) and physical beauty (1, 5, 18). He is a king (1, 27, 148; 1, 60, 334; 2, 51, 292) and is also a philosopher (2, 1, 2; the connection with Plato's 'philosopher kings' is explicitly made). The whole narrative is interspersed with philosophical platitudes, many of which would be completely unremarkable in any Greek work. The whole tenor of the work is that Moses is not just a better lawgiver and hero than those of the Greeks, he is better by the Greeks' own criteria.

Many newly hellenised cities were only too anxious to fabricate foundation legends which would fit in with Greek preconceptions and link them to the great centres of classical Greece. One solution was to claim to have been founded by settlers from Greece. In historic fact, Sparta originated only one colony, Taras (Taranto) in Italy. This did not deter a clutch of small places in south-west Asia Minor from claiming to be Spartan colonies by origin (Jones 1940: 50). At one point the political leaders at Jerusalem may have tried to go one better and claim that Sparta started as a colony sent out from Judaea (1 Maccabees 12, 5–23; cf. Josephus, *Ant.* 12, 225–7; 13, 166–70). A neighbouring Semitic people, the Phoenicians, had the advantage that there was a native Greek tradition that the city of Thebes had been founded by an emigrant from Phoenicia, Cadmus.

Another solution was to go back to Greek heroes of a legendary past, especially those who were supposed to have travelled very widely, such as Herakles or Perseus, or even the god Dionysos who had done the same. In this way Tarsus claimed a link of kinship with Argos. The geographer Strabo reports the legend: Tarsus is a foundation of the Argives who travelled with Triptolemos in search of Io (Strabo 14, 5, 12, 673c). The city's coins and inscriptions refer to 'ancestral and Argive Apollo'; the hero Perseus was supposed to have brought an image of Apollo to Tarsus from Argos (Robert 1977: 96ff.).

The same was done at Nicaea in Bithynia, which remained locked in bitter rivalry with its neighbour Nicomedia down to the third century. Both had been founded by kings in the third century BC; Nicaea (Nikaia) had been named by King Lysimachus, one of Alexander's generals, after his first wife. But the Nicaeans were not content with being named after a mere Macedonian princess, or to have a 'home-made' king as founder. The city's coins depict a goddess named Nicaea, and the fabricated legend which lies behind this was worked up in detail by a Greek poet from Egypt of the fifth century AD, Nonnus, in his immense poem on the escapades of the god Dionysos. Nicaea was a nymph, the daughter of the goddess Cybele and the river-god Sangarios; after being seduced by Dionysos by a trick (he turned the stream from which she drank to wine) she gave birth to Telete and then hanged herself; Dionysos founded the city in her honour.

Another royal foundation in north-west Asia Minor, Alexandria Troas (where Paul had his vision: Acts 16, 8–10), was fortunate enough to have in its territory a temple mentioned in the *Iliad* (1, 37–9) dedicated to Apollo with the epithet Smintheus. One account derived this epithet from the word *sminthos*, a mouse, and claimed that it recorded the destruction of a plague of field mice by the intervention of the god. The cult-image, made by the sculptor Skopas, represented Apollo crushing a mouse with his foot, and the city's coins showed Apollo holding a mouse (Head 1911: 540).

In other places novel cults enhanced a city's status. At Abonuteichos on the south coast of the Black Sea, in the middle of the second century BC, one Alexander (a charlatan according to the satirist Lucian, if we can believe him) presented himself as the interpreter of a new oracle, Glykon, which had the form of a huge snake with a head human or canine in appearance and long flowing locks of hair. This figure appears on the coins of the city, and portable images of Glykon discovered in places as distant as Athens and Tomis (Constanza in Romania, where a splendid statue of the 'god' is on display in the local museum) confirm Lucian's account of the spread of the new cult (Robert 1981: 513–35). Among those who consulted the oracle and were (according to Lucian) duped by Alexander was Rutilianus, who served as consul and governor of Upper Moesia; this interest by a senior Roman in a novel cult recalls the proconsul of Cyprus' interest in Elymas and in Paul (Acts 13, 6–8). Elymas is described as a *magos* and a false prophet, and the fact that Paul seems to regard him as a serious rival suggests that he was more than just a conjuror or an astrologer but, like Simon Magus (Acts 8, 9–24), a representative of an alternative religious cult (Wallace and Williams 1993: 47–8, 61–2).

A striking example of the conscious use of a religious shrine to enhance the status of a city is the oracle of Apollo at Klaros on the coast of Asia Minor just north of Ephesos. It was in the territory of Kolophon, a city of no particular distinction. Though the shrine was a very old one (it is mentioned in Homer) we really hear nothing of it until the emperor Tiberius' nephew, adopted son and designated successor, Germanicus, visited it in AD 19 (Tacitus, *Annals* 2, 54); it allegedly foretold, in the enigmatic style of oracles, his early death. Excavations have revealed that in the first and second centuries AD the site was developed into an oracle of international standing. A large Doric temple was built, underneath which were tortuous underground passages leading to mysterious chambers. Inscriptions tell us that visitors came from all over the world (including Dalmatia and Britain), and were received by the principal magistrates of Kolophon and by choirs of young men and women singing hymns to Apollo specially composed for the occasion. When the oracle was consulted, the answers were given in verse, as they were at the venerable oracle at Delphi, but they were given in a selection of complex metrical forms, rather than simple hexameters, and were sung rather than spoken. There were mysteries into which visitors could be initiated, and night-time ceremonies, in which the underground chambers surely played a part. The picture is of a local community developing and promoting its local shrine in competition with older (and more conservative) oracles and, by giving visitors a more exciting religious experience, achieving international renown and so enhancing the prestige and fame of the city. This is a period when we hear of the decline of shrines like Delphi. The example of Klaros should remind us that the explanation for the neglect of older sites is unlikely to be a decline of religious feeling (because this was by no means an irreligious age) but rather growing competition from shrines which were more imaginative, and more in tune with the religious mood of the day, helped on and encouraged by local patriotism.

These are but a few examples from a vast body of civic cults and foundation legends on record. They established the Hellenic credentials of a *polis*, boosted its standing in its rivalry with its neighbours and provided a focus for the loyalty of its citizens. One might compare this last function to that which is (or used to be) fulfilled in the education of British or American children by such stories as the enforced signing of Magna Carta by King John at Runnymede or Paul Revere's midnight ride from Boston to Lexington. In every city a sequence of festivals held every year or at four-year intervals would keep the legends firmly in the minds of the people. At Ephesos in the early second century an endowment by Vibius Salutaris provided funds for having twenty-nine figures made in silver of the goddess Artemis, of the emperor Trajan and his wife Plotina, and of numerous personifications (e.g. the Roman People). These would be carried from the great temple of Artemis through one of the city's gates, along one of its streets, and back through another gate to the temple; this happened, on average, about once every two weeks (Rogers 1991: 80–115). This emphasis on Artemis, and on Artemis in the quite distinctive form in which she was worshipped at Ephesos (cf. Wallace and Williams 1993: 104), illustrates the almost universal practice of each city having one particular and pre-eminent cult: that of Athena Parthenos at Athens, of Hera at Argos (where the count of years was calculated as the *n*th year of the tenure of office of the current priestess of Hera), and so on.

In the case of Rome the cult was that of Jupiter Capitolinus (the Jupiter whose seat was the Capitol Hill) and Roman victories were equated with the victory of this god over inferior deities, such as the god of the Jews when his Temple was destroyed in AD 70. The levy of two drachmas a year which adult male Jews had paid to support the Temple at Jerusalem was converted to a tax for the temple of Jupiter on the Capitol (Schürer 1973–87: 1, 513), and when a Roman colony was founded on the site of Jerusalem after the second Jewish revolt in 132–5 it was named Aelia Capitolina (Aelia after the emperor Aelius Hadrianus) and a temple to Jupiter Capitolinus was erected on the site of Herod's Temple (Schürer 1973–87: 1, 553–4).

For a Greek *polis* it would of course be a great source of prestige and profit if its local cult attracted the devotion of worshippers from a much wider area. The assertion of Demetrios in Acts 19, 27 (echoed in a decree of the city of Ephesos, see Wallace and Williams 1993: 105) is confirmed by a coin of Eumeneia (Wallace and Williams 1993: 105) and by the discovery of replicas of the curious cult-image, similar to those of Glykon mentioned above. Such replicas served as *hierōmata*, portable objects of devotion and sources of divine protection. If small enough, such *hierōmata* could be worn on the body as amulets; when the bodies of some of Judas Maccabaeus' men killed in battle were recovered for burial, 'under the tunic of every one of the dead they found *hierōmata* ['sacred tokens', RSV] of the idols of Jamnia [i.e. representations of the cult-images of the god Haurōnas, see Robert 1981: 517–20], which the law forbids the Jews to wear; and it became clear to all that this was why the men had fallen' (2 Maccabees 12, 40).

These are just some of the aspects of the religious life of the *polis*, of what Paul and the early Christians termed 'idolatry'. Besides acts of private devotion there were the regular ceremonies performed by representatives of the *polis* and associations within the *polis*. What would be most startling to modern Westerners would be the recurrent butchery of animals, sometimes on a large scale. For the priests and the magistrates of the Roman state this took the form of the routine fulfilment and renewal of a contract with the gods. For example, large sections survive in inscriptions of the 'minutes' of a minor college of Roman priests, the Arval Brethren. Two entries, for the 1st and 3rd of January AD 60 (the year when Paul may have arrived in Rome), record that the master of the college sacrificed on the 1st a bullock to Jupiter, a cow to Juno, a cow to Minerva and a bull to the *Genius*, or guardian spirit, of Nero on the occasion of his becoming consul, and that on the 3rd he renewed vows made a year before by sacrificing two bullocks to Jupiter and two cows to Juno, two cows to Minerva, two cows to Public Welfare, two bullocks to the deified Augustus, two cows to the deified Augusta, two bullocks to the deified Claudius – and so it went on, year in, year out (Smallwood 1967: 23). In this respect, of course, the cult practices at the Jewish Temple at Jerusalem were not significantly different from those at pagan temples. There too large-scale animal sacrifice was the normal way of honouring the god, and the environs of a temple (sacrifice took place outside the temple, which was regarded as the home of the god, rather than inside) would present the visitor with sounds, sights and smells which to us would have more in common with those of a slaughterhouse than a place of worship. In the case of the Jews, however, sacrifice could take place only at the Temple in Jerusalem, so that Jews of the diaspora had perforce to devise forms of worship which did not involve sacrifice, and which became the model on which Christian and other religious services were based (which is why the near-universal practice of antiquity now seems bizarre and disgusting to us).

Meat did not form a large part of the diet in the ancient Mediterranean, and most of the butchered meat available for sale consisted of those portions of sacrificial animals which were not burnt on the altars so that the aroma could ascend to the gods. While the offerings at the Temple of Jerusalem were 'holocausts', that is, sacrifices where the whole carcasses were burnt, this was done in Greek or Roman sacrifices only in exceptional circumstances. For Christians, therefore, buying meat would almost inevitably involve them in what might be seen to be some degree of compromise with pagan sacrifice, and hence 'idolatry' (see 1 Corinthians 8 and 10); the more established Jewish communities had made arrangements for the separate supply of foods acceptable to them. By the early second century a Roman governor was informed that after he had executed Christian confessors and spared apostates 'the flesh of sacrificial animals was being sold, for which very few purchasers could recently be found' (Pliny, *Letters* 10, 96, 10; cf. Wallace and Williams 1993: 70; see p. 116).

What is debatable is the extent to which scruples about 'idolatry' would inhibit Christians (or Jews) from enjoying the amenities of the communal life of the *poleis*, and in particular how far they attended or participated in the main cultural and recreational events held in those structures which are still such a prominent feature of the Roman sites of the East: theatres, concert-halls, running-tracks and gymnasia (see Part 4). Paul often uses imagery derived from public competition, e.g.:

> Do you not know that in a race all the runners compete, but only one receives the prize? So run that you may obtain it. Every athlete exercises self-control in all things. They do it to receive a perishable wreath, but we an imperishable. Well, I do not run aimlessly, I do not box as one beating the air; but I punish my body and subdue it, lest after preaching to others I myself should be disqualified.
>
> (1 Corinthians 9, 24–7)

You were running well; who hindered you from obeying the truth?

(Galatians 5, 10)

An athlete is not crowned unless he competes according to the rules.

(2 Timothy 2, 5)

Such references are, however, commonplace in the writings of most moralists, and may be regarded as simple platitudes (and later Christian writers, following Paul, routinely describe the faithful Christian as an athlete: e.g. Ignatius, *Letter to Polycarp* 1, 3). Even the implication that athletic glory is a poor second to spiritual glory has parallels in the writings of some philosophers who decry excessive attention to the physical. They certainly cannot be taken as evidence that people in Paul's circle were regularly spectators of (or participants in) competitions. In most Greek cities, however, theatres, gymnasia and running-tracks would be among the most prominent buildings, and would be the centre of the life of the community. Even in Palestine the hellenistic cities had such facilities (Schürer 1973–87: II, 44–8). Herod the Great held games in Caesarea and Jerusalem (Caesarea had in fact a theatre, an amphitheatre and a stadium: see p. 158). It is difficult to find firm evidence of Jewish participation in such public entertainments but there is some evidence that not all Jews rejected them. Josephus knew a Jewish actor in mimes, Aliturus, who was a favourite of the emperor Nero and who introduced him to the empress Poppaea (*Life*, 3, 16); however, the fact that Josephus describes Aliturus as a Jew 'by origin' (*to genos*) might suggest that he had given up the practice of Judaism. Philo admits to having seen a contest of pankratiasts (*That Every Good Man is Free* 5, 26) and a performance of the *Augē* of Euripides (*That Every Good Man is Free* 20, 141). There is an inscription in the theatre at Miletos which suggests that certain seats may have been reserved for Jews (Schürer 1973–87: III, 167–8; see pp. 201–2). It may be, then, that although the strictest interpretation of Jewish law excluded participation in Greek entertainments, individual Jews (possibly in large numbers) might well take part, especially if they were living in a highly hellenised environment (Schürer 1973–87: II, 54–5).

Performances of classical Greek plays and musical and athletic competitions were put on as part of the festivals dedicated to the gods. Professional actors and musicians belonged to an association of 'sacred victors and crown-winners and artists dedicated to Dionysos', just as professional athletes, boxers and wrestlers belonged to an association dedicated to Herakles (Millar 1992: 456ff.; Jones 1940: 230–1). That a highly privileged body of professional competitors eventually formed what were termed 'world-wide travelling' (*oikoumenikē peripolistikē*) associations which petitioned the emperors to protect those privileges illustrates the way in which such competitive 'games', all tied to pagan cults, multiplied in the hellenistic and Roman periods. To attract star performers cities competed to secure special status for their local festivals. Some are described as 'isolympian' or 'isopythian', which meant that athletic victories at such a festival entitled the victors to claim the same privileges from their home city as victors at two of the four games recognised as of the highest prestige in classical Greece. In the hellenistic age a city could obtain international recognition for its games only by widespread diplomacy (Jones 1940: 232), but from the time of Augustus all they required was the emperor's approval. The emperor Trajan evidently felt things had got out of hand and had pruned a list of games with 'eiselastic' status, ones where victors were not only entitled to make a triumphal entry (*eiselaunein*) into their native cities, but also to claim from them a subsistence allowance for life (Williams 1990: 156–7). Other 'games' had to attract competitors by offering cash prizes, and some of the travelling athletes did well out of them. Not that entrance was limited to visiting professionals, and the separate competitions for 'boys' (*paides*) and 'adolescents' (*ephēbeis*) were presumably included in the main for local boys and youths (at least those from the more prosperous families), for whom athletic training at the gymnasium was the main feature of education/ initiation into the distinctly Greek (male) way of life.

It should not be assumed, however, that the theatres possessed by virtually every city with any pretensions to significance were used exclusively (or even mostly) for the performance of serious works of literature like classical Greek tragedy. Apuleius' *Metamorphoses* depicts an entertainment in the theatre at Corinth which began with a dancing display (10, 29), including a Pyrrhic dance performed by boys and girls, followed by a pageant representing the Judgement of Paris, with spectacular special effects, and involving dancing and mime, as well as the display of a good deal of nudity on the part of Venus and her attendants (10, 30–2; 34), and culminating in a carefully orchestrated performance in which a female criminal was to be thrown to the wild beasts. Though allowance must be made for the fact that Apuleius was writing fiction, the general picture of the theatre as the scene for entertainments of all kinds, including executions, seems to be quite accurate. Religious performances might also take place there and, as we are reminded by Paul's experiences at Ephesos, it was the usual venue for public meetings. The Roman Cicero attributed the downfall of Greece to their habit of allowing ignorant people, 'sitting down' 'in the theatre', to make decisions (*Pro Flacco* 16), and it is certainly the case that the turbulence of the meeting at Ephesos was by no means unusual (compare Philo, *Against Flaccus* 41 and Josephus, *War* 7, 47–8). An ancient theatre was not a place devoted only to performances of the kind we now think of as theatrical. It was more of a general meeting place, an area which could be used whenever there was a need to accommodate a large crowd of people. It was not just for lovers of drama, but was one of the places where the community would come together for whatever purposes they chose. What is more, in most theatres seating was allocated to particular groups and statuses in the city, so that when the inhabitants gathered there the whole social structure of the community was visible to them.

THE POLITICS OF THE *POLIS*

Pausanias, the second-century author of a guidebook to Greece, asks whether it is proper to give the name *polis* to a community which has 'no offices for the magistrates, no gymnasium, no theatre, no *agora* [central square], no water brought down to a public fountain' (*Guide to Greece* 10, 4, 1). The provision and maintenance of all these essential attributes of the proper Greek *polis*, not to mention stadiums and prizes for athletic and other competitors, was an expensive business. It involved the leading families of a *polis* in large-scale giving, what was termed in Greek *philanthrōpia* (love of mankind) or being a 'do-gooder', a *euergetēs* (whence 'euergetism' as a synonym for 'philanthropia'). The evidence for this practice is very extensive, especially in the cities of western and southern Asia Minor. Apart from the public buildings for which such benefactors paid – the library at Ephesos, for example, recently reconstructed, built by Tiberius Iulius Aquila Polemaeanus in 110–20 in honour of his father Tiberius Iulius Celsus Polemaeanus, one of the earliest men of purely Greek origin to become a Roman consul – there are the statues erected in honour of such benefactors and the inscriptions on statue bases and elsewhere recording their services. One spectacular example is the ruined mausoleum at Rhodiapolis in Lycia of a local man named Opramoas, who must have been immensely wealthy. Inscribed on the walls were texts of no fewer than thirty-three decrees of the Lycian federal council and individual Lycian cities honouring him for his benefactions, as well as of twenty-three letters of governors of Lycia and thirteen letters of the emperor Antoninus Pius acknowledging receipt of messages in honour of Opramoas (see also p. 60). Such giving therefore differed from charity or almsgiving in the Jewish and Christian tradition. Even if wealthy Christians did not always live up to the commandment not to let their right hand know what their left hand was doing when they gave alms, the principle remained that no return should be expected or required in this world. Reciprocity, on the other hand, was an essential element of euergetism in the pagan world. Benefactors expected to receive, and beneficiaries felt obliged to confer, honours in return for gifts: votes of thanks, effusive praise, put on permanent display by being inscribed on stone, and, grandest of all, statues erected in the public spaces of the city. This was not only gratifying in itself, but was also an important element in the competition for status and prestige among the wealthy families of a city or region (Hands 1968: 26–61; Veyne 1990: 19–34).

Such reciprocity – favours evoking expressions of gratitude, with these in turn leading to claims for further favours – also characterised relations between individuals at different levels in a society best described as a steep pyramid of wealth and status. In Roman society such relationships were formalised as those between a *patronus* (the wealthier, more powerful, higher-ranking individual) and his *cliens* (a dependant of inferior status), whereas obligations incurred between social equals were described in terms of 'friendship' (*amicitia*). In a society without welfare services, effective police, paid lawyers, citizens' advice bureaux and even voluntary charitable organisations devoted to helping the needy (for euergetism benefited all citizens and, far from being targeted on the most needy, often conferred proportionately greater benefits on the better-off), there were numerous occasions on which an individual of lower social status would seek the help of a 'patron' of higher status. For example, a 'patron' with oratorical skills could speak in court on behalf of a 'client'. Such a favour would create a permanent mutual obligation, and at Rome clients would present themselves at their patron's home to greet him in the morning (the *salutatio*), and to escort him if he was going out to court, the Senate and so on. Since loyalty between patrons and clients was so important to the smooth running of Roman society there were the strongest social and moral sanctions for those who failed to carry out their obligations. How drastic the effect could be, at least at the very top, is illustrated by a story about Augustus in old age (technically this concerned a breach of friendship between equals rather than between patron and client, but 'friendship' with an emperor was a very unequal relationship). Augustus found out that a close adviser, Fabius Maximus, had 'leaked' a secret; when Fabius next attended the *salutatio* and greeted Augustus 'Ave, Caesar' ('Hail, Caesar') Augustus, instead of responding 'Ave, Fabi' ('Hail, Fabius'), said 'Vale, Fabi' (Goodbye, Fabius') and Fabius went home and killed himself (Plutarch, *Moralia* 508A). (The identity of the person involved is established as Paullus Fabius Maximus by Tacitus (*Annals* 1, 5), but see Millar 1992: 113 for a note of caution.)

Paul, as a visitor of not very high status in different cities, would have found useful the protection of 'patrons' (in the general, rather than the technical Roman sense): Jason at Thessalonika (Acts 17, 5 and 9), Titus Iustus at Corinth (Acts 18, 17) and the unnamed Asiarchs at Ephesos (Acts 19, 31) could be said to fill this rôle in their respective cities.

One region of the Roman Empire where this network of 'euergetism' and patronage failed to secure social cohesion and public order was Judaea. There, the local aristocracy had no legitimacy, being simply the courtiers of the Herodian dynasty, and the high priests were manifestly puppets of the current regime. The alternative source of authority, skill in interpreting the Law, had no integral connection with the wealthy landowning classes. Indeed, the prevailing ideology of Jewish society was egalitarian. The Temple and other religious institutions depended not on the benefactions of the wealthy élite but on the two-drachma tax paid by all adult male Jews. The belief that riches were morally and spiritually dangerous, and that only the poor are truly righteous, had deep roots in the prophetic tradition. The provision of charity and expenditure on public welfare was regarded as an act of piety, a duty, rather than a spontaneous and praiseworthy act of beneficence. There was no traditional wealthy élite to which the population in general looked as a natural ruling class. Elsewhere such a class, which would inevitably have a vested interest in good order and the maintenance of the status quo, could be cultivated by the Romans, protected by them and brought into the system. In Judaea the absence of such legitimate local authority resulted in breakdown and revolt in 66 (Goodman 1987: 109–33).

Whether the Jewish communities in the diaspora remained untouched by the euergetism/patronage system is another question. It has been argued (Rajak and Noy 1993: 84–9) that some movement in this direction can be detected in diaspora synagogues. The officials called *archisynagōgoi* whom Paul encounters at Pisidian Antioch (Acts 13, 15) seem to have responsibility for the conduct of the synagogue services, and elsewhere they are represented as having considerable status within their communities (Acts 18, 8; 18, 17). Other evidence, however, shows that the office was sometimes held by children (in one case as young as three years old) or by women, and occasionally appointments were made for life. In these cases it seems unlikely that real responsibilities went with the office. Often the *archisynagōgos* was a benefactor or a patron of the community, and might not necessarily have been Jewish. Rajak and Noy therefore argue that such communities had adopted the Greek practice of conferring titles which were purely honorific, and did not carry responsibilities with them.

To return to euergetism at the level of the city (and below this of associations within a city such as those of the Young Men (*Neoi*) and the Elders (*Gerousia*) attached to the gymnasium), where did the wealth for what were sometimes lavish displays of generosity come from? The most important source of wealth in the classical world, as in nearly all pre-industrial societies, was land. The leading citizens of the *polis* would be large landowners who derived most of their income either from rents from free tenants or from the sale of crops produced by the labour of slaves. They did not have the same incentives to save and invest part of their income that their counterparts in the modern world have; there were no secure forms of investment except land, no stocks or shares, no 'blue chip' companies, and opportunities to buy additional land seem to have been rare. There seems to have been little need to borrow for investment because in the province of Bithynia-Pontus the younger Pliny suggested forcing the city councillors to take out loans from city funds so as to provide the cities with the income (Pliny, *Letters* 10, 54; the emperor rejected the proposal: 10, 55). Rich men thus had little to do with their income except to spend it, and they would be under great pressure from their fellow-citizens to do so on 'philanthropy'. Indeed, rich men who were suspected of trying to enrich themselves by hoarding grain in times of shortage, for example, might find themselves the object of violent demonstrations, as happened to the orator Dio of Prusa in his native city (Jones 1978: 19–25). Unlike their counterparts in modern Britain (at least before the twentieth century) the aristocracies of the Roman Empire were based in the cities; their principal residences were in the towns, and country estates served only as places to go for holidays (Rawson 1976: 86–91). Unlike the first Lord Tollemache who, in the 'hungry forties' of nineteenth-century Britain, built himself a formidable castle in the country at Peckforton as a refuge from potential threats from industrial workers in the towns, the ancient notables wanted to continue living in the cities, and so the price of popularity with the poorer townsfolk (and even of personal safety) was expenditure on euergetism.

ECONOMIC LIFE

This brings us to the issue of the economic basis of urban life in the Roman world. Sir Moses Finley produced a very powerful explanatory model of the ancient economy. According to this ancient towns, unlike those of medieval and early modern Europe, did not have to earn their own living by producing and selling to the rural population goods and services which the latter wanted. In medieval and early modern Europe the nobility who controlled the countryside did not live in the towns, but in the ancient world they did, and spent the surplus produced by free peasants and slave labourers in the towns. In a sense ancient towns and their residents were parasitic on the countryside. Professor Keith Hopkins adduced some convincing evidence to support the argument that the Finley hypothesis, if put in this bald, extreme form, went much too far: a rural market for urban products did exist, and in the first two centuries AD sea-borne trade in the Mediterranean flourished as it had never done before and reached levels not seen again for a thousand years. The evidence of inscriptions reveals a high degree of craft specialisation, even in quite small cities. Paul and his fellow craftsmen were not therefore just catering for the needs and appetites of a small number of rich families and of an urban population subsidised by the former at the expense of the rural poor. Nevertheless, without the transfer of resources from country to town, not just by trade but also in the form of rents, the growth and prosperity of the cities, the splendid monuments and the urban amenities described above would not have been possible. (For a discussion of these issues, see Finley 1973: 35–61; Jones 1974: 35–60; Hopkins 1980: 101–25.)

ROME AND THE GREEK *POLIS*

What the civic aristocracies got in return for 'euergetism' was not just prestige and flattery, but also effective political control of their cities. Or rather internal developments and Roman pressure eliminated any effective popular participation in government but, since there was no equivalent of a police force or a gendarmerie at the disposal of the city authorities – the account in Acts of the demonstration at Ephesos, in which it is clear that the Clerk of the People has no resources on which to draw beyond his own capacity to persuade the crowd, reflects this state of affairs – 'voluntary' expenditure on what the Roman satirist Juvenal (10, 81) referred to as 'bread and circuses' (in relation to the urban poor of Rome itself) was a necessary method of appeasing the urban masses, whose volatility is well illustrated by the events at Philippi (Acts 16, 22), Thessalonika (Acts 17, 5), Corinth (Acts 18, 17) and Ephesos (Acts 19, 28–41). When Roman emperors or governors had occasion to send formal letters to a Greek *polis*, as they often did, the standard introductory formula was 'The Emperor so-and-so to the *archontes*, *boulē*, and *ekklēsia* of the Cyrenians, greetings'. These were the three main institutions of the self-governing communities of the Roman Empire. The *ekklēsia* was an assembly of all adult male citizens with full political rights (the equivalent bodies at Rome and in Roman citizen colonies were known as *comitia* in Latin). In theory an *ekklēsia* might consist of several thousand voters, and in the most fully developed democracy in the Greek world, that of Athens in the fifth and fourth centuries BC, it met at least forty times a year and was the supreme legislative and policy-making body. The Romans, however, did not look with favour on democracies in the Greek style, and under their suzerainty the meetings of the city assemblies did little more than rubber-stamp the proposals of the councils (Jones 1940: ch. 11; de Sainte Croix 1981: 518–37). It is doubtful whether Paul encountered any formal meeting of an *ekklēsia* – the *dēmos* at Thessalonika was no more than a mob (Wallace and Williams 1993: 83–4), while the meeting at Ephesos began as an unofficial mass meeting (Wallace and Williams 1993: 109–10).

The *boulē* or council of a *polis* consisted of up to six hundred members (at Athens in the first century); smaller *poleis* would have smaller councils, and the standard size for a Roman colony seems to have been a hundred (known in Latin as the *ordo* of *decuriones*). In democratic Athens the members of the *boulē* had been chosen by lot and replaced annually, and had acted as a steering committee of the *ekklēsia*; at Rome members of the Senate sat for life and were co-opted by special officers (the censors), and under the republic effectively determined the policy of the state. Again the Romans pushed the councils of the *poleis* away from the Athenian and towards the Roman model. Eventually in most *poleis* the council consisted of the members of a hereditary élite, sitting for life and running the affairs of the *polis*. The only two councils with which Paul was involved were both highly exceptional: the Areopagus at Athens (the smaller of two councils which carried out the same functions as the archons of other *poleis*) and the Sanhedrin at Jerusalem (a city which cannot really be characterised as a *polis*, though if it were, the Sanhedrin would be its *boulē* and the high priest its (sole) *archōn*).

Archontes, anglicised as archons, means 'rulers' or 'governors'; it was a general term for the chief executive officers of a city (the Latin equivalent was *magistratus*, 'magistrates') who were usually replaced every year. In Greek *poleis* their number and titles varied from area to area and city to city (e.g. politarchs (number unspecified) at Thessalonika; the Clerk of the People at Ephesos); in all Roman colonies the senior magistrates were *duoviri iure dicundo* ('two men for giving judgement'; the 'generals' at Philippi, see Wallace and Williams 1993: 78–9). The Roman preference was for the election of the archons by the Council rather than by the Assembly, and for the archons to be turned into mere agents of the Council. The eventual outcome of the 'Romanisation' of the institutions of the *polis* was that Councils composed of members of a hereditary aristocracy ran the cities, with members taking it in turn to serve as archons and carry out the Council's decisions, while meetings of the Assembly became purely ceremonial events. The same hereditary aristocrats engaged in euergetism and paid for the civic amenities.

They were also liable to be held responsible by Rome for the good behaviour of their *poleis*. The alarm expressed by the Clerk of the People at Ephesos (Acts 19, 40; cf. Wallace and Williams 1993: 170) was not misplaced. The governor might, for example, intervene to suspend the *ekklēsia* (assembly) of a city. Cities were also jealous of their status and rank in a province, and titles which were conferred by Rome could be taken away by her. The venom which could be expressed by rival cities is revealed in a nicely ironic letter from Antoninus Pius to the city of Ephesos:

> I welcome the news that the people of Pergamon in their letter to you used the titles I decided your city should use; and I think that it was by accident that the people of Smyrna omitted the titles in the decree about the joint sacrifice, and that in future they will be glad to co-operate if you in your turn, in your letters to them, remember the appropriate style of address which, it has been decided, belongs to their city.
>
> (*SIG*^{3} no. 849)

Clearly this had been a case of the pot calling the kettle black. A few cities were in theory outside the governor's control; such cities either had treaties with the Roman state dating back to the period of Roman expansion ('federate cities') or had received unilateral grants of freedom from Rome ('free cities'). Among the latter were Athens and Thessalonika (Wallace and Williams 1993: 16–17). But since ordinary provincial cities enjoyed a high degree of internal autonomy (unless they fell prey to riots, political cliques or financial mismanagement), and since both grants of freedom and treaties could be scrapped by Rome if the 'free' cities blotted their copy-books in any way, the distinctions were of more ceremonial than practical importance.

Not that the observation of ceremonial was regarded as unimportant by Rome in securing the peaceful co-operation of the local aristocracies and townsfolk; after all, in many of the provinces of the interior the Roman governors had no troops at their disposal to impose order. As late as AD 243 the emperor Gordian III was re-assuring the free city of Aphrodisias that 'the resolution of [the common council] of Asia ... was not a command, for it is not possible to use commands in respect of those who are free ... ' (Reynolds 1982: 133–5), and in the 180s Commodus was hesitant about even permitting the proconsul to visit Aphrodisias at that city's own request (Reynolds 1982: 119–24). Elsewhere visits from the governor were regarded as an honour (and in the case of assize centres were also a source of profit: see p. 81 above). The emperor Caracalla gratified the Ephesians by laying it down that 'a duty was imposed on the proconsul of approaching Asia by sea and of touching at Ephesos first of the *metropoleis*' (*Digest* 1, 16, 4, 5); there are actually coins of Ephesos with the proud legend 'Disembarkation of the Ephesians' (Head 1911: 577). The jurist Ulpian who cites this ruling also gives a proconsul the following advice:

> If he comes to a city other than a populous one or the provincial capital he should allow the city to be commended to him and should listen to his praises being sung without appearing bored, since the provincials claim this right for the sake of their honour. And he should grant a festival according to custom and previous practice.

> (*Digest* 1, 16, 7, pr.)

The kind of thing proconsuls would have to put up with is described in a handbook for Greek orators by Menander Rhetor. Prescriptions for the way to 'address a governor who has come to stay in the city' include: 'You should say at once, "With fortunate omens you have come from the emperor, brilliant as a ray of light from on high. Thus a happy report brought word of your fortunate arrival and the enviable lot of the subject peoples . . . " ', etc., etc. (Menander Rhetor, trans. Russell and Wilson 1981: 95). A very elaborate section is devoted to the speech in praise of the emperor (Russell and Wilson 1981: 77–95). A main feature of the diplomatic activity of the cities was the sending of embassies made up of leading citizens to deal with the emperor face to face. In some cases they would be appealing for favours – a separate section headed 'The Ambassador's Speech' begins: 'If you have to act as ambassador on behalf of a city in trouble . . . amplify at every point the topic of the emperor's humanity' (Russell and Wilson 1981: 181); in others they would simply be delivering the city's congratulations on the emperor's accession or his birthday (early in the second century an envoy was sent by Byzantium every year to greet Trajan and paid generous expenses, until a new governor in an economy drive put a stop to it, with Trajan's consent – Williams 1990: 39, 103–5). Of course a wealthy citizen could display his civic patriotism by waiving his claim for expenses (another form of euergetism). The sheer scale of these diplomatic and ceremonial journeyings is shown by an inscription which shows that in the early third century a citizen of Ephesos had travelled to Rome, Britain, Upper Germany, Sirmium (in modern Croatia), Nicomedia, Antioch and Mesopotamia (Williams 1990: 105), as the city's ambassador to the emperors.

In this way the city advertised its loyalty to the emperor, and hoped for its loyalty to be rewarded. Perhaps the most important way of displaying loyalty was to institute a cult and build a temple for the worship of the emperor as a god. Emperor-worship was by no means introduced to the cities of the eastern Mediterranean by the Romans, or imposed on the provincials by them. The origins of the practice went back to Alexander and his immediate successors, when it caused some shock to traditionally pious Greeks. By the time Roman power had expanded into the Greek world ruler-cult had become the accepted way of acknowledging the authority of a suzerain. Cities worshipped *Roma* as a goddess, but also deified individual Roman generals and governors. With the advent of Augustus as sole ruler the latter practice ceased. Individual cities founded local cults of individual emperors, but under Augustus there also developed the institutions of an imperial cult at the provincial level. Delegates from the cities of a province (Asia, for example) assembled once a year and elected a high priest for the cult to serve for a year (these high priests were associated in some way with the grandees known as Asiarchs: Acts 19, 3; see also Wallace and Williams 1993: 106; Kearsley 1986: 183–92; Kearsley 1994: 363–76). A new temple of the provincial cult of each new emperor was put up in different cities. Such a city was proud of its title of 'temple-guardian' of the imperial cult; the Greek term is *neōkoros*, which is also used of Ephesos by the Clerk of the People in Acts 11, 35, though there the city is the temple-guardian of the Great Artemis (see Wallace and Williams 1993: 107–8).

The modern reader is inclined to ask whether the imperial cult was a real religion, whether participants really believed that emperors, living or dead, were superhuman beings with supernatural powers. A modern scholar has recently condemned such questions because the use of emotions as a test of authenticity in rituals is 'covertly Christianising', because the search for the Greeks' real beliefs is a mistake since 'belief' as a religious term is Christian, and because they lay improper emphasis on individuals (Price 1984: 7–11). Yet there may have been some individuals at the time who engaged in theological speculations and, in any case, the greatest authority on ancient religion in an earlier generation, A. D. Nock, suggested a test based on instinctive, visceral reactions. Thousands of *ex voto* dedications survive from antiquity, recording that they were made to fulfil a vow (*ex voto* = 'from a vow'). Such a vow would be made in a prayer to a deity when the person involved was facing some grave emergency. Nock found only one such dedication made to a deified ruler, and that at a very early stage in the history of ruler-cult (King Ptolemy I, see Nock 1972: 834). Ancient pagans did not, it seems, pray to the emperor to rescue them from being drowned in a shipwreck.

Nor did the emperors (the sane ones) harbour any illusions about the limits of their powers. Vespasian is even said to have joked about his deification on his deathbed: 'I must be done for – I can feel myself turning into a god' ('Vae, deus fio, puto'; literally: 'Alas, I am becoming a god, I think': Suetonius, *Vespasian* 23, 4). It is therefore a mistake to think of the early Christian martyrs as victims of cruel megalomaniacs who resented the Christians' refusal to acknowledge their divinity. Ordinary people were not required to take part in the rituals of any of the official cults of the cities – that was a matter for the duly appointed priests or magistrates. A demand for sacrifices not just to the emperor but also to the traditional gods was first used as a test to discover whether those who said they had apostatised from Christianity were being truthful (Williams 1990: 141, with the references given there). Later, when governors tried to force Christian confessors to sacrifice, it was conformity to the traditional religion in general, not just to the imperial cult, which was being demanded of them. At any rate there is not one shred of evidence that emperor-worship was an issue in Paul's generation.

SUGGESTIONS FOR FURTHER READING

(full details of these works can be found in the Bibliography):

Though over fifty years old, A. H. M. Jones' *The Greek City from Alexander to Justinian* remains an incomparable quarry for information on all aspects of this subject.

On euergetism in general, see P. Veyne's *Bread and Circuses*, and on its failure in Judaea, M. Goodman's *The Ruling Class of Judaea*.

C. P. Jones' *The Roman World of Dio Chrysostom* offers a vivid picture of life in the eastern provinces.

8

THE INDIVIDUAL'S
SELF-IDENTIFICATION

Here there cannot be Greek and Jew, circumcised and uncircumcised, barbarian, Scythian, slave, free man, but Christ is all in all.

(Colossians 3, 11)

Now the first principle [of association among humans] is that which is seen in the connection between the whole human race; the bond of this is reason and discourse. . . . There are many levels of association among humans. Leaving aside that unlimited kind, the next one is that of the same people, tribe, language, by which humans are especially linked together; it is a still closer bond to be a member of the same state ['city']. For fellow-citizens have many things in common with each other: the forum, temples, porticoes, streets, laws, rights, courts, votes. . . . An even closer link of association is that between kindred . . .

(Cicero, De Officiis 1, 50, 53)

Paul lists distinctions which gave rise to exclusiveness and contempt: Greeks looked down on barbarians (i.e. those who did not speak Greek – Scythians would be one example of such a people, and one which was 'uncultured'); Jews excluded Gentiles (the uncircumcised), but were disliked by many Greeks, even if they spoke the Greek language; and anyone who was free could look down on and feel superior to any slave (even if some slaves were, in terms of intellectual attainments and/or material goods, better off than many of the free poor). There was therefore a variety of groups with which individuals in Paul's world could identify themselves; it was a much more complex pattern than that of the 'ideal type' of nation-state of the nineteenth- and twentieth-century West (an 'ideal type' to which hardly any real states conformed) in which language, culture and citizenship coincided.

117

RELIGION

Jews did not fit into either of Cicero's intermediate categories. With the growth of diaspora communities many Jews were monoglot Greek-speakers, whereas the majority of those in Palestine and Babylonia were Aramaic-speakers; nor were they members/subjects of a single political community. The Aramaic-speaking Jews of Jerusalem could be viewed (by Greeks or Romans) as citizens of a *civitas/polis*, or those of all Judaea as a 'nation/tribe' (*natio/ethnos*) which could possibly include the other Jews of Palestine (especially Galilee). What united all Jews in their own eyes (and what made them seem unique in the eyes of Romans, Greeks, etc.) was their religious allegiance to a god who was worshipped in the Temple at Jerusalem (it was the site of the Temple at Jerusalem which distinguished them from the Samaritans, who claimed to worship the same god and to follow the same Law, but whose temple was on Mount Gerizim). All male Jews bore the mark of their allegiance to that god, having been circumcised in infancy or as a condition of being converted to Judaism; all adult males were expected to (and most evidently did) support the costs of the elaborate daily sacrifices at the temple by paying a flat-rate tax (the *didrachm*, or 'two-drachma' payment) every year (Schürer 1973–87: III (1), 147–8). Jewish self-identification by religious allegiance rather than by political or ethnic ties was probably unique in the ancient Mediterranean world. There were of course numerous groups from one community living in other communities; indeed, there was a whole series of such diasporas. Such people did not forget the gods of their original communities. An inscription in Greek from the island of Delos, set up by three citizens of Jamnia in Palestine, reads as follows: 'To Herakles and Hauronas, gods dwelling in [or possessing] Jamnia, Zenodoros, Patron, Diodoros, citizens of Jamnia [set up] on behalf of [or for the sake of] themselves and their brothers and kinsfolk and their fellow-citizens dwelling with them, a thank-offering. To sacrifice all things except goat's meat' (Robert 1981: 517). The Jewish diaspora, however, differed from the other diaspora communities in at least three important ways: their regular financial contributions to the Temple; the sheer number and size of their communities; and their religious exclusiveness and refusal to show any respect for the local gods of the communities in which they had come to live.

The expansion of the Jewish communities in the Greco-Roman

world was noted late in the first century BC by the historian and geographer Strabo. Josephus quotes a passage from Strabo's lost history which referred to the city of Cyrene around 85 BC and to Jews as one of four classes of resident: 'This people had [or has] already made its way into every city, and it is not easy to find a place in the whole world which has not received this people and in which it has not made its power felt' (*Ant.* 14, 115). Other evidence of the range of the Jewish dispersion and the numbers involved is collected in Schürer 1973–87: III (1), 4ff. The revised Schürer raises, but does not attempt to answer, the question, 'Can this small population [of Judaea] have provided such multitudes of settlers . . . or was it greatly increased by converts to Judaism in the last centuries BC?' (Schürer 1973–87: III (1), 4). Schürer (or his revisers) neglect a point noted by the earliest Greek to describe the Jewish way of life in detail, late in the fourth century BC, Hekataios of Abdera: 'He [Moses] compelled those who lived in the land to rear their children and, since children were raised at little expense, the Jews were from the beginning a populous nation' (Diodorus 40, 3, 8; Stern 1974: I, no. 11). The Roman historian Tacitus recorded that among the Jews it was 'unlawful (*nefas*) to kill any of the new-born' (Tacitus, *Histories* 5, 5). This rule was in stark contrast to the practices of the classical world, where exposure of the new-born as a method of population control was widespread (Boswell 1988: 3–179). The historian Polybius deplored the depopulation of Greece in the mid-second century BC, and had no doubt about the cause: 'men who were not willing to marry, or, if they did marry, to rear the children that were born, or at best one or two out of many' (Polybius 36, 17, 7). Josephus, on the other hand, stressed that according to Jewish law the function of marriage was the procreation of children (*Against Apion* 2, 199), that it orders all children to be reared, and that abortion counts as infanticide, 'destroying a soul and diminishing the race' (*Against Apion* 2, 202). There is no need therefore to assume large-scale conversion (i.e. involving adult circumcision for men) to account for the growth of the diaspora, although the number of Judaising 'god-fearers' who did not take that final step (see p. 124) may have been large.

The large size of resident Jewish communities in Greek *poleis* will have exacerbated the hostility evoked by the exclusiveness of the Jews and their export of cash to Judaea. At the level of everyday social contact there were, for example, the difficulties which devout Jews would have in sharing a meal with Gentiles, and which clearly caused resentment: the historian Tacitus, in a long list of complaints against the Jews (*Histories* 5, 5) notes that 'they dine on their own' (i.e. they do not give or accept invitations to dinner). Strictly observant Jews took the view that Gentiles (and their homes) were unclean and defiling, and should be avoided altogether, but even Jews living in Gentile communities and perforce regularly doing business with them, would have had serious problems about accepting a meal in a Gentile home, for two reasons. First, it would be improbable (and unsafe to assume) that such a meal would conform to the dietary rules laid down in Leviticus 11 and subsequently elaborated. Presumably this was the objection of those who complained about Peter's visit to Cornelius: 'Why did you go to uncircumcised men and eat with them?' (Acts 11, 3). Second, there was the problem of food offered to idols. In pagan religion, a sacrifice was a meal shared between the god and the worshippers. An invitation to a social meal might well be an invitation to a shared sacrifice, and surplus meat from public sacrifices would be disposed of in the market-place (see p. 103). A Jew could not be sure that accepting a meal offered to him by a Gentile would not imply involvement with idolatry. This was a problem for Christians also, and Paul discusses it in 1 Corinthians 8, taking the view that food offered to idols is not objectively polluting (since idols have no power) but that it should be avoided so as not to give offence. The problem of diet may lie behind the curious set of rules laid down by the apostles and elders in Jerusalem in response to complaints from rigorists about the admission to the church of uncircumcised converts. The rules do not mention circumcision at all, but Gentile converts are enjoined to 'abstain from what has been sacrificed to idols and from blood and from what is strangled and from unchastity' (Acts 15, 29). Though even in antiquity attempts were made to give these instructions more moral content, they look like a set of guidelines to enable Jewish and Gentile Christians to share meals by avoiding problems arising from food offered to idols, and at any rate the most serious violations of Jewish dietary laws. Certainly by the time we reach the period when the co-existence of Gentile and Jewish Christians had ceased to be an issue, the ruling of the Jerusalem council seems to have remarkably little effect on Christian practice (for a discussion see Wallace and Williams 1993: 70–2 and Wilson 1983: 68–102).

A minor but telling instance of the prejudices which developed in the Greco-Roman world is the sour remark of the Roman satirist

Juvenal (early second century): 'They learn and observe and fear Jewish law, whatever Moses handed down in his secret book, not to show the way to anyone but a fellow-worshipper, to lead only the circumcised to a drinking fountain when asked to do so' (*Satires* 14, 101–4). That this reflected widely held beliefs is shown by the efforts of the Jewish apologist Josephus to rebut the charge: 'He [Moses] defined other things which it was obligatory to share: to supply to all who ask fire, water, sustenance; to point out the road . . . ' (*Against Apion* 2, 211). Josephus even interpreted Deuteronomy 27, 48, 'Cursed be he that maketh the blind to walk out of the way', in these words: 'One must point out the way to those who do not know it, and not seek entertainment in impeding someone's business by leading them astray' (*Ant.* 4, 276).

At the community level, Greek *poleis* resented the outflow of money which resulted from the *didrachma* paid by adult males (see p. 118); at Cyrene, even after Augustus had instructed that the Jews should be allowed to send money to Jerusalem without hindrance, attempts were made to frustrate this by false allegations that the Jews owed taxes to the city, so that Augustus' right-hand man Agrippa had to intervene. This is one of a series of announcements by Augustus and proconsuls of Asia quoted by Josephus as evidence of the protection offered by the Roman authorities, especially in the province of Asia. One of the main focuses of the communal loyalties of the Greek *poleis* was the cult of their local gods (see p. 101), so that the Greeks of Cyrene and Asia may well have felt that money earned in their cities should be devoted to the cult of the civic gods. Other immigrants would have had no difficulty about supporting local cults and would expect to do so as a matter of courtesy. This was the convention of classical polytheism: one showed special devotion to the particular gods of one's own ancestors (or to new cults which inspired special enthusiasm), but one would never insult or fail to show respect for other gods, especially the presiding deities of whatever place one might be visiting (see MacMullen 1981: 2–4). But for pious Jews, the fundamental principles of their religion (including two of the Ten Commandments: 'You shall have no other gods before me. You shall not make to yourself a graven image . . . ; you shall not bow down to them or serve them', Exodus 20, 3–4) made it impossible to engage in any such acts of courtesy, and even the Hellenisers in Jerusalem in the 170s BC jibbed at this point; a delegation sent to the Phoenician city of Tyre with money to pay for a sacrifice to

Tyre's patron deity, Herakles/Melkart, used it instead to pay for building a warship (2 Maccabees 4, 18–20).

This clash between a monotheist and a polytheist view of the world explains why Gentiles so often charged Jews, and subsequently Christians, with 'atheism'; Dio Cassius (early third century) wrote of the Jewish people that 'it is split off from the rest of mankind both in virtually every aspect of daily life and especially in that they honour none of the other gods, but show extreme veneration for one particular god' (37, 12, 2). Nevertheless, the Roman imperial government in general upheld the right of the Jews to lead their way of life, not just in their homeland but also in the various parts of the Empire where they had settled. Josephus collected a large body of documents which testified to this tradition of protection in *Antiquities* 14, 185–267 and 16, 160–78. There is no surviving detailed discussion or explanation of this policy from a Gentile author. Some factors which contributed to it may be outlined. The Jews (until AD 66) were anxious not to appear politically disloyal; from the time of Augustus down to the rebellion in 66 a sacrifice (of two lambs and a bull) for the emperor and the Roman People was offered twice daily in the Temple at Jerusalem (Josephus, *War* 2, 197, 409–10; *Against Apion* 2, 77; Philo, *Legatio* 157, 317). Roman administration was highly conservative, so that where it found that the hellenistic dynasties had granted the Jews privileges, it maintained them. Judaism had 'friends in high places' (Sherwin-White 1967: 96) in the shape of the Herodian dynasty who kept well in with Julius Caesar, Antonius, Augustus, Gaius (Caligula) and Claudius, and generally maintained good relationships with the Julio-Claudian dynasty. Suetonius tells us that, after the assassination of Julius Caesar, 'foreigners gathered in groups lamenting him, each according to their own custom, especially the Jews who crowded round his pyre for entire nights' (*Divus Iulius* 84, 5). But, above all, the Romans were devoted upholders of the *mos maiorum*, 'the custom of the ancestors', especially in matters of religion, and believed that their subject peoples should be the same. They had a healthy respect for the local supernatural powers of the places on which they made war, and had an old religious ritual for inviting such powers to desert the enemies of the Romans in return for Roman favours, 'making them an offer they could not refuse'; the *evocatio* ceremony was being performed as late as the 70s BC (Hall 1973: 570). Therefore the God of the Jews and his exceptional demands had to be respected. As Tacitus puts it, 'these ceremonies, whatever their origin, are protected by their antiquity' (*Histories* 5, 5), and in an edict quoted by Josephus the emperor Claudius said, 'It is fitting that the Jews also throughout the whole world under our rule should follow their ancestral customs without hindrance' (*Ant.* 19, 290). Gentile converts to Christianity, however, could expect no such tolerance; in Roman eyes, as Gibbon put it, 'the Jews were a people which followed, the Christians a sect which deserted, the religion of their fathers' (*Decline and Fall*, Table of Contents, ch. 16).

As we have seen, for non-Jews the worship of the gods was very much tied up with the life of the city, and attachment to particular gods was a way of expressing loyalty to one's community (which is not to say that pagan worship was not a genuine expression of religious feeling). Similarly membership of a family or a profession might bring with it an obligation to a special god. Worship of this kind, however, was just one expression of a broader loyalty, and is not comparable to the Jewish self-identification through religion. The same may be said for the cults of foreign (non-Greek) gods which are frequently found in the cities of the Roman Empire. Though it was undoubtedly the case that there were individuals with a taste for such things who might attach themselves to foreign cults, in almost all cases their presence in a city meant foreign worshippers (MacMullen 1981: 112–18). So the strong presence of Egyptian cults in Ephesos (and the dearth of other foreign cults) is to be accounted for not by mass conversions among Ephesians to the religion of the Egyptians, but by the city's trading links with Egypt. Similarly, dedications to Artemis of Perge found in a number of Asian cities simply mark the presence of Pergeans in those cities. Even those who chose a foreign cult out of personal preference will have done so in addition to, rather than instead of, the cult of their native gods. There is no question of conversion from one religion to another; one did not identify oneself as a worshipper of Isis, in the same way that Jews identified themselves as Jews. A small number of people were devotees of 'invented' cults like that of Mithras (which, despite its Persian trappings, seems to have originated not in Persia but in the European provinces of the Roman Empire), but their number was very small, and devotion to such cults did not exclude other forms of worship (MacMullen 1981: 118–26; Lane-Fox 1986: 35–6, 82–3).

It is, however, more difficult to categorise those Gentiles who attached themselves to Judaism. Proselytes, of course, who simply became Jews, raise few problems. They joined the Jewish *ethnos*, and presumably cut their ties with their previous community. The historian Tacitus complained that the first lesson such people learned was 'to despise the gods, to cast off their native land, and to consider their parents, children, and brothers as worthless' (*Histories* 5, 5). There was, however, also a group of Gentiles who were attracted to Judaism and attached themselves to Jewish communities without fully becoming Jews. Josephus claims that 'for a long time the masses have been eager to imitate our religious practices, and there is no city, Greek or barbarian, and no nation to which our custom of resting on the seventh day has not spread, and where our feasts and lighting of lamps and many of our food prohibitions are not observed' (*Against Apion* 2, 282; see also Persius 5, 179–84; Seneca, *Moral Epistles* 95, 47; Horace, *Satires* 1, 9, 68–72; Juvenal 14, 96–106). He knows of 'judaisers' in every city of Syria (*War* 2, 463), and especially in Antioch (*War* 7, 45). These are the people Acts refers to as *phoboumenoi* or *sebomenoi ton theon*, 'god-fearers' (e.g. 13, 6; 13, 26; 17, 4; 17, 17) and to whom Paul's message was particularly attractive. These terms were also applied even to full Jews, but the existence of this group of sympathisers with Judaism is now guaranteed by the discovery of an inscription at Aphrodisias (Reynolds and Tannenbaum 1987) where the *theosebeis* (another term for them) are included in a list of synagogue members separately from proselytes and those born Jews (Schürer 1973–87: III (1), 160–72; Trebilco 1991: 145–66). No doubt there was considerable variation in the degree to which 'god-fearers' conformed to Jewish practice. An inscription of the first century AD from Acmonia records the building of a synagogue by one Julia Severa, who we know from other evidence had served as a high priestess in the cult of the emperor. She cannot, then, have been a Jew, and if she had retained her connection with the synagogue she is unlikely to have been an apostate. This may be a case where sympathy with Judaism was not thought to be incompatible with participation in pagan cults (Trebilco 1991: 58–60). It impossible to know to what extent people of this kind had taken on the Jewish self-identification through religion.

PHILOSOPHY

Though it would be an exaggeration to claim that no ancient religion (apart from Judaism and Christianity) gave any guidance about the conduct of life at all, in general it is fair to say that their adherents did not expect to get much in the way of moral instruction from the worship of the gods. For the educated classes that rôle was filled by philosophy, which offered an understanding of the nature of the world, of humanity's place in it and of the implications of this understanding for the behaviour of the individual. For many, adherence to a philosophical 'school' will have been a significant part of their identity. Consequently Jews and Christians sometimes found it useful to present their beliefs and teachings not as pure religions in the sense in which religion was usually understood in the ancient world, but as a sort of amalgam of religion and philosophy.

It must be stressed, however, that when we talk about a philosophical 'school' we are not talking about an organisation which had a membership and which one could join (any more than the worshippers of the conventional gods formed a congregation or a denomination in the modern sense). Philosophical allegiance was self-defined, based partly on 'a virtually religious commitment to the authority of a founder figure' (Sedley 1989: 97), and partly on reliance on a set of texts which were regarded, if not as authoritative, at least as central to the school (Sedley 1989: 99–102). There was no orthodoxy which the believer had to accept (nor any way of forming one), and the range of opinions held by supposed adherents of a school might be quite wide. An individual's philosophical allegiance might be formed by attending lectures at intellectual centres such as Athens, Rhodes or Tarsus, by attendance at schools like that run by the Stoic Epiktetos in Nikopolis, or by association with individual philosophers. The central texts of the school were usually complex works of a highly technical nature (this is especially true of the Stoics, whose works were notorious for their aridity), and would certainly not be part of the regular reading of any but the most devoted followers of the school. There were, however, popularising versions of the school's teachings (examples being Seneca's *Moral Epistles*, Epiktetos' *Discourses* and perhaps the versification of Epicurus' physics by the Latin poet Lucretius) which were more widely read. All of this would naturally be accessible only to the intellectual élite (or those who chose to think of themselves as such); of the mainstream schools only the Epicureans seem to have made a serious attempt to broaden their appeal. Nevertheless, many of the shared assumptions of philosophers were widely disseminated through society, in part through the activities of popular moralisers such as the Cynics.

What the Roman world knew as philosophy, however, was quite different from the critical academic discipline we know today. The first philosophical system-builders were probably Plato and Aristotle, working in Athens in the fourth century BC. It was at the end of the fourth and the beginning of the third centuries BC that the distinctive philosophies of the hellenistic and Roman periods began to take shape. The two schools mentioned at Acts 17, 18, the Stoics and Epicureans, were certainly the most successful, though by Paul's day their members were probably not at the forefront of new developments in philosophy. Both schools were originally founded in Athens, Epicureanism by an Athenian citizen (originally from Samos) called Epicurus who set up his school there in 306 in a house with a garden quite near the Academy, and Stoicism by Zeno from Kition in Cyprus, whose school got its name from the *stoa poikilē*, the 'painted stoa', a covered arcade on the north edge of the *agora* in which he used to teach. Both had disciples who took over and developed their doctrines, and in particular Chrysippus, the head of the Stoic school at the end of the third century, reformulated the doctrines of the school on a firmer philosophical basis (Zeno seems to have been more of a charismatic teacher than a technically minded philosopher).

Though the followers of these two schools regarded them as being absolutely opposed to one another, to the modern observer they seem to have had a great deal in common, at least in terms of what they were trying to achieve for their followers. Ethics was at the centre of both systems, and in each case was supported by an elaborate structure of physics, cosmology and epistemology. Both schools believed that there was a single goal which was the aim of all activity, and whose achievement constituted the supreme fulfilment of human nature. Both regarded it as intolerable that the achievement of this goal should be at the mercy of fate or chance, or should be dependent on anything but the individual's unfettered choices, and consequently both regarded the individual's internal state as all-important, and his (or her – both schools had female adherents) external circumstances as insignificant. Both in practice recommended a morality of moderation and self-control, differing only in details: an Epicurean would avoid marriage, while a Stoic would marry out of duty; an Epicurean would avoid politics, while a Stoic would regard it as a duty to participate in the affairs of the city. These general prescriptions could be modified in particular circumstances, so that there were plenty of unmarried apolitical Stoics, and married Epicureans who were deeply involved in politics. In fact there was nothing in the doctrines of either school which prevented their adherents from living the conventional life of the gentleman or lady. It could be argued that both systems were simply elaborate ways of justifying conventional morality.

The way in which they each arrived at these positions was, however, completely different. For Epicureans, the goal was pleasure, but they defined pleasure as the removal of all pain (which included all wants), a state which, they argued, was achievable only when all unnatural desires (i.e. those like ambition and greed, which are not related to natural bodily needs) had been eliminated. Hence they recommended a simple life, because it is only if we limit ourselves to those desires which are capable of being satisfied without excessive effort that the highest pleasure can be achieved (and that our ability to achieve happiness can be kept entirely under our control). Their view was that the major obstacle to this life of simple pleasure was fear, and particularly fear of death and of punishment by the gods after death. They argued, then, that since death consisted of the complete dispersal of the parts of the body, and so the total destruction of the person, death was not to be feared because it is something which we will never experience ('when death is, we are not; when we are, death is not'). They supported this view by arguing that the world is explicable as the product of the random collisions of tiny particles of pure matter called atoms, and that the intervention of the gods is therefore not required. They did believe that the gods exist (for we see them in visions and dreams) but that they are perfect beings (and so perfect Epicureans) who live in eternal contemplation of their own happiness, and do not concern themselves with the running of this world. (For a fuller account, see Long 1974: 19–74.)

The Stoics, like the Epicureans, had a physical theory which was totally materialistic, but for them the cosmos consisted of a mixture of two kinds of material being, formless matter and a creative force which they referred to by a variety of names, including world-soul, Zeus, and God, and of whom they sometimes speak in terms reminiscent of Judaeo-Christian ethical monotheism, as in the *Hymn to Zeus* of Zeno's pupil Cleanthes (though it would be more accurate to describe their system as pantheistic). This creative force was both purposive and benevolent, but was not the sort of being with which

127

one could have a personal relationship; it could not be influenced by prayers or sacrifices (because it would always do what was for the best). Everything is controlled by this force, and the individual human being cannot control what is going to happen in the world, but can choose whether to accept the world-soul's plan willingly or unwillingly. The end for a human being was to function as a healthy human being ought to function, which meant to exercise the distinctive capacity of humanity – reason – without the interference of the passions, which were regarded as diseases of the soul, to be eliminated entirely. (For a fuller account see Long 1974: 118–209.)

It is worth noting that the adherents of neither school held that popular beliefs about the gods were acceptable, or that their cults had any effect on anything but the worshippers (though Stoics interpreted stories about the gods as symbolic of truths about the universe). They supported, and participated in, traditional religious practices because they were good for society, and simply because they were traditional. Certainly no Stoic or Epicurean seems to have been deterred by his or her beliefs from accepting magistracies and other offices which involved religious cult. Indeed, a high proportion of the ruling class of the Roman Empire held views of this kind. Towards the end of the republic we hear of a number of prominent Epicureans, including Cassius, the assassin of Julius Caesar, and Cicero's friend Atticus; later, Stoicism is more visible – in Paul's day notable Stoics included Seneca, the tutor and adviser of the emperor Nero, and brother of the proconsul Gallio before whom Paul appears at Acts 18, 12–17.

Jewish writers, when trying to explain their religion to Gentiles, sometimes did so using the language of philosophy. Josephus calls his own sect, the Pharisees, a *hairesis* (the normal world for a philosophical school), and says it is 'very similar to what the Greeks call the Stoic school' (*Life* 12), and in three other places in his works he describes three groups within Judaism – the Pharisees, the Sadducees and the Essenes – in terms which make them seem comparable to Greek philosophical schools (*War* 2, 119–66; *Ant.* 13, 171–3; *Ant.* 18, 11–25). The differences in terms of which he classifies them were ones about which Greek philosophers also argued, such as the question of fate and free will, and the immortality of the soul. In doing this, Josephus achieves two things. First, he conveys to the Gentile audience the fact that there are differences between Jews, just as there are between philosophers (which is important for him since he wants to argue that the blame for the outbreak of the Jewish revolt lay with a section of the Jews, not the Jews as a whole). Second, he suggests that Judaism should be associated with philosophy, highly respected and full of prestige, rather than classified as a strange foreign superstition.

Of the Greek philosophies, it was with Stoicism, rather than Epicureanism, that both Jews and Christians wished to associate themselves. So Josephus described his own sect, the Pharisees, as Jewish Stoics, while the Sadducees were credited with views (belief in the mortality of the soul and rejection of retribution in the afterlife) which were characteristic of the Epicureans. Elsewhere he speaks disparagingly of the Epicureans because of their rejection of divine providence (*Ant.* 10, 278). For Philo also the Stoics were a school of which he could approve. He even produced a Jewish treatment of a traditional Stoic theme *That Every Good Man is Free* (and claimed to have produced another on its counterpart, *That Every Bad Man is a Slave*, which has not survived). Even the author of 4 Maccabees, a graphic account of martyrdoms of Jews at the hands of the Seleucid king Antiochos IV Epiphanes, perhaps written in Paul's lifetime (Bickerman 1976: I, 281–2; Schürer 1973–87: III (1), 588–91), described their heroism as the victory of reason over the passions in terms reminiscent of (and probably derived from) Stoicism. Christian writers also wanted to claim an affinity with Stoicism. In the early third century Tertullian asserted that the Stoic Seneca is 'often on our side' (*De An.* 20, 1), and in the fourth century someone took the trouble of forging a correspondence in Latin between Seneca and Paul, in the course of which he was converted to Christianity (a view which has found supporters surprisingly recently: for references see Colish 1992: 335–6). Even Epiktetos, who wrote quite disparagingly of the Christians (4, 7, 6) was claimed as a convert by an anonymous commentator on one manuscript.

The Epicureans, on the other hand, had many points of resemblance with Christianity. Like the Christians, Epicurus' followers were enthusiastic proselytisers, and they alone among philosophical schools seem to have made a real effort to spread their message to a wider public (Long 1974: 17). The Roman writer Cicero, in the first century BC, complained that they were the only school to try to communicate with Romans who did not speak Greek, by producing Latin accounts (bad ones, according to Cicero) of Epicurean philosophy, as a result of which 'they have taken possession of the whole of Italy' (*Tusculan Disputations* 4, 3, 2–7). Cicero revealed an attitude which is perhaps closer to that of the general run of philosophers when he argued that the very popularity of Epicureanism with the uneducated proves that it must be wrong. The passionate enthusiasm which Epicureanism could inspire in its followers is revealed in a remarkable inscription put up in the second century in the small Lycian town of Oenoanda by one of its prominent citizens, Diogenes. In one of the stoas of the city he set up, for the edification of his fellow citizens, a vast inscription, perhaps as much as 100 metres in length (Clay 1990: 2478), containing an account of the Epicurean philosophy and incorporating complete transcriptions of whole works by Epicurus himself. To date, more than two hundred fragments have been recovered and published (Smith 1993), perhaps less than a quarter of the whole (Clay 1990: 2478). Diogenes himself explained his motive for undertaking this enormous enterprise:

> For now, on account of our advanced age, we have come to the sunset of our life, and as we are at the point of departing from life, [we leave] with a fine hymn of rejoicing, [and, having enjoyed] our fill [of good things], we wanted to help those who are naturally capable of philosophy now before we are cut off. Now if only one man were in a bad condition, or two, or three, or four, or five, or six, or, reader, any number greater than this you like – provided they are not too many – I would have called aside each individually, and I would have done all in my power to give him the best prescription. But since the fact is, as I have said before, that the majority of mankind is affected by an epidemic of false opinions concerning the world, just as if they were suffering from a plague – and their number is increasing, for out of their emulation of one another one person catches it from another like sheep, and since it is right and proper to help those who live after us, for they too belong to us even if they are not yet born, and in addition it is humane to come to the aid of strangers who visit our city – now, since the kinds of remedy [I offer] have extended to a greater group, I wanted, by making use of this stoa, to set out [the remedies] which bring health and safety.
>
> (trans. Clay 1990: 2457)

Evidence of this kind is a salutary corrective to the common belief that Epicureanism was a philosophy of egocentric hedonism. In the same century, the satirist Lucian linked Epicureans and Christians as the opponents of the charlatan Alexander (Lucian, *Alexander the False Prophet* 25; 38). Nevertheless, the Epicurean doctrine that the world is not divinely created or governed, coupled probably with the feeling that an association with the moral seriousness of Stoicism rather than the apparent hedonism of Epicureanism was a safer strategy for a new religion bidding for respectability, meant that without exception Christian writers aligned themselves with the opponents of Epicureanism (Ferguson 1990: 2297–326).

Though everyone with a literary education (a very small proportion of the population) would have had at least some contact with philosophy, it is difficult to assess how seriously they took it. A small minority became enthusiasts; probably more held on to some vague feeling that philosophy is a 'good thing'; the majority will have regarded it as no more than the sort of knowledge which you can bring out when appropriate to display your culture, except perhaps (like the nominally religious) when you needed it to give you consolation in times of adversity. The Roman élite might use philosophy to reconcile them to administrative chores:

> I am completely occupied by my duties, which may be important, but are very tiresome. I sit in court, countersign petitions, make up accounts, write many letters (of no literary merit whatsoever). Sometimes (whenever I can) I complain about these chores to [the philosopher] Euphrates. He consoles me by saying that these duties, conducting public business, presiding over trials and passing judgement, expounding and administering justice, and putting into practice what philosophers teach, are part of philosophy, and indeed its finest part.
>
> (Pliny, *Letters* 1, 10, 10)

to strengthen them to face the vicissitudes of life:

> 'So what should we have prepared to meet circumstances like this?' It's obvious! A knowledge of what is mine and what is not mine; what I can do and what I cannot do. I must die. But I need not die complaining. I must be put in prison. But I need not weep in prison. I must go into exile. So who will prevent me going laughing, cheerful, and happy? 'Tell me the secrets.' No, it is within my power to refuse. 'I'll put you in chains!' Don't be silly! Me? What you will chain is my leg! Even Zeus himself has not the power to constrain my free will. 'I will throw you into prison!' No, you will throw my poor

little body into prison. 'I will cut your head off!' Well, when did I ever tell you that my neck was the only one which could not be cut through? This is the sort of thing which students of philosophy ought to practise, this is what they should write every day, this is the training they should do!

(Epiktetos, *Discourses* 1, 1, 21–5)

and to convince themselves that their moral superiority fully justified their positions of extreme privilege:

If people visit us at home, they should admire us rather than our furniture. He who can use earthenware as if it were silver is a great man. But equally great is the man who uses silver as if it were earthenware. It is the sign of a weak mind not to be able to endure wealth.

(Seneca, *Moral Epistles* 5, 6)

From antiquity down to the present day, a resemblance between the moral teachings of Christians (and Jews) and of philosophers has been noticed, and attempts have been made to find explanations for it. In antiquity Christian writers (following Jews like Philo and Josephus) claimed that the original source of these ideas was Moses, from whom the philosophers had borrowed them; alternatively, later Christian writers like Clement of Alexandria and Eusebius of Caesarea argued that the high moral standards and near-monotheism of the philosophers was the result of a real (but secondary and inferior) revelation of God to the Gentiles designed to prepare them for the Gospel of Christ. More recent writers have been more inclined to see the relationship as one of Christian dependence on philosophical influence, sometimes with polemic intent (for a full account of post-medieval views on the subject in so far as it concerns the Stoics, the usual candidate for the position of the philosophical mentors of the early Christians, see Colish 1992: 339–79). Though there clearly is a relationship between the work of Paul and his Christian contemporaries and the thought of the philosophers, often in the past too much reliance has been placed on the spotting of alleged 'parallels' (Malherbe 1992: 277–8), and too little on the common culture in which both Christians and philosophers lived. One of the striking developments in philosophy in the hellenistic period was the growth of a consensus on a wide range of philosophical and moral issues, and the creation of literary forms in which to express these ideas at a more popular level. There is no need to suppose a special relationship between any individual Christian and a particular philosophical school to explain the fact that the content and form of their writings have points in common. For example, although Paul's city Tarsus was famous for its philosophers, there is no reason to suppose that a Jewish tentmaker born in Tarsus would therefore have a better than average knowledge of philosophical ideas, any more than we would expect someone who worked in a car factory in Oxford to have for that reason a better knowledge of Wittgenstein than one whose workplace was in Coventry.

In so far as philosophical ideas did spread beyond the educated élite to the lowest level of society, the credit probably belongs most of all to the group of philosophers (or, more accurately, popular moralisers) usually referred to as Cynics. It is difficult to be precise about what exactly a Cynic was. Ancient writers on the history of philosophy make them into a proper philosophical school with a pedigree going back to Antisthenes, one of the disciples of Socrates, but it seems more likely that they were a group of individuals united only by the fact that they were devoted to a life of extreme virtue and total self-sufficiency, a 'life according to nature'. Their teaching was marked by a complete rejection of all of the conventions of society (which is why they were called Cynics, which means 'dog-like'), absolute freedom of speech, rejection of all wealth and possessions, and a desire to shock respectable society which bordered on exhibitionism. In some ways Stoicism was a tamer form of Cynicism (Zeno started his philosophical career as a follower of the Cynic Krates), and by the second century BC Cynicism had been absorbed into the Stoic movement (Billerbeck 1991: 148–9). It left behind, however, not only a concept of a way of life totally opposed to society's norms, but also a series of literary forms – the diatribe (or popular moral discourse), the parody, the philosophical letter, the fable and the satire – which were taken over and developed by mainstream authors (Dudley 1937: 110–16). By the first century AD we begin again to find references to people calling themselves Cynics, usually in the writings of respectable Stoics trying to distance themselves from them (Billerbeck 1991: 153–66). Though there cannot have been many Cynics, their extravagantly unconventional behaviour will have made them very noticeable, and their preaching was simple and direct, of a kind which would appeal to, and be understood by, anyone (Goulet-Cazé 1990: 2760–3). As the satirist Lucian puts it, in a parody on philosophical schools:

It's very easy, and anyone can follow it without trouble. You
don't need education and books and rubbish like that; this is a
real short cut to glory. Even if you are completely uneducated
– a tanner or a fishmonger or a joiner or a money-changer –
nothing will stop you becoming a celebrity if only you are
shameless and uninhibited, and learn how to abuse people
properly.

(Lucian, *The Auction of Lives* 11)

This radical rejection of the world may have appealed to some of the
same sorts of people who later found Christian asceticism attractive,
but it would be interesting to know whether there was an early
connection between the two movements. Gadara in the Dekapolis
(not very far from Galilee) had a strong Cynic tradition (Downing
1993: 292–3), and in the second century we hear of one individual,
Peregrinus, who abandoned Christianity to become a Cynic of the
most outrageous type (Lucian, *On the Death of Peregrinus* 11–16;
Hornsby 1991: 165–81). Even if we do not accept the case (argued,
for example, by Downing 1993: 281–304) that aspects of
Christianity were modelled on Cynicism, there can be little doubt
that the Cynic movement was an important channel through which
radical philosophical ideas and a philosophical style of moral exhor-
tation entered the general pool of ideas, from which Christians like
Paul could draw.

Though the Stoics, Epicureans and Cynics are undoubtedly the
philosophical schools of which the ordinary educated person of the
first century was most likely to have heard (which is why they are
the ones mentioned at Acts 17, 18), at the period when Paul was
active a new philosophical movement, the revival of Platonism, was
gathering strength, and was to have a decisive influence on the
development of Christian theology. Plato had tried to solve a range
of philosophical problems by arguing that the physical world was
not fully real, but was an imitation or reflection of a more funda-
mentally real level of existence in which 'things in themselves'
existed in an absolute and unconditional sense, and which was in
some way the cause of the physical world. After Plato's death, other
philosophers (and especially his pupil Aristotle) showed that Plato's
problems could be solved much more simply without assuming the
existence of this 'real world', which in any case generated more
problems than solutions. Plato's school, the Academy, played down
his distinctive doctrines (if it did not abandon them altogether) and,

perhaps as a result of polemic against the Stoics and Epicureans, took on a sceptical character. The works of Plato, however, continued to be widely read, partly because of their excellence as works of literature, but mainly because Plato was one of a handful of authors who were regarded as models of good Greek.

The process by which, from the first century BC onwards, Plato's doctrines began to be taken seriously again as philosophy is completely obscure, but the first surviving works which reflect this new movement are those of the Jew Philo of Alexandria. Philo was attempting to show that the 'truths' of Greek philosophy can be discovered in the Pentateuch (if it is interpreted correctly), and the philosophy he discovered there is a form of the revised Platonism. For Philo, the ultimate first principle of the world is that which alone really exists, the One, or God. From God comes the *Logos*, the formative principles on which our world is based and the equivalent of Plato's 'real world'. Philo's philosophy is eclectic, with a good deal of Stoic influence, but it is recognisably the same sort of Platonism which we find in later authors. The process by which we can discover these philosophical 'truths' in the Pentateuch is the application of allegorical interpretation, which is based on the belief that underneath (and perhaps as well as) the literal meaning of the text there was a deeper, spiritual or philosophical, meaning. This was by no means a new way of approaching the scriptures (and Paul himself used it : Galatians 4, 22–6); if these works were really God's revelation to his people, then every detail, however apparently trivial, must carry some important message, if only we interpret it correctly. The Stoics also had used this method to give philosophical meaning to mythology and works of literature. So the feats of the Greek hero Herakles were interpreted by them not as victories over actual monsters or wicked men, but as expressing allegorically the good man's defeat of his irrational passions, so that Herakles became a sort of Stoic 'saint'. Using these techniques, Philo was able to discover the doctrines of current philosophy in the works of Moses, who, he concluded, must have been the ultimate source of Plato's ideas (for a full account, see Dillon 1977: 115–83). The extent to which this variety of Platonism influenced such texts as the opening of John's Gospel remains a matter of controversy, but when a distinctive Christian theology began to develop in the second century, it was heavily dependent on these concepts and methods.

LANGUAGE AND CULTURE

To identify oneself as a 'Hellene' (= Greek) was in the first instance to claim membership of an association bound together by a common language. But the long-established distinction in the Greek language between 'Hellene' and 'barbarian' carried the implication that all those who did not speak Greek were uncivilised. Conversely a mere ability to speak Greek without following the Greek way of life, the customs of the *polis* (training in athletics in a gymnasium and so on) did not qualify one as a true Hellene. Being a Hellene also implied acknowledging the pantheon of Olympian deities, first made canonical in the Homeric epics. Of course in the hellenistic and Roman periods many individuals not born and reared as 'Hellenes' adopted hellenism, and migrated into the heart of the Greek world (the philosopher Kleitomachos from Carthage, for example, and the poet Meleager from Gadara in Transjordan). Whole communities, as we have seen (see pp. 62–4), were remodelled as Greek *poleis*. But an element of ethnic prejudice against such 'home-made' Hellenes persisted and came to the fore when the emperor Hadrian (117–38) created a *Panhellēnion*, a 'council of all the Hellenes', with its headquarters at Athens – cities had to prove that they were 'Hellenic' by descent to secure admission. A similar desire to claim ties of kinship with the Greek homeland explains the fabrication of foundation legends by numerous communities in Asia Minor (see pp. 98–9). For most Hellenes, however, their primary method of self-identification would have been as citizens of one of a large number of *poleis*. This overriding loyalty to the face-to-face community described by Cicero was firmly established in the Greek world before its 'Classical Age' in the fifth and fourth centuries BC, many *poleis* at that time being independent states, with greater or smaller scope for independent action according to their size. Even after the loss of political independence they continued to attract fervent loyalty. How the peasants living in remote parts of extensive civic territories in the East (the *chōra*, see pp. 65–5, 95) would identify themselves is a subject about which there is little evidence – probably just as residents of a particular village or tenants of a particular imperial estate.

It is interesting to compare the case of the Greeks, of whose identity the Greek language was an indispensable component, with that of the Jews, for whom language does not seem to have been important at all. The original language of the Jews was Hebrew, but, as we have seen (pp. 35–8) by about 300 BC Hebrew was being replaced by Aramaic, a related language which originated among the tribes of the Syrian desert and which became the administrative language of the Assyrian and Persian empires. Aramaic was adopted by Jews not just as a vernacular, but also as a language of literature (parts of Ezra/Nehemiah and Daniel are in Aramaic). Later the Jewish diaspora in the hellenistic world adopted Greek, which they used for all purposes, including literature and religion (the Septuagint translation of the Pentateuch was supposed to be authoritative because of its divine inspiration, see pp. 48–9. Though it is possible that Hebrew survived as a vernacular, that case has to be argued on linguistic grounds, on the basis of claims that when the Hebrew of the Mishna appears later there are signs that show that it has been developing as a living language. What there is not, however, is any sign of any controversy about the use of languages other than Hebrew, or any claim (until after AD 70) that only Hebrew was the real language of the Jews. Language does not seem to have been an essential part of Jewishness (Schwartz 1995: 3–47). Indeed, some Jewish commentators regarded the divine revelation as being essentially multilingual (Fraade 1992: 267–71): though Hebrew had a special status, God did not confine himself to a single language. When the Septuagint went out of use, it was not because it was in Greek rather than in Hebrew, but because the process of stabilising the Hebrew text (which eventually led to the production of the Masoretic text, the one still used today) had the result that readings were regarded as standard which were different from the readings found in the text on which the Septuagint translation was based (so that it was no longer a translation of the accepted Hebrew text). A new Greek translation, therefore, that of Aquila, was produced around 125, followed by two others, by Theodotion and by Symmachus (Bickerman 1976: I, 157–8). Though the abandonment of the Septuagint may also have been encouraged by the fact that Christian interpretations of the Old Testament sometimes relied on ways of understanding the Septuagint translation (which Christians continued to use) which could not be supported by the Hebrew original, language (Greek or Hebrew) was not an issue in itself.

ROMAN CITIZENSHIP

To identify oneself as a Roman (Roman citizen = *civis Romanus*) was not to claim membership of a nation or tribe (although the total body of Roman citizens was by the first century larger in size than most 'nations' of the ancient world) nor of a body linked by a common language – all Roman citizens were supposed to be able to speak Latin, but by the first century there were many of them whose first language was not Latin, and some of those can have had little or no knowledge of it; '[Claudius] not only removed from the list of judges but actually deprived of citizenship a distinguished man who was one of the leading inhabitants of the province of Greece, but did not know Latin' (Suetonius, *Claudius* 16, 2) – but to claim a political and legal status. In a technical sense this amounted to membership of a 'city', the kind of face-to-face urban community which Cicero had described – and this is how Rome had begun in the fifth and fourth centuries BC. But this 'city' had expanded and incorporated numerous independent cities without obliterating the identity of these communities (these were the self-governing 'municipalities' of Roman Italy) and it had also hived off new self-governing cities, the *coloniae*, whose citizens were also all Roman citizens from the early second century BC. This was a complex and prolonged historical process lasting over three centuries from the fourth to the first century BC (see p. 87). The end result was that by the middle of the first century BC the whole free population of Italy south of the foothills of the Alps enjoyed Roman citizen rights, lived under Roman law and used Latin. Not that the Roman citizen body had ever consisted of all or only Latin-speakers. The identification of 'Roman' (legal status) with 'Latin' (linguistic identity) is an error; many of the communities which had received Roman status at an early date had been Oscan- or Umbrian-speaking, while the last of the original Latin-speaking communities to receive Roman citizenship did so only in 90 BC.

A hundred years later (in Paul's lifetime) the process of extending Roman citizenship had continued in the subject provinces beyond Italy. There was a crucial difference between this process and the earlier enfranchisement of Italy. Outside Italy, apart from a few exceptions and apart from the new *coloniae* of citizens planted in the provinces, it was not entire communities but individuals and their families which received the citizenship. In the western half of the Empire subject communities received 'Latin rights' under which the leading local families which filled the local offices received full Roman status, but in the eastern provinces the extension was in the main the result of grants to individuals. Under the republican system of government such grants had been rare because they required a vote by the Roman citizen assembly, the equivalent of a 'private' Act of Parliament in Britain. But the mighty generals in the decades when the republic broke down arrogated this right to themselves, and Augustus and his successors monopolised this power and made grants of citizenship on a very large scale.

An inscription from Morocco has revealed that there was an immense register of such grants made by successive emperors and the formula in which they were made:

> At the request of Aurelius Iulianus, chief of the tribe of the Zegrenses, by petition, with Vallius Maximus [the local governor] giving his support by letter, we have granted to the above [the names and ages of Aurelius Iulianus' wife and children had already been listed] Roman citizenship, the rights of the tribe being preserved, without reduction of the taxes and dues of the people and the exchequer.
>
> (Sherwin-White 1973: 88–95; Williams 1975: 56–78)

The emperors would have been anxious to honour provincials who had done them service (especially in war) and those whose local influence was such that they were worth conciliating (such as this chief of a frontier tribe), but they must also have received numerous applications backed up by the support of influential people. One compensation the emperors offered to senators for their loss of any real political power was this opportunity to act as 'brokers of patronage' (Saller 1982: 74–5) by securing from the emperor favours for their dependants. The younger Pliny, for example, got Trajan to make Pliny's Egyptian physiotherapist and some relatives of his Greek doctor Roman citizens (Pliny, *Letters* 10, 5–7, 10–11). But under some emperors, such as Claudius and Nero, it was the imperial freedmen-secretaries who were the most influential 'brokers of patronage' and who used this influence to enrich themselves. It is in this context that Claudius Lysias' words to Paul, 'I bought this citizenship for a large sum' (Acts 22, 28), should be set. Lysias must have been a Greek who took the name of Claudius after receiving citizenship from the emperor Claudius as a result of a bribe to one of the imperial freedmen. The historian Cassius Dio recorded that the freedmen sold citizenship on such a scale that the price fell and there was a popular jibe that 'you could become a citizen by giving pieces of glass' (Dio 60, 17, 5f.; see Wallace and Williams 1993: 117).

It must in the main have been provincials of high status, wealth and education who became citizens in this way (the grandest of all being the ruling dynasties of client kingdoms, see p. 74–5). This undoubted truth must be the basis for the argument sometimes put forward (e.g. Lentz 1993: 23–8) that it is highly improbable that Paul was a Roman citizen. Nevertheless there was a minority of Roman citizens with provincial ancestry who were neither very rich nor highly educated nor grandees in their own communities.

There were two main routes by which individuals of this kind could attain such a status. One was military service: by the mid-first century at least half of Rome's fighting men were not citizens enrolled in the legions but provincials enrolled in much smaller 'auxiliary' units of infantry or cavalry, and from the reign of Claudius onwards it was universal practice to grant such soldiers who had completed twenty-five years service Roman citizenship on discharge. There is no likelihood at all that Paul's ancestor who had received the citizenship had been a soldier – apart from problems of chronology, service in the army involved pagan observances, and indeed during the civil wars of the 40s BC Jews who were Roman citizens were exempted from conscription, according to a series of official rulings preserved by Josephus (*Ant.* 15, 220–37), on the grounds that 'they cannot undertake military service because they may not bear arms or march on the Sabbath, nor can they obtain the native foods to which they are accustomed' (*Ant.* 15, 236).

The other route to citizenship for the 'less than grand' was, ironically, slavery; and in this connection it is Paul's profession, that of skilled craftsman, a leather-worker (Acts 18, 3; cf. Wallace and Williams 1993: 97), which is significant given that, like his citizen status, it had probably been passed down to him from his ancestors. The wars of conquest and the civil wars of the second and first centuries BC had resulted in the sale into slavery of vast numbers of people living round the eastern Mediterranean, especially the residents of towns, since it was the standard Roman practice to sell off the entire populations of cities which had resisted them. A high proportion of these slaves were exported to Italy, the unskilled majority of whom became labourers on the rural plantations of the rich with no prospect of freedom. The minority, however, who had special skills or aptitudes either joined the (often huge) slave households of the rich (see pp. 82–3, 66) or were set up in business in the towns plying their specialised trade – as it might be, leather-working. The owner would take the profits of a business, and such skilled craftsmen needed some incentive other than fear to maximise their return – in fact, the prospect of freedom. An owner could either (a) set a slave free on condition that he still carried out so many days' worth of work for the benefit of his former owner, or (b) permit his slave craftsman to keep an allowance (a *peculium*) from which he could save enough to buy his freedom, thus enabling the owner to invest in a replacement (Roman law forbade an owner both to extract a fee and to require compulsory work). That manumission of domestic slaves and urban craftsmen took place on a large scale is indicated both by such anecdotes as that about Scipio already quoted (see p. 66) and, more importantly, by the legislation brought in by the emperor Augustus to limit the freedom of Romans to free as many slaves as they liked, when they liked. Paul's advice to Christian slaves, 'if you can gain your freedom, avail yourself of the opportunity' (1 Corinthians 7, 21), makes it clear that he too regards manumission as a real possibility for slaves. Corinth, a colony under Roman law with a large proportion of slave craftsmen, was just the sort of place where such a slave might gain his or her freedom, and with it Roman citizenship. Besides, the extensive discussion of legal problems arising from such manumissions by Roman jurists is also evidence that they were fairly common.

What worried Augustus was probably not that slaves became free men but that slaves manumitted by Roman owners themselves became Roman citizens. This very ancient practice (whose origins can only be a matter of speculation) had no parallel in the Greek world, where a freed slave counted merely as a resident alien of the *polis* where the slave had been freed. Augustus insisted that only slaves who had been freed by a formal ceremony before a Roman magistrate or by a will should become citizens, and separate legislation was needed to regulate the status of the very large number who continued to be freed informally by their owners. This provides a very plausible context for the acquisition of citizenship by Paul's father or grandfather, or by an even remoter ancestor: taken prisoner of war, sent as a slave to Italy and set up in business, then freed and so given Roman citizenship, and eventually migrating back to the East and settling in Tarsus, a centre of skilled crafts (cf. Acts 18, 1–3 for the migration from Italy to Corinth of Aquila and Priscilla who seem to have been craftsmen like Paul). The argument that a servile ancestry for Paul is incompatible with the claims for relatively high status made on his behalf in Acts (in associating with the best class of people in the towns he visits, like the Asiarchs at Ephesos at 19, 31, or his claim that unlike Claudius Lysias he was born a citizen) is based on a misunderstanding of the position of ex-slaves and their descendants (e.g. Lentz 1993: 48). It was certainly the case that there was a good deal of snobbery about slavery in the family, for which reason it is not surprising that neither Paul nor Acts ever mentioned that he received citizenship as a result of the manumission of an ancestor; one did not advertise servile ancestry. Nevertheless, ex-slaves not uncommonly became successful in business and individuals of some prominence in their communities, and some rose to positions of considerable power. Such people would certainly be in a position to associate with the upper echelons of society. In any case, what is claimed for Paul is not that he belongs to the élite class, but simply that he is not one of the urban rabble.

Paul's claim to citizenship of Tarsus (Acts 21, 39) is more of a problem, if only because we know very little about how one could become a citizen of Tarsus, apart from the fact that one group, referred to by Dio of Prusa as 'the linen-workers' (34, 21), were excluded from citizenship, perhaps as a result of the substantial fee of 500 drachmas levied for the exercise of citizen rights (Jones 1940: 174). It is unlikely that the Jews of Tarsus as a group were citizens, and it is certainly not the case that Paul's Roman citizenship would have brought him Tarsian citizenship automatically. Nevertheless there is no reason to suppose that individual Jews could not become citizens. It may have been the case (as argued by Lentz 1993: 36–7) that the worship of the city's gods, and participation in festivals associated with the gods, was 'fundamental to civic identity'. It was not, however, compulsory for anyone except those who accepted civic office (though refusal to participate might cause offence). There were certainly arguments about the collective rights of Jews (Schürer 1973–87: III (1), 126–32), but nothing precluded an individual like Paul having citizenship of his native city. Given the lack of information, it is pointless to speculate on how his family acquired it. There is certainly evidence from the third century of Jews in cities in Asia Minor holding civic offices, and they must have been in some sense citizens; there is no reason to believe that the situation was different in Paul's day (Trebilco 1991: 167–85).

How would Paul, given his modest social status, have been able to convince sceptical officials that he really was entitled to claim the rights of a Roman citizen? He could very well have had the equivalent of a modern birth certificate. Newly enfranchised citizens certainly had documentary proof of their status: the chieftain

Aurelius Julianus was supplied with a copy of the entry in the imperial register, attested by the seals of twelve eminent imperial advisers (see p. 139). 'Auxiliary' soldiers were routinely issued with similar copies of the entries relating to their own enfranchisement inscribed on the interior and exterior surfaces of a pair of bronze plates. Under the republic those who were citizens by birth were supposed to have their status recorded by their fathers when the citizenship rolls were revised every five years by the two censors elected for that purpose. By the time of Augustus, however, the huge expansion of citizen numbers and the extension of citizenship to the provinces made this process hopelessly cumbersome, and he instituted a system of birth registers kept by local authorities (by the governors in the provinces); a parent (father or mother) appeared before the authority and testified to the birth of a legitimate child, an entry was made in the register, and a certified copy could be obtained; a number of such documents are preserved among the papyri from Roman Egypt (Crook 1967: 47). Such documents could be produced as evidence in court; when the stepchildren of the writer Apuleius took him to court alleging that he had used magic to get their mother, at the age of sixty, to marry him (so that he could get his hands on her fortune) he produced her birth certificate: 'Hand Aemilianus the tablets, let him examine the binding, identify the seals, work out the age . . . ' (Apuleius, *Apology* 89, trans. Crook). People did make bogus claims to Roman citizenship, as well as, more subtly, conveying a misleading impression by adopting a set of three names which, in a world of patronymics, were distinctive of Roman citizens (Wallace and Williams 1993: 25–6). Claudius had offenders of both kinds executed (Suetonius, *Claudius* 25, 3).

The normal practice in the ancient world was for a man to be identified by the name of his father (i.e. 'son of x') and for a woman to be identified by the name of either her father or her husband. Roman men, however (but not Roman women, whose nomenclature follows the more usual pattern), normally had a characteristic set of three names, the *tria nomina*: the first, the *praenomen* or personal name, was usually selected from a very restricted (in contrast to the large choice available in other communities) list of about a dozen boys' names, some of which display no great imagination (e.g. Quintus = 'number five'; Sextus = 'number six'; Decimus = 'number ten'); next came the name of the 'clan', the *nomen* or *gentilicium*, which might be shared by many families; finally the *cognomen* marked out a family or branch among those sharing the same *gentilicium* (some of these seem to reflect distinguishing 'nicknames' given to particular members of families, e.g. Flaccus = 'big-eared', Cicero = 'chick-pea', Naso = 'big nose'). A newly enfranchised citizen would usually keep his own name (or a Latinised version of it) as his *cognomen*, and would adopt the *praenomen* and *gentilicium* of whichever Roman was responsible for his enfranchisement (his former owner in the case of a freed slave, the reigning emperor or the patron who had intervened on his behalf in the case of the free-born). Excluding the proconsuls, only Titius Iustus has a standard *gentilicium* and *cognomen* in Acts (18, 7); if he is the Gaius of 1 Corinthians 1, 14, then we have a convincing set of three names, Gaius Titius Iustus. A number of other individuals in Acts and in Paul's letters have Roman names, but this is not in itself evidence of citizenship; provincials often adopted Roman names for reasons of convenience or vanity.

What were the obligations and privileges of Roman status? There was no obligation to take part in any particular religious rituals if one was an ordinary civilian. The rituals of the Roman state religion were purely the concern of the colleges of priests, who did not form a separate profession but were 'part-timers' drawn from the ranks of the Senate, or magistrates such as provincial governors – that was why the Jew Tiberius Julius Alexander, the nephew of the philosopher Philo, who pursued an official career which elevated him to the office of Prefect of Egypt, had to apostatise. Under the republic conscription had placed heavy burdens on adult male citizens below the age of 46, but under the emperors the size of the army was limited and voluntary enlistment was used as far as possible. Conscription was still used, especially in the provinces. As far as Paul was concerned, it is unlikely that as an urban craftsman he would have been in any danger (peasants were preferred as recruits); and in any case, as a Jew by birth, he may well have been able to claim exemption (see p. 140). Roman citizens resident in Italy enjoyed a great advantage over provincials, for they did not pay the *tributum*, a land tax and a poll tax, levied in the provinces. Roman citizens resident in the provinces were not exempt from paying it, and even citizen colonies settled in the provinces had exemption only if they received special grants of 'Italic right' (the right to treat their territory as equivalent to Italian land). Nor were they exempt from paying local taxes or performing compulsory services in the cities where they resided (see the provision of the grant to Julianus' family quoted above). Under the Republic the right to vote in elections and legislative assemblies had been the privilege of citizens, but since it required personal attendance at Rome it would have been of no practical value to citizens in the provinces; in any case the voting assemblies had become purely ceremonial gatherings by Paul's day.

The great advantage of citizenship had been a degree of protection against having capital sentences or corporal punishment inflicted by Roman magistrates in the way they could inflict them on foreigners and slaves. Under the republic citizens had had a theoretical right of appeal to the assembly of fellow-citizens; under the rule of the emperors this was changed to a right of 'appeal to Caesar'. It was this right that Paul appears to have invoked before the procurator of Judaea, Festus (Acts 25, 11–12), but precisely what he was entitled to under Roman law at this time and whether Festus was respecting a constitutional right or acting out of political prudence is almost impossible to establish. The problem is that, according to Roman legal authorities, the right of appeal was against sentence after a trial (Ulpian, *Digest* 48, 6, 7; *Sententiae Pauli* 5, 26, 1). Paul on the other hand appeals to Caesar in order to *avoid* a trial in Jerusalem (Acts 25, 9). Besides, no reference is made to Paul's citizen status in this section of the narrative, and Festus' words, 'as he himself appealed to the emperor, I decided to send him' (Acts 25, 25), suggest that he was granting a request which he was empowered to reject, rather than respecting a right for disregarding which he could have been prosecuted. The fact that he consulted his council of advisers before making the decision (Acts 25, 12) points in the same direction. A governor seems to have had the discretion to refer cases to the emperor for judgement when it seemed appropriate. So Quinctilius Varus, the governor of Syria, intervened in an insurrection in Judaea and sent the ringleaders to Augustus to be judged (Josephus, *War* 2, 77–8); Julius Civilis, charged with rebellion, was sent for trial to Nero (Tacitus, *Histories* 4, 13, 1). In these and other similar cases there are obviously special reasons why the emperor might be thought to want to deal with the matter personally, but they establish that a governor might, in the right circumstances, decide that it was prudent not to handle a case himself. In Paul's case Festus, anxious on the one hand not to offend the Jewish authorities in Jerusalem by dismissing the case against Paul, and on the other hand apprehensive of the trouble which might be caused for him if it were claimed that a Roman citizen had been condemned to gratify the provincials, might well have thought that sending the case to Rome was the easy way out. If this is true, Festus would not be acknowledging Paul's legal rights, but making a prudent political decision.

There are in fact no other known cases of a right of appeal to the emperor being claimed before sentence. In an apparent parallel reported by Tacitus (*Annals* 16, 8, 2–3), where a group of distinguished Romans charged with black magic and incest appealed to Nero, it is unclear whether the appeal is to a legal right or to the emperor's discretion (the case in fact never came to trial). When Pliny as governor of Bithynia under Trajan, confronted by Roman citizens accused of being Christians, sends them off to Rome (Pliny, *Letters* 10, 96, 4), he may simply be acting in anticipation of an appeal to the emperor if he himself were to condemn them (Williams 1990: 141). If the narrative in Acts is accurate, we may have in this episode not an instance of the exercise of a citizen's legal rights, but a striking illustration of the 'clout' carried by Roman citizens in the provinces, and the power of the emperor's name. (For discussion of the issues, see Jones 1960: ch. 4; Jones 1973: 101–2; Sherwin-White 1963: 57–70; Garnsey 1966: 167–89; Garnsey 1970: 71–9; Millar 1992: 507–16; Wallace and Williams 1993: 122–3). An episode in Apuleius' comic novel *Metamorphoses* illustrates the way in which the emperor's name might be invoked. The narrator has been magically (and accidentally) transformed into an ass, and then stolen by robbers. When passing through a small town he gets the idea of appealing to the authorities for help. He tries to do so by 'calling upon the August name of Caesar'. Unfortunately when he attempts to cry 'O Caesar' only an ass's bray comes out (*Metamorphoses* 3, 29).

OUTSIDERS

It is paradoxical that foreigners, women and slaves, groups which between them must have made up by far the greater part of the population of all cities, can be classified as outsiders. And yet, in different ways, each of these groups was kept outside the mainstream of civic life.

In most ancient communities, citizenship went by descent. One was a citizen of the city of one's ancestors. Naturalisation was unusual, and being born in a city gave no claim to citizenship to those whose parents were not citizens themselves. Craftsmen and traders moved freely from city to city, and such people would remain resident aliens in all but their 'native' cities. In this way, a substantial section of the population of most cities (and perhaps especially Roman colonies, see Sherwin-White 1963: 177) would be non-citizens.

We have already noted the increasing visibility of women, at any rate in the élite class, in the hellenistic and Roman periods. A few women certainly did reach positions of prominence, especially in religious associations (Meeks 1983: 23–5). It is, however, important not to draw too broad conclusions from what may be isolated incidents. The prevailing ideology remained strongly unsympathetic to the involvement of women in public affairs, and in most cases the participation of women in religious cult reinforced rather than challenged traditional rôles (Kraemer 1992: 80–92).

In the account of Magna Carta in Sellar and Yeatman's *1066 and All That*, each clause of that document ends with the proviso 'except the common people'. Everything which has been written hitherto about self-identification must be qualified with the proviso 'except for the slaves'. Some would have been born in slavery or brought up as slaves after being rescued when they had been put out to die when new-born (the standard form of population control in the classical world: see p. 119). Such slaves, if living under the same roof as their owners, would never have known any focus for loyalty other than the household (*familia*); this may explain the conversion of entire households along with the mistress or master (Acts 16, 15 and Wallace and Williams 1993: 78; Acts 16, 33; 18, 8). Slaves kidnapped or taken as prisoners of war beyond the frontiers when adults would be completely separated from all that was familiar to them; whether they could ever develop any loyalty to the household seems very doubtful.

Slavery is one of the aspects of the ancient world which look very alien from the perspective of the twentieth century. Though we cannot be sure of exact numbers (and slavery is another of those facts of ancient life which were so obvious and mundane at the time that our sources rarely bother to tell us much about them), it has been calculated that in some areas, such as Italy, they may have made up as much as 35 per cent of the population (Hopkins 1978: 99–101). The great majority of these will have been engaged in hard manual work in agriculture, but there were few jobs which could not be done by a slave. Many (though by no means most) slaves could hope to be freed at some time during their lives, and ex-slaves formed a significant proportion of the population, especially in the cities. Some of them became involved in commerce, becoming very rich (Hopkins 1978: 116–17), and the case of the ex-slave Felix, who became governor of Judaea, has already been mentioned. An intriguing case is that of Epaphroditus, the emperor Nero's ex-slave and secretary (who thereby exercised considerable power), who had one of his own slaves, Epiktetos, educated as a Stoic philosopher; Epiktetos himself was eventually freed, and set up as a teacher of philosophy to young aristocrats, a rôle in which he achieved considerable distinction – his works were admired by, among others, the emperor Marcus Aurelius, and remain among the most exciting and inspiring works which have survived from antiquity. This was a world in which slaves and ex-slaves were successfully performing the same functions as the freeborn, and yet the rightness of slavery was never seriously questioned. Neither Christians nor Stoics (both groups which regarded social distinctions as ultimately unimportant, and who stressed the brotherhood of mankind) challenged it. True, both asserted that slaves should be treated humanely. Paul, for example, says, 'Masters, treat your slaves justly and fairly, knowing that you also have a Master in heaven' (Colossians 4, 1), while Seneca wrote that 'they should respect their masters, not fear them. . . . He who is respected is loved, and love and fear cannot go together' (*Moral Epistles* 47, 18). But both believed that slavery was not so much immoral as irrelevant in comparison with the greater slavery which we all share, and from which their creeds could save us:

> Do you not know that if you yield yourselves to anyone as obedient slaves, you are slaves of the one whom you obey, either of sin, which leads to death, or of obedience, which leads to righteousness? But thanks be to God, that you who were once slaves of sin have become obedient from the heart to the standard of teaching to which you were committed, and, having been set free from sin, have become slaves of righteousness.
>
> (Romans 6, 16–18)

Show me a man who is not a slave. One man is a slave to lust, another to greed, another to ambition, and all are slaves to fear. I will show you an ex-consul who is a slave to an old woman, a rich man who is a slave to a little servant girl, and young men from the best families who are slaves to stage entertainers. No slavery is more shameful than the one we choose ourselves.

(Seneca, *Moral Epistles* 47, 17)

Neither suggested that slaves should stop being slaves. There is no reason to believe that the attitudes of Christians to slavery in antiquity were ever significantly different from those of their non-Christian neighbours (MacMullen 1986: 324–5).

SUGGESTIONS FOR FURTHER READING

(full details of these works can be found in the Bibliography):

Racial Prejudice in Imperial Rome by A. N. Sherwin-White is a brief introduction to some of the themes of this chapter; J. A. Crook's *Law and Life of Rome* deals with citizenship, slavery and questions of status in general.

The essays in the volume *The Jews Among Pagans and Christians* edited by J. Lieu *et al.* deal with a number of issues arising from the question of how Jews established a relationship with Gentile society.

Stoics, Epicureans, and Sceptics by R. W. Sharples is an approachable and sympathetic account of the main hellenistic philosophical schools. No similarly accessible account exists of the philosophies developing in Paul's day, but J. Dillon's *The Middle Platonists* probably makes the subject as comprehensible as it is capable of being, and contains a substantial section on Philo.

Part 4

PAUL'S CITIES

The entries in this section have three purposes:

1 to illustrate the great variety in status, history, tradition, local government and relationship with Rome which existed in the cities of the Roman Empire (which is one of the themes of this book);

2 to give (brief) guidance to those travelling in the eastern Mediterranean lands, and wishing to visit the sites associated with Paul, about where significant remains from Paul's time survive, and how each site got into the state in which we find it today;

3 to 'place' Paul within the history and geography of his world, which is perhaps also why the author of The Acts of the Apostles chose to record his visits even to quite insignificant places.

They do not aspire to be complete histories of the places, or full guides to archaeological sites.

9

PALESTINE, SYRIA AND ARABIA

JERUSALEM

When David captured Jerusalem from the Jebusites and made it his capital (2 Samuel 5, 6–9) it was not because of its strategic or economic importance, but simply because, being part of the territory of none of the Israelite tribes, it was neutral. Although Jerusalem is reasonably conveniently situated on the north–south route through the hill-country and has an adequate water supply, it is not otherwise in an obvious site for a great city. Despite Josephus' encomium (*War* 5, 136–76) on the strength of the site and its fortifications (which was presumably largely designed to magnify Titus' achievement in capturing the city) Jerusalem has not had a good record in resisting attacks. Josephus himself (*War* 6, 435–42) records five previous occasions on which it had been captured before its capture by Titus. Later it was taken by Hadrian in 135, by the Persians in 614, by the Arabs in 638 and by the crusaders in 1099. More usually, however, the city passed without resistance to whoever controlled the region. Situated in the hills at the edge of the Judaean desert, in an area with poor agriculture, on no important route, Jerusalem has been an important centre only when religious or political motives have taken precedence over economic or strategic considerations. The key to its significance was that the Temple there was the only place in the world where it was possible to sacrifice to the god of the Jews, which guaranteed its unique importance for Jews throughout history. Indeed, the religious significance of the city probably tended to inhibit its development as a centre of economic activity; the need to preserve the purity of the city by, for example, prohibiting the bringing in of any but sacrificial animals will not have encouraged traders (Hengel 1989:

74). Nevertheless, its religious importance meant that it supported a substantial population – according to a recent estimate more than 60,000, and perhaps as many as 120,000 (Reinhardt 1995: 263) – augmented by perhaps a million pilgrims during the major festivals (Reinhardt 1995: 262).

The Jerusalem of Paul and his contemporaries was essentially the creation of the Hasmoneans and (most of all) Herod the Great. Although, as we have seen (see p. 68), earlier attempts to turn Jerusalem into a hellenistic city were violently resisted, and ultimately unsuccessful, Herod did equip the city with a theatre and an amphitheatre (Josephus, *Ant.* 15, 268), though the site of neither has been identified, and he instituted athletic contests and games. The limitations within which he was constrained are illustrated by the protests which were raised by the trophies commemorating Augustus' victories with which he had decorated the theatre: they were objectionable because they carried human figures (Josephus, *Ant.* 15, 276–9). Similarly, when the governor Pontius Pilate later brought military standards bearing the image of the emperor into the city, serious disturbances followed (Josephus, *War* 2, 169–74). These incidents illustrate the difficulties faced by secular authorities within a sacred city, and explain why both Jewish kings and Roman governors preferred to operate from Caesarea. Herod's greatest contribution to the city was certainly the rebuilding of the Temple, which began in about 20 BC, and was probably not finished much before its destruction by the Romans in AD 70; a small section of the wall supporting the platform of this Temple survives under the name of the Western (or 'Wailing') Wall. The actual form of the Temple was not very different from that of many temples in the East and in North Africa. It consisted of a central shrine surrounded by a complex of courtyards. Indeed, Josephus tells us that at least some of the architecture was influenced by hellenistic models (e.g. *Ant.* 15, 414), and archaeology confirms that the international hellenistic style was extensively used even in Jerusalem (Lifshitz 1977a: 448).

To an outsider, the Temple and its practices would have been recognisable as an extreme form of what was normal elsewhere. In most temples sacrifice took place, not inside, but outside the main shrine, and worshippers would not normally expect to enter the innermost shrine, though few other temples absolutely prohibited entry, as was the case with the Holy of Holies in Jerusalem (indeed, it was surrounded by a series of enclosures, allowing only priests to approach the immediate vicinity of the Holy of Holies, with male Jews allowed into the next, all Jews including women into the third, and Gentiles being permitted only in the outermost court-yard); though it was unusual, several pagan cults did not have anthropomorphic images of their gods, but only the Jews banned any physical manifestation whatsoever of their god; temples regu-larly maintained their ritual purity by restricting access to certain classes of person, but only the Jews regarded the whole of the human race apart from themselves as polluting, and were prepared to defend the purity of their temple by lynching intruders (cf. Acts 21, 27–31; Wallace and Williams 1993: 113).

The most substantial remains of the Jerusalem Paul knew are those of the fortress adjacent to the temple, the Antonia, which was built by Herod and named after his friend and patron Marcus Antonius, the eventual loser to Augustus in the civil war (this was one of Herod's few serious political miscalculations, see p. 77). Paul will have been taken here when the Roman garrison rescued him from the Jerusalem mob (Acts 22, 24), and kept here until he was sent to the governor in Caesarea. The Herodian fortress was badly damaged during the Roman assault in 70, and most of the surviving masonry probably belongs to a second-century rebuilding. Today it is on the traditional Via Dolorosa, where it is shown as Pontius Pilate's Praetorium, where the trial of Jesus took place. It is more likely, however, that when Roman governors visited Jerusalem they stayed in one of Herod's palaces rather than a barracks, and the most likely is the one on the site of the Citadel, where some Herodian masonry can still be seen in the lower courses of the outer walls.

CAESAREA MARITIMA

Though Jerusalem is, in terms of world history, unquestionably by far the most important city in Judaea (as well as being of unique significance for both Jews and Christians), it is by no means obvious that to most people in the Roman period Caesarea would not have seemed at least as, or even more, prominent. Jerusalem, up in the hills, looked inland to the desert and the roads north and south along its fringe; communications with the coast were not especially good. When the region became attached to the Roman Empire, however, an orientation towards the Mediterranean became more important and, though Jerusalem retained its spiritual significance, politically, socially and geographically it became a backwater; indeed, as we have seen, the city's religious importance tended to hamper its development as a focus for trade and government, apart from what concerned Jews alone. Its political and commercial rôle was taken over by Caesarea, described by the historian Tacitus as the chief city of the province (*Iudaeae caput*: *Histories* 2, 78). This is the place to which Paul was sent to be judged by the governor Felix (Acts 23, 23) and where he was imprisoned until his transfer to Rome; it was the regular point of entry to and departure from Judaea (Acts 9, 30; 18, 22; 21, 8). Members of the early Christian community tended to gravitate there: Philip went to Caesarea after his encounter with the Ethiopian eunuch (Acts 8, 40), and clearly remained there for some time (Acts 7, 8); it was visited by the prophet Agabus (Acts 7, 11); and it was the home of an early Christian community (Acts 21, 16). More importantly, it was in Caesarea that Peter met the centurion Cornelius, the first Gentile convert, who was there presumably because the city was the normal residence of the governor, so that the greater part of the Roman garrison would be stationed there.

Unlike Jerusalem, an ancient and venerable city, Caesarea was a new town. The site had originally been occupied by a stronghold and trading post called Strato's Tower, which had been founded in the fourth century BC by Strato, one of two rulers of that name (it is not known which one) of the Phoenician city of Sidon. The settlement, which may at some stage have adopted the institutions of a Greek *polis*, survived under the Ptolemies and the Seleucids until, with the collapse of Seleucid power, it was taken by the Hasmonean king Alexander Jannaeus at the end of the second century BC. The Roman general Pompeius, arriving in 63 BC, made it independent again, but at some time around the end of the first century BC the emperor Augustus allocated Strato's Tower to Herod the Great.

Herod needed a suitable port on the Mediterranean, and, in a coastline where natural ports are hard to find, all the alternatives were either not in his control or disaffected, so the development of the derelict facilities of Strato's Tower was an attractive option. What is more, the opportunity of founding what was effectively a new city gave Herod the opportunity of behaving like a real hellenistic king unfettered by Jewish sensitivities. Although, as we have seen, almost all major building of the period in Jerusalem bears the unmistakable mark of the influence of the international hellenistic style, pagan temples were out of the question, statues and other images were liable to provoke protests, and even theatres and amphitheatres would be resented because of suspicions of their links with pagan cult. So in Jerusalem even the most commonplace facilities of a typical hellenistic city were controversial. In his rebuilding of Strato's Tower, however, which had no status in Jewish tradition, Herod needed to have no inhibitions and it could be developed into a kind of showplace for his kingdom to the Greco-Roman world. This may be the point Josephus is making when he says:

> In his ambition he founded cities and raised temples (not in the land of the Jews, for they would not have tolerated the kinds of things which are forbidden to us, like honouring in the Greek manner statues and sculptured images, but he built them abroad and in the neighbouring lands), giving the Jews the excuse that he was acting not by his own choice, but as a result of instruction and command, trying to please the emperor and the Romans.
>
> (*Ant.* 15, 329)

Though this new city, like many hellenistic cities, attracted a large Jewish population, it was never a Jewish city.

Josephus gives us long and elaborate descriptions of Herod's constructions:

> He adorned it with a sumptuous palace, public buildings, and, the greatest work of all which required most labour, a sheltered harbour as big as the Piraeus . . . Surrounding the harbour was an unbroken row of houses of polished stone, and in the middle a hill on which stood a temple of the emperor, which could be seen at a distance from approaching ships, containing statues of Rome and Caesar . . . He also built a stone theatre, and an amphitheatre south of the harbour and further back, big enough to hold a large crowd and offering a good sea-view.
>
> (*Ant.* 15, 331–41; see also *War* 1, 408–15)

He also goes into details of the enormous effort of construction which went into creating harbour moles, involving sinking masses of rock as foundations, and an elaborate sewage system flushed by the action of the sea. The whole project, he tells us, took only twelve years to complete. Recent archaeological work on the site has revealed that, although Josephus is occasionally carried away by his rhetoric, essentially the harbour installations were as impressive as he describes them, though not really as big as the Piraeus, the harbour of Athens (Holum *et al*. 1988: 90–105). Much of the southern mole is still visible, and remains of the northern break-water and other installations can be seen below water. The theatre, just to the south of the city, was excavated from 1959 to 1963, and although it had been rebuilt and enlarged several times in the period after Herod, substantial parts of the original building can be distinguished; it seems to have been capable of holding about 3,500 spectators. Little remains of the amphitheatre though the site, north-east of the city, has been identified; it seems to have been a large structure, perhaps even bigger than the Colosseum at Rome. Josephus' description of the sites of these two buildings seems to have confused the one with the other (unless there is a corruption in the text); it is the theatre, not the amphitheatre, which is south of the city. The theatre has the better sea view. Herod's palace has not been securely identified, but there is speculation that it may be a structure found on a promontory quite near the theatre (Holum *et al*. 1988: 82–6). Elsewhere on the site a number of vaulted build-ings have been excavated, which may have been granaries and warehouses, though some of them may have formed the substruc-ture of the platform on which the temple of Rome and Augustus was built.

Herod called his new city Caesarea, a compliment to the emperor of a kind which client-kings frequently found expedient. Other examples are Caesarea Philippi (more properly Paneas) founded by Herod's son Philip, Caesarea (Mazaca) in Cappadocia founded by Archelaus, and Caesarea in Mauretania founded by Juba. To distin-guish it from the others, Herod's city had the official name 'Caesarea beside the harbour of Augustus' or, more concisely, 'Caesarea-by-the-sea' (*Caesarea Maritima*). Herod paid a further compliment to the emperor by establishing in his honour quin-quennial games on the hellenistic model.

We have no firm information on how the internal government of the city was organised. If Caesarea was like Herod's other cities, we can infer that it had some sort of constitution and a body of magis-trates (Levine 1975: 17), and Josephus (*War* 1, 550) speaks of Herod summoning an assembly (*ekklēsia*) there. Providing the city with the status of a proper *polis* would be in line with Herod's adoption of a hellenistic style, but there is no doubt that real power would always remain in the hands of the king or one of his officials (an *archōn* or *stratēgos*).

After the exile of Herod's son Archelaus in AD 6, Caesarea retained its importance. Though the Roman procurator, like all governors, will have been peripatetic, the attractions of Caesarea as a pagan city, with all the amenities of urban life, and good port facilities, meant that it would be his most usual residence, and Herod's palace (where Paul was imprisoned) his normal home. Excavations in the theatre have revealed an inscription (on a block of stone used as building material during later construction) recording a dedication, whose details are obscure and controversial, by the best known of them, Pontius Pilate (Lifshitz 1977b: 501). In 41–4 it briefly became part of the kingdom of Herod Agrippa I, who spent much time there. It was the theatre at Caesarea which was the scene of the events reported in Acts 12, 21–3 and Josephus, *Ant.* 19, 344–6 where he appeared dressed in splendid robes and was hailed (perhaps) as a god, an event promptly followed by his death. For some reason, Agrippa seems not to have been very popular with the citizens of Caesarea. At any rate, Josephus tells us (*Ant.* 19, 356–7) that on his death they hurled abuse at him and 'went home and, taking the statues of the king's daughters, carried them to the brothels and set them up on the roofs, where they insulted them in ways too indecent to describe'. The fact that Agrippa seems to have had statues of his daughters set up is a striking indication of how far he had absorbed hellenism.

After the restoration of direct Roman rule, tensions between the Jewish and Gentile sections of the population became more evident. Josephus (*War* 2, 266–70) reports a dispute over citizen rights, in which the Jews claimed that the city was theirs because its founder, Herod, was a Jew, while the Gentiles responded that if Herod had intended it for Jews he would never have built temples or erected statues there. The dispute eventually led to street fighting and serious disorder, until the governor Felix intervened. He referred the matter to the emperor Nero in Rome, where the Jews took the opportunity of accusing Felix of misgovernment – they lost on both counts. The issue here, the status of the Jewish community in an essentially Gentile city, is one which arose in a number of cities in the hellenised East and indicates that, whatever rights the constitution of Caesarea gave to citizens, they were worth having. This episode also gives the background to Felix's sensitivity to Jewish opinion when Paul was in his hands (Acts 24, 27). Trouble between the two communities continued until in 66 a dispute over the erection by a Gentile of some buildings which seemed to restrict access to a Jewish synagogue led to serious fighting, in the course of which the Jews were, according to Josephus (*War* 2, 285–92), driven from the city. By the beginning of the Jewish revolt later that year, however, sufficient numbers had returned for 20,000 of them to be massacred in the city, so Josephus claims (*War* 2, 457). During the Jewish War, Caesarea was the Roman army's principal base, and the headquarters of the general (and future emperor) Vespasian.

After the suppression of the first Jewish revolt, Caesarea was given the status of a Roman colony (Colonia Prima Flavia Augusta Caesariensis) by the emperor Vespasian (Pliny, *Natural History* 5, 14, 69), perhaps as a settlement of Roman veterans of the war (Levine 1975: 35–6). Presumably from that point it had the institutions typical of Roman colonies everywhere; certainly an inscription datable shortly after the establishment of the colony refers to a *duovir*, one of the two chief magistrates of any colony (Levine 1975: 37; Holum *et al*. 1988: 118). The city was now wholeheartedly pagan, and there is abundant evidence (Holum *et al*. 1988: 142–53) of the cult of a wide variety of deities (including the Artemis of Ephesos). We hear little of any Christian community in Caesarea until, in 231, the great Alexandrian Christian theologian Origen, having quarrelled with his local bishop, migrated to Caesarea, bringing with him his famous school. There he completed work on his monumental *Hexapla*, an immense critical work on the Old Testament, which arranged in six columns the Hebrew text in Hebrew and Greek letters and four Greek translations. Origen's work established Caesarea as one of the intellectual centres of Christianity (Levine 1975: 119–27). Perhaps the best-known of the products of the city's schools was Eusebius, the bishop of Caesarea from about 314 to about 340 and the author of the famous *Ecclesiastical History*, our principal source for the history of the early church.

In late antiquity the city was in relative decline. It is important, however, not to exaggerate. The harbour was certainly deteriorating, partly through subsidence – the present level of the sea floor is now more than five metres lower than it was in antiquity (Raban 1992: 113) – and the breakwaters may have been breached through this process as early as the third century; on the other hand, the massive harbour installations built to serve Herod's kingdom would no longer have been appropriate to the local needs of Caesarea and its immediate hinterland, and there would have been no incentive to invest in the level of maintenance necessary to keep the Herodian port in operation. Lesser facilities would be quite sufficient (Raban 1992: 119–23). In fact, recent excavation has revealed abundant material remains from the Byzantine period (on which evidence an estimate of a population of about 100,000 is based, making it one of the larger cities of the Empire), and a fortification wall built in the fourth or fifth century enclosed a very substantial area of urban settlement. In the sixth century part of the theatre (now in ruins) was adapted as part of a fortress (Holum *et al.* 1988: 164–76). A church was built on the site of Herod's temple to Rome and Augustus. From the fourth century onwards the growth of religious tourism, pilgrimages, brought more income to the city, both in its own right (the alleged houses of Cornelius and Philip were shown to visitors) and as a port for Jerusalem. The conquest of Palestine, first by the Persians in 614 and then, following a Byzantine reconquest in 627, by the Arabs in 638, and the disturbances which accompanied these events, resulted in the sudden depopulation of the city. The site was occupied in the early Muslim period as a fortress, and the fertility of the hinterland guaranteed a degree of continuing prosperity, but Caesarea did not regain its former importance until it was seized in 1101 by the First Crusade. The new Kingdom of Jerusalem again looked west to the Mediterranean, and Caesarea's crusader fortifications, completed in 1252, are today the site's most prominent and impressive feature. The return of Muslim rule under Baibars in 1265 brought the city's history to an abrupt end. The fortress, like the other crusader strongholds along the coast, was destroyed as part of a deliberate policy of removing all possible footholds which might be seized by new invaders. By the fifteenth century the site was reduced to uninhabited swamps.

DAMASCUS

Damascus claims to be the oldest continuously inhabited city in the world. This is a plausible claim, for the name of the city is found in archives as early as the third millennium BC, but the fact that it continues to be a densely inhabited and flourishing capital city has inhibited the kind of archaeological investigation which would be needed to establish how old it really is. Though it has had periods of greater or lesser prosperity, Damascus has consistently been an important centre almost irrespective of the political situation in which it has found itself at any period, because of its geographical situation. Essentially it is a large oasis, a region of high fertility created on the edge of the desert by the waters of the river Barada, which flows from the Anti-Lebanon mountain range. It lies on the innermost of the north–south routes through Syria and Palestine running from the Red Sea through Petra and Amman, and then to Palmyra and beyond. The history of Damascus in the hellenistic period is confused and obscure. It passed from the control of the Seleucids to the Ptolemies and back again, but it is not always clear who had it when. In the chaotic period before the coming of the Romans it was, at different times, independent, the capital of a small state, and under the control of Tigranes of Armenia and the Nabataean king. In 65 BC one of Pompeius' officers occupied the city, and it became a part of the province of Syria.

Despite its antiquity, and the fact that the inhabitants on the whole continued to use Semitic names, the city became thoroughly hellenised. At any rate, only Greek inscriptions have survived (Millar 1993: 310–11). The architecture too was entirely Greek. In the Roman period it was one of the loose grouping of cities called the Dekapolis, a term which means 'the ten cities', though the membership of the grouping seems not to have been fixed, and the cities listed by various authors hardly ever come to ten. The status of the group is uncertain, but they seem not to have been a formal federation (because they do not mention it on their coinage) so much as an informal association of hellenised cities between northern Palestine and the desert (they included Philadelphia, which is modern Amman, Gerasa and Gadara).

The city as it is today has, of course, grown much larger than its ancient or medieval predecessors, but the walls of the old town, though largely eleventh-century in date, preserve some traces of Roman masonry and many of the Roman gates; the grid-plan of hellenistic Damascus can still be seen (with difficulty) underlying the modern city. The centrepiece of the Roman city was the temple of Zeus, who may possibly have been identified with the Semitic Hadad (for discussion see Millar 1993: 312–16). Like many eastern and North African temples (and like Herod's temple at Jerusalem) it consisted of a central shrine enclosed within a large and imposing courtyard (the *temenos*). That at Damascus was exceptionally large, and the temple complex seems to have been under construction for most of the first century AD (so work was being done on it when Paul was in Damascus). The temple itself was destroyed in the reign

of Theodosius I (shortly after 379) when the Christian church of
John the Baptist was built in its place. After the Arab conquest the
church was replaced in 708 by a splendid mosque, perhaps the most
magnificent early mosque still surviving (it still contains the
alleged burial place of the head of John the Baptist). Some traces of
the *temenos* wall can be seen in the wall of the courtyard of the
mosque, but the temple enclosure was bigger still, and another
fragment of the wall can be seen standing (rather incongruously)
among modern buildings in a street just west of the mosque.

When Paul came to Damascus (blinded after his vision on the
Damascus road) he was taken to 'the house of Judas' in 'the street
called Straight' (Acts 9, 11) which is usually identified with the
modern street running across the old city from the Bab al-Jabiye to
the Bab Sharqi, called Madhat Basha Street at its western end, and
Bab Sharqi Street at the eastern. It was part of the hellenistic 'new
quarter' of Damascus, just south of the ancient city centre, and
presumably got its name from the fact that this area was laid out on
a grid, and its straightness contrasted with the unplanned streets of
the older town (although it was never absolutely straight, and these
days encroachments on what was a broad thoroughfare in antiquity
have left it narrow and not strikingly straight at all). The gate
usually associated with Paul's visit to Damascus is the Bab Sharqi –
which of all the gates probably best preserves its Roman form,
though it is likely that this dates from around 200 AD, rather than
Paul's day – presumably because it is at one end of 'the street called
Straight'. To the north is a chapel which is allegedly on the site of
the house of Ananias, who met Paul in Damascus (Acts 9, 10–19);
some of the masonry incorporated in it may indeed be very old, but
nothing links it positively with Ananias. The place where Paul was
lowered over the wall in a basket (Acts 9, 25) is supposed to be
marked by a chapel south of Bab Sharqi, at a place where there
probably was a Roman gateway (of which no traces now survive); it
is completely modern, and the identification of the spot does not
seem to rely on any old tradition.

Unfortunately, we know very little about the internal affairs of
Damascus in Paul's day. It is therefore difficult to know how to
make sense of Paul's commission from the High Priest to seize and
carry to Jerusalem 'any belonging to the Way' (Acts 9, 2). Since
Acts says quite clearly that the letters Paul was carrying were to the
synagogues at Damascus (9, 2) and not to the Gentile authorities,
whatever he was doing must have been an entirely internal Jewish

affair. Since it is unlikely that the arrest and extradition to Judaea of dissenters was one of the privileges enjoyed by diaspora communities (for discussion see Wallace and Williams 1993: 51–2), what Paul was engaged in must have been unauthorised; that is to say, kidnapping. So why was he not stopped? Such evidence as there is suggests that no Roman forces were stationed in or near Damascus (Millar 1993: 37), so that unless an appeal was made to the governor, or serious disorder broke out, the Roman authorities would not have become involved. As for the city authorities, if the business was done discreetly without causing public disturbances they might well have taken the view that what went on in the Jewish community was none of their concern, especially if those involved were not citizens of Damascus, but incomers. There were many Jews in Damascus; Josephus gives the number massacred after the outbreak of the Jewish revolt as 10,500 (*War* 2, 561) or 18,000 (*War* 7, 368). If 2 Corinthians 11, 24, 'Five times I have received at the hands of the Jews the forty lashes less one', really shows that local synagogues could have dissidents flogged, it is perfectly possible that the local authorities would also have turned a blind eye to the removal by Jews of Jewish troublemakers (even supposing they ever found out about it), provided that the affair was kept within the community.

Later Damascus continued its relatively uneventful existence as a point of contact between the settled lands and the desert, and it is no surprise that after the Arab conquest of 635 it readily accepted the new rulers, and indeed for almost a hundred years in the seventh and eighth centuries under the Umayyad caliphs it was the capital of the Muslim world until, with the replacement of the Umayyads by the Abbasids, the capital was transferred to Baghdad.

ARABIA

Although it is not mentioned in Acts, in Galatians (1, 17) Paul tells us that after his conversion on the road to Damascus he spent some time in Arabia. In 2 Corinthians 11, 32 he tells the story of his escape from Damascus over the wall in a basket, but in this account, unlike that of Acts 9, 24–5, those watching out for him are not 'the Jews' but the ethnarch of King Aretas. The two reports may be connected. Arabia must be the kingdom of the Nabataean Arabs, whose king at the time was Aretas IV. (Aretas is a hellenised form of a name written in Aramaic as *ḥrtt*, and which is related to the Arabic name Ḥarith; like many such hellenised names, it has the advantage of seeming to be related to a genuine Greek root, *aretē* = virtue).

The Nabataeans first appear in history in 312 BC when, using their mobility and skill in desert warfare, they resisted an attempt by Antigonos I to conquer them (Diodorus Siculus 19, 94–7). At that time they were still semi-nomadic and indeed, according to Diodorus Siculus (19, 94), they counted planting crops or trees, drinking wine and building houses as crimes punishable by death (see Jeremiah 35, 6–10 for a Jewish group similarly trying to cling to the nomadic life). With the coming of the Romans they became a client kingdom – one of the most successful client kingdoms, in fact. They were not brought directly under Roman rule until the emperor Trajan (for reasons which we do not know) annexed the kingdom in 106 and turned it into the province of Arabia.

By Paul's time the Nabateans had established a number of substantial urban centres. The best-known of these is the city of Petra, whose spectacular rock-cut tombs have made it a popular tourist site. Bostra, however, in the north of the kingdom, was growing in importance and was to become the capital of the kingdom by the end of the first century. Since it is quite close to Damascus, Paul's activity in Arabia is as likely to have taken place here as anywhere else. Though Arabia was never part of any of the kingdoms founded by Alexander's successors it was deeply influenced by hellenistic culture and, if a recent reconsideration of the sequence of the monuments at Petra is correct (McKenzie 1990: 33–56), the Nabataeans were already in the first century BC building structures modelled on the architecture of Ptolemaic Alexandria. Aretas IV himself was responsible for the building of the theatre in Petra (McKenzie 1990: 35). But though they were sometimes willing to use hellenistic artistic forms in their depiction of their gods, elsewhere they represented them aniconically, as blocks or slabs without features (Gawlikowski 1990: 2662–8). Like the Jews, then, they combined an openness to Greek influences with an attachment to their own traditions, especially in religion.

The wealth of the Nabataeans probably depended on their control of the overland trade in perfume and spices coming up from south-western Arabia. They also had great skill in water management, as the surviving remains at Petra demonstrate. The reign of Aretas IV saw a considerable extension of irrigation-based agriculture (Bowersock 1983: 64–5), and their reputation as agriculturalists survived at least as late as the fourteenth century in the name of a famous treatise, *Nabataean Agriculture* (Ibn Khaldûn, *Muqaddimah* 6, 25).

Relationships between the Nabateans and the Jewish kingdom were very stormy. At the end of the first century BC open warfare broke out between them, almost provoking Roman intervention. Perhaps in an attempt to improve matters, Herod Antipas married the daughter of Aretas. Herod, however, returned his wife to her father when he fell in love with Herodias, his niece and the wife of his half-brother (in about AD 27; this is the Herodias who was implicated in the death of John the Baptist (Mark 6, 17–28; Matthew 14, 3–11; Luke 3, 19–20)). Aretas responded by attacking Herod and defeating him in battle. Vitellius, the governor of Syria, was on the point of intervening when he was distracted by the death of the emperor Tiberius in 37 (Josephus, *Ant.* 18, 109–24; Bowersock 1983: 65–7). Since Aretas IV died in 39 or 40, it is likely that these events (which illustrate both the reality and the limits of the independence of client kings) were very close to the time of Paul's stay in Damascus and Arabia.

The question of what a representative of Aretas IV was doing in Damascus in Paul's time is not an easy one to answer. Some have concluded that Damascus must have been temporarily under Nabataean control (e.g. Bowersock 1983: 68–9; Taylor 1992: 727; more cautiously Millar 1993: 56–7). There is, however, no evidence whatsoever for Nabataean control of Damascus at this period. Even Josephus has nothing to say on the subject. The fact that there is no surviving dated coinage of Damascus between 33/4 and 65/6 means no more than that we do not have one of the bits of evidence which would positively exclude Nabataean control; in itself it establishes nothing. Though this was a period of some chaos in the region, it would have been an act of lunacy for a client king to take advantage of it to seize part of the province of Syria (for discussion see Taylor 1992: 726–7). Nor is there any obvious reason why the Romans would have wanted to cede the city to Aretas. So who was the Nabataean representative who tried to catch Paul at Damascus? Paul used the term *ethnarchēs*, 'ethnarch' (translated 'governor' by the RSV). The literal meaning is 'ruler of a nation', but the term is applied widely and with no consistency. Josephus (*Ant.* 19, 283) uses it of the leaders of the Jewish community in Alexandria, but there is no reason to suppose that there was a similar organised Nabataean community in Damascus. Despite what is sometimes asserted (e.g. Taylor 1992: 720) there is nothing in what Paul says to lead us to suppose that the ethnarch was watching from the inside rather than the outside of the city, or that (despite Bowersock 1983: 68) he was guarding the city in a permanent sense; Paul says simply that he was guarding the city *to catch Paul*. Sense can be made of the episode, however, if the ethnarch was simply a local tribal chief (Taylor 1992: 722–4), who had the job of protecting trade routes running through his tribal territory from robbers. His responsibilities might well have extended as far as the gates of Damascus; the Nabataeans would have had an interest in protecting the passage of goods all the way to a city which was an important link in their trade and, in the absence of permanent Roman troops, the city authorities might well have welcomed such an arrangement – the use of local forces to protect desert trade routes is attested later in the case of Palmyra (Millar 1993: 134). It is possible to reconcile the statement of Acts 9, 23–5 that Paul's danger came from the local Jews with his own claim that it came from the ethnarch of Aretas. If Paul had come on a strictly unauthorised mission from Jerusalem to get hold of troublemakers and take them back, when he defected to those same troublemakers the local Jews would surely have wanted him too sent back to Jerusalem. They would not have had facilities to do this themselves, and could hardly have approached the city authorities for help, but the local sheikh who guarded the caravans would certainly have had the means both to capture Paul and to transport him to Jerusalem. So they simply hired him to do the job. This is, of course, pure speculation, but it is no more speculative than a completely unattested period of Nabataean control of Damascus, and has the advantage of being compatible both with Acts and with Paul's account.

ANTIOCH

Though it became one of the greatest cities of the ancient world, Antioch's rise owes much to accident. It was founded in about 300 BC by Seleukos Nikator, the first of the Seleucid dynasty, and named after his father. This did not stop later Antiocheans claiming that their real founders were a group of settlers brought by the hero Triptolemus, whom they honoured with a cult and a festival (Strabo 16, 2, 5). When Alexander arrived in Syria the area, which had had a long history of culture and urbanisation, had been largely depopulated by four centuries of alien rule, and no cities had survived (Grainger 1990: 7). After Alexander's death his general Antigonos, who had included Syria in his domain, founded a new city, Antigoneia, to consolidate his control of the region and, presumably, to settle his retired soldiers. When Antigonos was replaced by Seleukos after the battle of Ipsus in 301 Antigoneia was abandoned (apparently for no other reason than that it had been founded by Antigonos) and replaced by four new foundations, of which Antioch was one. Originally, Antioch seems to have had no particular status among them and Seleukia, on the coast, may have been designed as the principal city in the region. The site of the city is not especially favourable. It is built at a point where the river Orontes turns away from the mountains, and the main area of settlement in ancient times was between the mountain and the river. It had some advantages, however. It was at a junction of routes (between the plains and the hills, and along the Orontes to the sea), controlled a crossing of the river, and had a good water supply and a pleasant climate (aided by breezes from the mountains). On the other hand, it was liable to flooding during the heavy rains which are frequent from October to April – Procopius in the sixth century tells us that one stream could become so torrential that it was called *onopniktēs*, 'the ass-drowner' (*On Buildings* 2, 10, 16, 4) – unless the canalisation of the watercourses was carefully maintained (Grainger 1990: 74). What is more, the city was built in a region liable to severe earthquakes, which regularly throughout its history caused widespread devastation. The main problem with the site, however, is that, being overlooked by Mount Silpius, it could not easily be made defensible. Indeed, on every occasion that the city has faced serious assault, it has fallen (Downey 1961: 15–17). The Orontes seems to have been navigable by large ships only as far as Antioch and a little beyond, but smaller boats could bring in produce from the fertile hinterland, which would supplement what the immediate vicinity of the city yielded (Liebescheutz 1972: 73–4).

The original population was composed in part of retired soldiers (including some of those whom Antigonos had settled at Antigoneia), and in part of immigrants brought in from Greece. In addition, Josephus claims (*Ant.* 12, 119) that Seleukos also settled Jews in the city, and that he or his successors gave them citizen rights, or something like it, and other privileges which were inscribed on bronze tablets on public display (*War* 7, 110). They included a cash allowance to buy oil for those Jews who could not, for religious reasons, accept the free olive oil allocated to the city's gymnasia (*Ant.* 12, 120). Later these rights were strongly contested by the non-Jewish population, but they were regularly upheld by the Roman authorities (*Ant.* 12, 121–2; *War* 7, 111). Antioch was a Greek-speaking intrusion in a countryside where the rural population spoke Syriac, the local dialect of Aramaic, though no securely dated document or coin with writing in any Semitic language survives from before AD 337 (Millar 1993: 242). This Syriac culture had virtually no influence on the life of the city until, with the rise of Christianity in late antiquity, the creation of a Christian literature in Syriac and the growth of the popularity of hermits, many of whom seem to have been monoglot Syriac-speakers from the villages, gave the city-dwellers an incentive to come to terms with the local culture. When this happened, they seem to have had no difficulty in communicating, which suggests that even earlier there had been a good deal of unreported practical bilingualism (Liebescheutz 1972: 62).

Like many hellenistic cities, Antioch was laid out on the fashionable grid-plan. The traces of this layout are still visible in the modern city, but this is the result of the nineteenth-century rebuilders making life easy for themselves by using ancient foundations and roads rather than a sign of continuity from antiquity; indeed, in the oldest part of the city, round the bridge, the ancient city-plan is completely lost (Grainger 1990: 74).

Antioch became the principal city of the Seleucids largely by default. Seleukia was occupied by Ptolemy III Euergetes in 241 BC and held by him until 219. After their defeat by the Romans in 190 most of Asia Minor was lost to the Seleucids (see p. 72). In these circumstances, there were few alternatives to Antioch as a relatively secure capital in touch with the Mediterranean. It was Antiochos IV Epiphanes (175–164 BC) who, perhaps in an ultimately unsuccessful attempt to rival Alexandria, began the process of enlarging and adorning the city. Under him, it doubled in size, and he equipped it with splendid new public buildings. With the decline of Seleucid power the city fell first to Tigranes of Armenia and was then, after the intervention of Pompeius, taken over by the Romans. But even before Antioch officially came under direct Roman rule the proconsul of Cilicia, Q. Marcius Rex, visited it in 67 and built a palace and a circus. As a reward for backing the right side in a civil war, Antioch received from Julius Caesar a new theatre, a basilica (the first in the East), an amphitheatre (Roman-type games had already been introduced by Antiochos IV – Livy 41, 20), an aqueduct and public baths (Lassus 1977: 68). This pattern continued under Augustus. Indeed, Herod the Great, wishing to ingratiate himself with the emperor, himself funded the construction of part of a splendid colonnaded street (one of the first examples of the kind of monumental road which later became common in Roman cities) through the centre of the city (Josephus, *Ant.* 16, 148). Strabo, writing at this period, tells us that it was the metropolis of Syria, and puts it in the same league as Seleukia-on-the-Tigris and Alexandria (*Geography* 16, 5).

When Pompeius came to Antioch in 64, he gave the city its 'freedom'. Presumably, this means that he restored the city's *polis* institutions. Strangely in view of Antioch's importance, we know very little of its internal affairs until the fourth century AD, when the writings of the Antiochean rhetorician Libanius give a great deal of information. So far as we can tell, Seleucid Antioch had been governed by a *boulē* (council) of six hundred citizens from the wealthiest families (Lassus 1977: 81–2), though in reality the king or his local representative must have made all but the most trivial decisions. Under the Romans, the *boulē* continued to function (Josephus, *War* 7, 107), and there seems also to have been an assembly which met in the theatre. Titus, the son of Vespasian, addressed the people there (Josephus, *War* 7, 107); a renegade Jew called Antiochos entered the theatre during an assembly (*ekklēsia*) to stir up the people against the Jewish community (Josephus, *War* 7, 47); and the governor of Syria, Licinius Mucianus, addressed the crowd in the theatre 'where they usually held assemblies' in an attempt to win support for Vespasian's bid for the throne (Tacitus, *Histories* 2, 80). On this last occasion one of the arguments which Mucianus used was the claim that Vitellius, Vespasian's rival, was intending to transfer the Syrian legions from Antioch to Germany. Tacitus tells us that this was as unpopular with the civilian population as it was with the army, because 'they enjoyed having dealings with the soldiers they knew, and many of the provincials were linked with them by marriage and family ties'. This is a reminder that, as the principal base for the legions stationed in Syria to confront Rome's main rival in the East, Parthia, Antioch must have experienced a much greater Roman presence than most cities in the Empire, and the money brought in by the army must have greatly increased the prosperity of the city.

The Jewish community continued to flourish, and Josephus tells us that, despite friction with the local Gentiles, 'they regularly attracted large numbers of Greeks to their worship, and they had, to some degree, made them a part of their community' (*War* 8, 45). It is therefore not surprising to find that Antioch was one of the earliest centres of the new Christian church (Acts 11, 19; 11, 22; 13, 1) or that the first Christian Antiochean of whom we hear was Nikolaos, a Gentile converted to Judaism (Acts 6, 5). It was, of course, in Antioch that the conversion of Gentiles first gave rise to controversy (Acts 11, 20; 14, 26–15, 1), and where the new group were first given the name Christians (Acts 11, 26), a curious Greek word with a Latin adjectival ending, perhaps indicating the mixture of cultures in the city. Indeed, Antioch features so prominently in Acts that some have been led to speculate that its author was an Antiochean, though apart from a certain amount of name-dropping we are actually told very little of the detail of what was going on in the city.

The importance of Antioch increased further when, from the middle of the third century, the revival of the Persian empire put Rome on the defensive in the East: Antioch became a frontier city, and a frequent residence of emperors. The Persians captured and sacked the city in 256, and again in 540, when it was burnt to the ground and depopulated. Nevertheless, the importance of the city as a military base guaranteed that it continued to flourish. As one might expect, the Christian community there was always large and, indeed, turbulent – their quarrel with their bishop Paul in the 260s led to the deposition of the bishop and the referral of the question of the ownership of the church buildings to the emperor Aurelian, the first instance of an emperor, a pagan one in this case, being invited to arbitrate in an ecclesiastical dispute. Local tradition (Malalas 242, 11–12) had identified a street (called Singon or Siagon; the word seems to mean jaw-bone) where Paul and Barnabas had preached (Downey 1961: 275). They claimed that the first bishop of Antioch was Peter, and a mile or so out of the city is a rock-cut church in which he is alleged to have taught. Most of the surviving fabric is from the crusader period, but some mosaics of the fifth or sixth centuries survive, suggesting that the tradition may go back to late antiquity. Local Christians also contested with the Jews possession of the tomb of the seven brothers whose martyrdom under the Seleucids is narrated in 4 Maccabees 8–13; it was finally allocated to the Christians some time after 363. It was, however, Antioch's political prominence, rather than its possession of important religious sites, which made the bishop of Antioch one of the most powerful leaders of the church; by the fifth century the theological schools of Antioch were rivalled only by those of Alexandria.

After the Arab invasions of the seventh century, Antioch continued to exist as a frontier fortress, and for a while it was the centre of a crusader principality. The city was in decline, however, and when the frontier moved away after the Muslim reconquest in 1268, it dwindled rapidly to a small village round the bridge over the Orontes. With its military and administrative functions removed, there was nothing to sustain a large town on the site. Before it was excavated in 1932–9 all that was visible from its ancient past were sections of the city wall built by Justinian in the sixth century, the ruins of the crusader citadel, the ancient bridge, fragments of an aqueduct (built by Trajan) and of the hippodrome, and a curious rock carving, the Charonion, on a hill nearby which may represent Charon, the ferryman of the dead, and may have been executed in the time of Antiochos IV Epiphanes (which would make it the only visible relic of Seleucid Antioch). Excavations have turned up, among other things, a splendid series of mosaics (on display in the city museum) mostly from the second to the fourth centuries AD, which are striking evidence of the wealth and prosperity of the city in its greatest days. The city is now an administrative centre. Modern urban development on the site began during the French occupation of the region after the First World War, before, following a referendum in 1939, it was handed over to Turkey.

SELEUKIA

Paul's only visit to Seleukia, when he and his companions travelled there from Antioch to take ship to Cyprus (Acts 13, 4), accurately reflects the city's rôle in his day as simply the port of Antioch. It is, however, not very conveniently situated for travel from Antioch. The mouth of the river Orontes is several miles south of the city, whose precise site was chosen, apparently, by observing the flight of an eagle which had carried off meat while Seleukos was sacrificing. Strabo (16, 2, 7) says that it was possible to leave Antioch and reach the sea on the same day by sailing down the river. It is hard to reconcile this with Pausanias' claim in the second century (8, 29, 6) that because of waterfalls the river was not navigable along its whole length until an unnamed Roman emperor diverted it into a canal. It is likely that the emperor in question was Vespasian (Millar

1993: 87). Pausanias was probably exaggerating, but the fact that Vespasian was prepared to invest money and labour in this project suggests that the natural waterway was at least unsatisfactory. In fact, Seleukia was designed not to serve Antioch, but to be Seleukos' western capital (which is why it, like his eastern capital Seleukia-on-the-Tigris, is named after him), a plan which was abandoned only when Ptolemy Euergetes' occupation of the city demonstrated that the Seleucids did not have the power to guarantee its security. The walls of which traces are visible today are probably Roman, but they seem to follow the lines of the Seleucid walls, and enclose an enormous area, including both the port and an acropolis, though it is most unlikely that all the land within the walls was built up (Grainger 1990: 84). By the second century (and perhaps earlier) it was a Roman naval base (Millar 1993: 103–4). Like Antioch it ceased to function in the thirteenth century and today the site, though attractive, is entirely abandoned, with very few visible remains.

TYRE

Paul visited Tyre only once, when the ship in which he was sailing from Patara to Caesarea made a seven-day stop to unload some cargo (Acts 21, 3–4); he found a Christian group there. Elsewhere in the New Testament we are told that Jesus spent some time in the vicinity of Tyre and Sidon, though not in the cities themselves (Mark 7, 31); it is here that he encountered the woman who 'was a Greek, a Syrophoenician by birth' whose daughter he healed (Mark 7, 26; cf. Matthew 15, 21–2). Otherwise it appears, linked with Sidon, in a saying of Jesus where it stands as one of the representatives of the Gentile world, in language reminiscent of the Old Testament (Matthew 11, 21–2; Luke 10, 13–14). Tyre had once been one of the great cities of the Mediterranean. Together with the other Phoenician cities it dominated sea-borne trade from the eleventh century BC (with their greatest period being perhaps the ninth to the seventh centuries), and sent out a number of settlements to the West, the most famous of which was the Tyrian colony of Carthage (*Qart-ḥadasht* = 'New Town'; now in Tunisia). Though historians looking at the Tyrians from the point of view of the Greeks and Romans tend to think of them (rightly) as great seafarers, they also had an interest in the trade by land to the East (perhaps the most vivid ancient account of the extent of Tyrian trade is to be found in Ezekiel 27). The Greeks had early links with the Tyrians. In their mythology Europa (the mother, by Zeus in the form of a bull, of a number of Greek heroes) and Cadmus, the mythical founder of Thebes, both came from Tyre (though Sidon also claimed them), and the Greeks believed, probably correctly, that it was from Phoenicia that they had learned the alphabet (Herodotos 5, 58). As a consequence, the Tyrians had no difficulty in establishing respectable Greek connections in the hellenistic period.

The city of Tyre itself was built on an island equipped with artificial harbours; the structures are still visible, though largely under water (Grainger 1991: 13–14). The Tyrians resisted Alexander fiercely, and the city was taken – and brutally sacked – only after a long siege, in the course of which Alexander constructed a causeway linking the island to the mainland. This causeway remained in place, and silting widened it until the city became a promontory rather than an island. Today Alexander's causeway lies underneath a section of the modern city. Despite this, and further disruption during the wars of Alexander's successors, the city recovered. Its most famous product was a scarlet dye (sometimes called purple) which was derived from a local shellfish. The increase in prosperity and the proliferation of kings in the hellenistic period meant that the demand for this product, which was associated with royalty, was very strong (Grainger 1991: 70–1), and Tyre became a substantial market city (though Strabo remarks that the dyeing industry made the city a very unpleasant place: 16, 2, 23). Tyrian trade was certainly active: we hear of communities of Tyrian traders in Delos and in Puteoli (Schürer 1973–87: III (1), 108, 111). It was, however, on a small scale compared to what it had been in the great days of Tyre. As Pliny the Elder put it (*Natural History* 5, 17, 76): 'All that Tyre is famous for now is a shellfish and scarlet dye.' In the third century Tyre did produce a famous son, Domitius Ulpianus, the most voluminous of Roman jurists, and ruler of the Empire as adviser to the boy emperor Severus Alexander for a short period before he was murdered by the Praetorian Guards in 223. Continuous occupation of the site has inhibited archaeological investigation. There are today substantial remains of Roman Tyre (which developed largely on the mainland), including part of a colonnaded street and a splendid, well-preserved, hippodrome, of doubtful date but certainly later than Paul. The colonnaded street continues to the harbour on a separate site (Fig. 9.1).

Figure 9.1 The road to the port at Tyre

SIDON

Much of what has been said about Tyre could be said also of Sidon, the second of the great Phoenician cities. In Paul's activities it was not an important centre; his ship simply called in there on his way to Rome, and he stayed with friends in the town until they resumed their journey (Acts 27, 3). Sidon seems to have been receptive to Greek influences from the very beginning of the hellenistic period. Some twelve years before Alexander's invasion the Sidonians had rebelled against the Persians, and the revolt had been crushed with great brutality. As a consequence when Alexander approached they threw out their Persian-appointed king and welcomed him into the city (and the support of their fleet was crucial to his success in the siege of Tyre). Alexander appointed a member of the old royal family, Abdalonymus, as king of the city; it is probably his sarcophagus, the so-called 'Alexander sarcophagus', which was discovered in 1887 in a tomb-complex near Sidon (it is at present in the Archaeological Museum in Istanbul). This remarkable work, decorated with scenes of Alexander in battle and taking part in a hunt, uses Greek sculptural techniques with an un-Greek exuberance (Smith 1991: 190–2). It was presumably designed to signal the Sidonians' enthusiasm for the new regime. Sidon contested Tyre's claim to be the home city of Europa and Cadmus, and seems to have cultivated its Greek connections. In about 200 BC, for instance, we hear of a Sidonian winning the chariot race at the Nemean Games in Greece (Millar 1993: 265). Like Tyre, by Paul's day it was a thriving industrial and market city. It was particularly famed for its glass (Strabo 16, 2, 25; Pliny, *Natural History* 5, 17, 76), and it is possible that glass-blowing was invented in Sidon in about 50 BC (Grainger 1991: 182–3).

Today little survives of Sidon's ancient past. It remained a prosperous port serving Damascus until the seventeenth century, when the harbour was allowed to silt up to forestall Turkish attacks. The most prominent monuments are a crusader castle (built in the thirteenth century and subsequently modified), and the Great Mosque, essentially of the fifteenth century but incorporating crusader masonry. There is, however, a large rubbish-tip overlooking the southern harbour which consists mainly of the remains of the shell-fish used to make purple dye.

PTOLEMAIS

Another of Paul's ports-of-call, Ptolemais (where he stayed with 'the brethren' one day: Acts 21, 7), held the same position in the Galilee as Caesarea did in central Palestine, in that it was the most important city in the region, was the principal port and was completely hellenised (Kashtan 1988: 38–40; Millar 1993: 267–8). Unlike Caesarea, however, it was an ancient Phoenician city, occupying one of the very few good natural harbours on the coast. Its old name was Akko (or Akē); it acquired the name Ptolemais when it was refounded by Ptolemy II Philadelphos, though the old name remained in use. It passed from the control of the Ptolemies to that of the Seleucids in 219, and was greatly favoured by them, being a frequent royal residence and sometimes the capital of pretenders to the Seleucid throne; the citizens were given the privilege of referring to themselves as 'Antiochenes in Ptolemais' – a title reminiscent of that requested by the Hellenisers in Jerusalem (see p. 63) – and continued to use this name even under Roman rule (Schürer 1973–87: II, 123). One of the reasons for the city's importance was that it was a natural base for armies campaigning from Syria into Palestine and Egypt. It was the base for the Persian army in the invasion of Egypt in 374 BC, and for Antiochos III in 219–217 BC. During the Maccabean revolt the city was notably hostile to the Jewish rebels (Kashtan 1988: 46–8). Under Roman control it became one of the principal gateways to the Galilee, and the emperor Claudius recognised its importance by making it a Roman colony under the name of Colonia Claudia Stabilis Germanica Felix Ptolemais (Millar 1993: 268). We know very little of the life or institutions of Ptolemais in Roman times. Presumably a city as important as this would have had at least a theatre and a stadium, but none has been found (Kashtan 1988: 49–50). With the decline of Roman power it reverted to its old name, and under the crusaders (who knew it as Acre) it became the principal port for the kingdom of Jerusalem, and was their last foothold in Palestine until it was taken by the Mamluks in 1291. What can be seen in the city today is almost entirely what has been left by the crusaders and their successors.

JOPPA

When Peter was called to Caesarea by Cornelius the centurion, he was staying with one Simon the tanner in Joppa (Acts 9, 43), where he had also healed Tabitha (Acts 9, 36–42). The history of Joppa vividly illustrates the vicissitudes of many settlements in Palestine in the hellenistic and Roman periods. It had one of the few natural harbours in the region, though it was not safe in bad weather (Josephus, *War* 3, 421–3; Theoderich, *Libellus de Locis Sanctis* 51), and had been an important port even before the time of the Persians (Schürer 1973–87: II, 110–11). It was known to the Greeks even before Alexander's conquests, for the mythical story of the exposure of Andromeda to the sea-monster and her rescue by Perseus was located here (Schürer 1973–87: II, 33–4). Visitors were shown the marks of her chains on the rock to which she had been bound (e.g. Pliny, *Natural History* 5, 69), and in 58 BC Pompeius' lieutenant Marcus Scaurus had brought back from Joppa and exhibited in Rome the skeleton of a monster forty feet long, allegedly the remains of the beast from which Perseus had saved Andromeda (Pliny, *Natural History* 9, 11). Ptolemy I abandoned the city in 312 BC, and destroyed it to prevent it being occupied by Antigonos. The Ptolemies were occupying the city again in the third century BC. The Jewish leader Judas Maccabaeus attacked it and destroyed its harbour (2 Maccabees 12, 3–7). Later the Hasmoneans occupied Joppa, expelled all the inhabitants and turned it into a Jewish city (1 Maccabees 13, 11). Subsequently it was fought over in the wars with the Seleucids, but remained Jewish (Schürer 1973–87: II, 111–13), and it was in a Jewish city that Peter was staying – hence his visit to Cornelius in Caesarea was a transition from the Jewish to the Gentile world. When the Jewish revolt broke out in AD 66 Joppa was a centre of resistance, and it was destroyed by Cestius Gallus, with the massacre of the entire population of 8,400 according to Josephus (*War* 2, 508), but reoccupied, so that Vespasian had to capture it again, killing 4,200 inhabitants (*War* 3, 414–30). Thereafter Joppa was a thoroughly Greek city (Schürer 1973–87: II, 113–14). Today, as Jaffa, it is an appendage of the modern city of Tel-Aviv.

LYDDA

The city from which Peter travelled to Joppa, Lydda (Acts 9, 32–8), was also predominantly Jewish, and had been since Seleucid times (Schürer 1973–87: II, 1–2). It lies on the road between Joppa and Jerusalem (its modern name is Lod). Josephus (*Ant.* 20, 130) says of it that though it was a village, it was as big as a *polis*. Early in the Jewish revolt Cestius Gallus captured it, but most of the inhabitants were not at home, since they had gone to celebrate the Feast of Tabernacles in Jerusalem, and he could find only fifty people to massacre (Josephus, *War* 2, 516). Refounded as Diospolis ('city of Zeus') it was in the late third or early fourth century the site of the martyrdom and burial of St George.

10

CYPRUS AND SOUTHERN ASIA MINOR

TARSUS

Since citizenship in the ancient world went by descent rather than domicile, there is no intrinsic reason why Paul, the citizen of Tarsus (Acts 21, 39), need ever have visited the city, much less lived there. Paul's obvious connections are all with Jerusalem: he was educated there (Acts 22, 3), and at least some of his family lived in the city (Acts 23, 16). The fact that, when he was driven from Jerusalem shortly after his conversion, his fellow-Christians sent him for safety to Tarsus (Acts 9, 30), where he stayed until brought to Antioch by Barnabas (Acts 11, 25), suggests only that some of the family still lived there, rather than that it was Paul's own home town. In short, attempts to throw light on Paul's character and teaching from speculations about the environment he experienced in his supposed childhood in Tarsus are built on insecure foundations. Though it is in Cilicia, in Paul's day Tarsus was part of the province of Syria. This made sense, because Tarsus's natural communications are with Antioch. It is situated in a large, fertile plain at an important road junction, for it is on the route which leads from the 'Cilician Gates' (one of the few passes giving access to the Anatolian plateau) down to Syria. Though it lies some way from the sea, the River Kydnos, which runs through it, was navigable right up to the city, and a lake just south of Tarsus formed the city's harbour. Most famously, when Kleopatra VII met and captivated Marcus Antonius here in 41 BC her splendid royal barge made this river journey from the sea to the city in great style (Plutarch, *Antony* 26). Strabo says of the river:

> The river Kydnos flows through it [Tarsus] right by the gymnasium of the young men. Since the source is not far away and immediately before it enters the city the river passes

through a deep gorge, the stream is cold and fast. For this
reason immersion in it is beneficial both to beasts and to men
who suffer from swollen sinews.

(Strabo, *Geography* 14, 12)

We do not know whether it was reasons of health which persuaded
Alexander of Macedon to take a swim in the Kydnos when he
passed through on his way to Syria (Arrian, *Anabasis* 2, 4), but the
result was a serious illness, which ancient writers attributed to the
coldness of the water, and which almost cost him his life. In Paul's
day the Tarsians claimed that their city was an ancient Greek one
founded in mythical times by the Argives (Strabo 14, 12) or by the
demigod Herakles (Dio of Prusa 33, 47; see p. 99). Whatever may
lie behind these stories, at the outset of the hellenistic period the
city (which had existed at least as far back as the third millennium
BC) retained few traces of a Greek origin. Indeed, even at the end of
the first century AD the rhetorician Dio of Prusa, in a speech given
in Tarsus, could tease the Tarsians for their un-Greek habits by
calling them Phoenicians (33, 41–2). He goes on to commend the
custom of the women of Tarsus of dressing so modestly that 'no-one
can see any part of them, neither of their face nor of the rest of their
body, and so that they themselves can see nothing but the road' (33,
48). This, however, is not a sign of oriental influence. Women in the
East at this period did not in general cover themselves more
comprehensively than women elsewhere, and the custom Dio
mentions seems to have been found also in Perge (see p. 189). Like
the other cities in the region, Tarsus was thoroughly hellenised after
Alexander's conquests; it came under Roman rule in 67 BC as a
result of Pompeius' campaign against the pirates (see p. 28). The
Tarsus of Paul's day was the *metropolis* of Cilicia (Dio of Prusa 34, 8)
– the title was an honorific one given to prominent cities – and the
largest city in the region. According to Strabo, it was notable also
for the number of philosophers it produced:

Such is the enthusiasm of the people of Tarsus for philosophy,
and indeed for the whole educational syllabus, that they have
surpassed Athens, Alexandria, and any other place you can
mention where there are philosophical schools and lectures.
They are so superior that in Tarsus the scholars are all natives,
and foreigners do not readily settle there. Indeed the Tarsians
do not stay at home but finish their education abroad, and
when they have done so they are happy to live abroad, and few

of them return home. . . . They also have schools of rhetoric of
every kind.

(Strabo, Geography 14, 13)

Strabo goes on to give an impressive list of Tarsian philosophers,
but no explanation of why the city became such a philosophical
centre. Whether this has any relevance to Paul's life and teaching is
doubtful. Though Paul does show signs of some acquaintance with
philosophical ideas, they are mostly the sort of thing that any
reasonably educated persons in the ancient world might have as part
of their general knowledge; they do not need to be explained by
elevating Tarsus into some sort of 'university city', which it was not.
Dio of Prusa gives us an intriguing glimpse into what seems to have
been a turbulent political situation in the city (34, 19). Not only
was there discord in the *boulē* (council) and the *dēmos* (the assembly),
but there was also some sort of dispute about 'the linen-workers'
(*linourgoi*), whom Dio describes as 'a sizeable group which is, as it
were, outside the constitution (*exō tēs politeias*)' (34, 21), and whose
status and right to attend the assembly seem to have been dubious
(34, 21–2). Later he seems to suggest that they were excluded from
the public life of the city because they could not afford the fee of
500 drachmas for citizenship (34, 23) – about half a year's pay for a
soldier, so a substantial sum to a poor man (Jones 1978: 81). So, if
Paul really was a citizen of Tarsus, he was a member of a relatively
privileged group. Tarsus continued to be a prosperous city until it
was sacked by the Arabs in 641. Thereafter it passed from one ruler
to another until it was taken into the Ottoman empire in 1515.
However, unlike many of the other cities of Asia Minor which had
similar experiences, it has always remained a fair-sized town.
Perhaps for this reason, few vestiges of Paul's city now survive. The
remains of one ancient gate, now called Kancık Kapısı ('bitch's
gate'), and some fragments of what may have been a bath-house,
plus a few other pieces of masonry, are all there is to see. The spring
in the city centre called St Paul's Well was certainly used in antiquity, but there is no reason to believe that it has any special
connection with Paul.

CYPRUS

Paul's visit to Cyprus is notable for his conversion of the governor
and his confrontation with the magus Elymas (Acts 13, 5–12; for a

discussion of the episode see Wallace and Williams 1993: 60–3), but otherwise his stay there is passed over rather cursorily. Cypriot Jews, however, feature prominently in the earliest history of Christianity (Acts 4, 16; 11, 20; 21, 16). Cyprus had always had close relationships with Palestine, and perhaps as early as the ninth century BC there had been a Phoenician kingdom at Kition, which was extinguished only when Ptolemy I captured the island and executed the last Phoenician king of Kition, Pumiathon. By the Roman period the island was completely hellenised, and very few traces of surviving Phoenician culture can be observed (Mitford 1980: 1319). We have already described the peculiar circumstances of the Roman annexation of Cyprus in 58 BC (see p. 79). Initially it was administered as part of the province of Cilicia, but from 22 BC (after a brief period of restored Ptolemaic rule) it became a province in its own right. Cyprus was governed by proconsuls, chosen annually by lot from ex-praetors. It was a province of no significance and little importance (apart from its copper mines); there is no evidence of substantial Roman settlement; it guarded no important route, and was not on a frontier, so the governor commanded no military forces. As a consequence it was not a province which ambitious men sought. If Sergius Paulus, the governor Paul met (Acts 13, 7), is to be identified, as seems probable, with the senator L. Sergius Paullus who was a member of the board charged with the care of the bed and banks of the Tiber in Claudius' reign (*CIL* 6, 31545; see Mitchell 1993: II, 6–7), then he was one of a very small number of governors of Cyprus to go on to achieve the rank of consul. There is no independent Cypriot evidence for this governor, but that is not surprising. Nor is there anything surprising in his taking an interest in exotic religions (see Wallace and Williams 1993: 61–2). There has been some speculation that the change of name from Saul to Paul which takes place at Acts 13, 9 means that Paul had taken the governor's name to honour his first prominent convert (Mitchell 1993: II, 7: Mitford 1980: 1381). This cannot be positively excluded, but is an unnecessary hypothesis. As a Roman citizen by birth, Paul would presumably already have had a name in Roman form. Though Paulus is not a common Roman name, it is a real one, and sufficiently like Saul to make it a plausible *cognomen*. In the earlier sections of Acts Paul is represented as acting as a Jew, as part of a picture of Jewish hostility to the early church, so he is appropriately referred to by his Jewish name. Now, as he is about to move into the region in which there were churches which regarded him as

their founder, naturally the name by which they knew him is introduced (actually before, not after, the conversion of Sergius Paulus is
reported).

Paul and Barnabas landed at Salamis, just north of modern
Famagusta, and the nearest port to Seleukia. Later tradition (incorporated in the *Acts of Barnabas*, a work perhaps of the fifth century)
made Barnabas a native of Salamis, and claimed that he was later
martyred there at the hands of the other Jews. Salamis was one of
the oldest Greek cities on the island. It claimed as its founder the
hero Teucer, and in the fifth and fourth centuries BC under its king
Evagoras it grew rich and powerful. Under the early Ptolemies,
however, the old harbour appears to have become unusable because
of silting, and Paul's Salamis was a new city on a different site to the
north. It grew and prospered under the Ptolemies, and remained
important under Roman rule. Excavation has revealed at least one
impressive gymnasium of hellenistic date (which was further
enlarged in Roman times), and inscriptions indicate the existence of
three others. The theatre there, which has been excavated and
restored, is probably later than Paul's time; an inscription tells us
that the costs of the building were paid by a local benefactor, Ser.
Sulpicius Pancles Veranianus, of the Flavian period. The temple of
Olympian Zeus is hellenistic with Roman additions, and was one of
only three in Cyprus with the right of asylum (Mitford 1980:
1322).

Paphos, where Paul and Barnabas meet the governor, is at the
other end of the island and was founded in 312 BC to replace Old
Paphos, just to the north, the site of the famous temple of
Aphrodite, the main religious centre of Cyprus. (One of the versions
of the myth of the birth of Aphrodite had her rising from the sea-
foam near here; she is often referred to simply as Kypris or Paphia.)
The goddess was worshipped here aniconically, in the form of a
large pointed stone (Spivey 1996: 46). The confused remains of this
temple, whose surviving masonry is of various periods, can be seen.
The city had a small harbour and the usual facilities of a *polis*;
among structures which have been excavated are a theatre of
hellenistic date and a first-century odeum. There is an extensive
excavated area, whose main features are two houses, probably of the
third century, with splendid floor mosaics (Mitford 1980:
1309–15).

Little is known of the Jewish population of Cyprus, but it must
have been large, for when, in 115, a number of Jewish diaspora

communities revolted, we are told that on Cyprus they slaughtered 240,000 Gentiles, under the leadership of one Artemion. Following the suppression of the revolt Jews were apparently banned from the island altogether (Dio Cassius 68, 32). Despite the activity of Paul and Barnabas, we hear nothing certain of Christians on the island until the appearance of a bishop of Paphos at the Council of Nicaea in 325 (Mitford 1980: 1381–20).

ATTALEIA

Presumably Paul sailed from Cyprus to the port of Attaleia (modern Antalya) in Pamphylia; at any rate, he sailed from there when he returned to Antioch (Acts 14, 25). Attaleia was named after its founder, King Attalos II of Pergamon (reigned 158–138 BC), who needed a port on this coast after his conquest of much of Pamphylia. It came under Roman control as a result of their campaigns to suppress piracy in the first century BC. Little now remains of its Roman past. The major Roman monument is a well-preserved gateway in the form of a triumphal arch put up to commemorate the visit of the emperor Hadrian in 130; some parts of the walls adjacent to it may be earlier, though much changed in the medieval period. On the cliffs overlooking the harbour are the remains of a round building which may be a Roman tomb of the second century. The present form of the older part of the city goes back to the period after it was taken by the Selçuk Turks in 1206. Nowadays Antalya is the administrative capital of the region, and a major centre for industry and agriculture; it also has an excellent archaeological museum. The present port is to the west of the old town. The ancient and medieval port, and the old buildings surrounding it, have been carefully preserved (in the interests of tourism). It is possible to get a good sense of how this port must have looked when Paul sailed from it (Fig. 10.1) (Bean 1979a: 21–4).

PERGE

Though Paul and his companions stayed only briefly at Perge, first on the way to Pisidian Antioch (Acts 13, 13–14), and then on the way home again (Acts 14, 25), the fact that the remains of the city are very well preserved (because Arab raids from the seventh century onwards led to its abandonment), and that much of the central area,

Figure 10.1 The harbour at Attaleia

including the gateway and the main colonnaded street, has recently been excavated by Turkish archaeologists, makes it a very good site from which to get an impression of the sort of cities Paul was visiting. In some ways, the site at Perge embodies in condensed form the history of the Roman Empire in the East.

The first Greek settlement (traditionally founded immediately after the Trojan War) was in a well-defended position on a hill now at the north end of the colonnaded street which later ran through the city and which is now the most prominent feature of the site (Fig. 10.2). By the hellenistic period it had outgrown this site, had spread out into the plain and was defended by an impressive wall (sections of which are still standing) equipped with towers and gates which represented the best of current military technology. Hellenistic Perge was a prosperous city in the mainstream of Greek culture; one of her citizens was Apollonius of Perge (about 200 BC), a brilliant mathematician and the author of a book, much of which is still extant, on conic sections. The stability of Roman rule led to the abandonment of the walls, the settlement of several prominent Roman families in the city and the erection of a number of impressive buildings. The first of these buildings was a large square structure, probably a *palaestra* (an exercise ground), built by the Roman Gaius Julius Cornutus and dedicated to the emperor Claudius, and so of the same sort of period as Paul's visit (MacKay 1990: 2079; Bean 1979a: 35). The main streets were built in about AD 80.

At the beginning of the second century (around 120) there was a great burst of new building. This is true of most cities in the eastern Roman Empire, but at Perge it is, unusually, associated with a woman, Plancia Magna. She not only held several priesthoods but was also *dēmiourgos* (holder of the highest civic office in Perge) and clearly a woman of some importance (Boatwright 1993: 204); her family was a distinguished one, for members of it were active politically under Nero and Vespasian. The probability is that they had migrated from Italy in the first century BC (Bean 1979a: 32–3). Plancia Magna's most outstanding contribution to the city was the restructuring of the hellenistic south gate into a sort of sculpture gallery carrying in niches representations of various gods and imperial personages, the mythical founders of Perge and members of her own family (as 'second founders'). All of this was put up in her own name and, what is quite extraordinary, inscriptions define her father and her brother in terms of their relationship to her ('father of

Figure 10.2 Perge: the main street from the acropolis

Plancia Magna', 'brother of Plancia Magna'), the opposite of what is normally expected (Boatwright 1993: 192–7). Plancia asserts her Roman identity by putting up her inscriptions in both Greek and Latin. Though she was probably not unique as a woman who achieved prominence in her city (Boatwright 1993: 204–5), there is no other case where the evidence is preserved so well. As it happens, we are given another glimpse of women in Perge at about the same period in a work on physiognomy (preserved only in Latin and Arabic translation) by the orator Polemon, who says: 'In Perge women put on a white and a red garment and so on, and cover it all with a great cloak which covers every part of them so that nothing can be seen except their eyes and their nose' (Polemon, *De Physiognomia* 68). Polemon's skill in physiognomy enabled him, by examining the nose and eyes of a woman he observed at the temple of Artemis, to predict that some disaster was about to befall her, and he was vindicated when the news promptly arrived that her daughter had fallen down a well. Reports like this, when set beside the activity of Plancia Magna, should lead us to be cautious in inferring from similar reports about Tarsus (see p. 181) that women there were kept in some sort of 'oriental seclusion'. Later in the second century the theatre and stadium outside the walls, and a nymphaeum, bringing water down to a channel which carried it along the main street, were built. Perge flourished well into the third century, but by the end of that century disturbed conditions in the region made it necessary once again to fortify the city and, perhaps in the fourth century, a new gate was built just outside the hellenistic south gate. Finally, in the Byzantine period, before it was finally abandoned, the last occupation of the site was a citadel on the acropolis, where the city had started.

In antiquity Perge was perhaps most famous for the temple of Artemis of Perge, which Strabo (14, 4, 2) tells us was situated on a hill near the town. The site has yet to be found (Bean 1979a: 35–8). In the local Pamphylian dialect she was called *Vanassa Preia* ('Queen of Perge') and appears to have been worshipped in the form of a stone (Bean 1979a: 27); she was presumably a form of a local Anatolian goddess. Like her counterpart at Ephesos, though on a smaller scale, she was worshipped outside her native city (MacKay 1990: 2059), and like her she is often represented adorned with jewels and symbolic figures.

PISIDIAN ANTIOCH

As its name suggests, Pisidian Antioch was a Seleucid foundation of the mid-third century BC (made by either Seleukos I or his son Antiochos I). It is not actually in Pisidia – its name is more properly 'Antioch-next-to-Pisidia' (Strabo 12, 569) – but to the north of it, in a region where the culture was Phrygian. It originated in a settlement of colonists from Magnesia on a site already associated with a major shrine of the Phrygian god Men, put there to act as a check on the tribes of Pisidia proper which the Seleucids were never able fully to control (Levick 1967: 17–18). More significant in Paul's day, however, was the fact that it was the most important Roman colony in Asia Minor. It had been refounded as a colony by Augustus probably in 25 BC (but see Mitchell 1993: I, 76) when Galatia was occupied by the Romans following the death of its king Amyntas at the hands of a local tribe, the Homanadenses (see p. 75). The original settlers were veterans of two legions, V Gallica and VII, and so were mostly Italians (Levick 1967: 58–67). Like all colonies, Antioch was set up as a sort of miniature Rome, originally Latin-speaking (and in Paul's day, though it was under pressure from Greek, Latin seems still to have been holding its own in Antioch, see Levick 1967: 130–44), and with political institutions which were modelled on those of Rome herself (Levick 1967: 78–83). The city's territory seems to have been widespread and fertile, and its position on the road from Ephesos to Syria meant that it had an important rôle in trade (which is presumably what attracted the substantial Jewish community Paul found there: Acts 13, 14). He will have travelled up from Perge on the Via Sebaste, 'the Augustan Road', which was built in 6 BC to link the Augustan foundations in Galatia with one another and the coast (Mitchell 1993: I, 76–7). This journey takes him, however, further inland than he normally went, and would involve travelling through the dangerous mountain country of Pisidia; we are not told why he went in this direction rather than concentrating on the populous cities of the Pamphylian plain. The clue to the solution of this puzzle may lie in the fact that Sergius Paulus, the governor of Cyprus whom Paul had just left, was a native of Pisidian Antioch, and still had close family connections there (Mitchell 1993: II, 6–7). If Paul had an introduction to the best families in the city from Sergius Paulus, it would have been too good an opportunity to miss.

Pisidian Antioch remained the most important city of its region until it declined in the twelfth and thirteenth centuries, and the site was abandoned when the region was occupied by the Turks. Today remains of various Roman structures can be seen, including a theatre, a city gate, baths and an aqueduct. The general outline of the layout of the streets can be made out. From late antiquity there are two large fourth-century churches. On a hill nearby there are the remains, some of them hellenistic in date, of the sanctuary of the Phrygian god Men.

ICONIUM

Paul's journey through difficult territory further along the road to Iconium can be explained by the fact that he was in flight from Antioch, and was being pursued (Acts 13, 50; 14, 19). The city was a very old one and the site seems to have been inhabited as far back as the third millennium BC. In the hellenistic period it adopted Greek institutions, and came under direct Roman control in 25 BC. Under Augustus a Roman colony was set up there, coexisting with the hellenised *polis* (Mitchell 1993: I, 77, 91), which, shortly before Paul's visit, had been allowed to rename itself Claudiconium in honour of the emperor Claudius. The Roman colony seems to have absorbed the native *polis* in the next century under the emperor Hadrian. Settlement has been continuous at Iconium, and it remains prosperous today under its modern name, Konya. Traces of its Roman past are few and insignificant, and it is visited today mostly because of the splendid Turkish monuments of the Selçuk period.

LYSTRA

Now being pursued by irate Jews from both Antioch and Iconium, Paul took the southern branch of the Via Sebaste to the small town of Lystra, a rather remote place up in the hills. The fact that there appears to have been no synagogue there, and that the Lycaonian language was still widely spoken (Acts 14, 11), suggests that it was a place well out of the mainstream, and one to which Paul would not naturally have gone to preach had he not been on the run. Lystra (or to give it its proper name, Colonia Julia Gemina Felix Lystra) was another of Augustus' colonies in this region, and seems to have been established for the sole purpose of protecting the highway and acting as a base for operations against the Homanadenses (Levick 1967: 51–2). There is no evidence of a settlement on the site before the colony, but the name suggests a Lycaonian origin, despite attempts in coins and inscriptions which use the form Lustra to suggest a derivation from the Latin *lustrum* (Levick 1967: 155). It was a reasonably prosperous rural community of no special significance. So far as we can tell, it continued to exist at least as late as the thirteenth century (Levick 1967: 183).

DERBE

When his pursuers drove him from Lystra (Acts 14, 19–20) Paul fled to the obscure town of Derbe, on the fringes of the Taurus mountains. It may have been originally a Macedonian colony founded in the early hellenistic period (Mitchell 1993: I, 85), and in the middle of the first century BC it was the centre of a small kingdom ruled by one Antipater, which lasted until it was annexed by Amyntas the Galatian king. Unlike the other cities visited by Paul in this stage of his travels it was not a Roman colony, but the emperor Claudius had allowed it to change its name to Claudioderbe (Levick 1967: 28). Its site was identified only in the 1950s (Levick 1967: 165).

MYRA

On his way to Rome, Paul and his companions put in at Myra, where they picked up a ship to Italy (Acts 27, 5). Myra was an important Lycian city from at least the fifth century BC, and a series of impressive rock-cut tombs, markedly influenced by hellenistic art, indicate a city which was doing well. The major structure from the Roman period so far excavated is the theatre. The original theatre had been destroyed in an earthquake in 141, and its replacement was paid for by Opramoas of Rhodiapolis (see pp. 60, 107). The rest of the city has not been systematically investigated. Myra is best known for its fourth-century bishop, St Nicholas. A small church associated with him may well have had its origin in Nicholas' day, but it has been so changed since that it is hard to be sure. The traditional site of the saint's tomb is inside this church, but his remains were stolen by Italian merchants in 1087 and taken to Bari. Saint Nicholas is the original of Santa Claus, and an odd statue of him in this guise has been erected outside the church.

Myra is actually a little way from the sea, and Paul will have put in at Myra's port, Andriace, where traces of a number of Roman buildings can be seen, including a granary built in the reign of Hadrian. Myra remained an important city until the eleventh century, when constant Arab raids led to the depopulation of the area (Bean 1989: 120–30).

11

WESTERN ASIA MINOR

EPHESOS

Greeks may have settled at Ephesos as early as 1000 BC, and the native Carians were certainly there before them (Bammer 1988: 127–41), but the original site of the city has not yet been identified with certainty. The city whose remains we can see today was first built by Lysimachos, one of Alexander's successors (who induced the inhabitants to move from the old site by blocking the city drains during a rain storm, and flooding them out – Strabo 14, 21). Ephesos came under Roman control in 133 BC with the death of King Attalos III of Pergamon who left his kingdom to the Roman People in his will. It was a 'free city', and one of the assize centres (see p. 81) of the new province of Asia. The unscrupulous behaviour of Roman tax-collectors and businessmen soon made Roman rule in Asia deeply unpopular, and when the king of Pontus, Mithridates, invaded and occupied Asia in 88 BC, the Ephesians welcomed him and enthusiastically joined in a massacre of all Italians in the city. When Mithridates had been defeated the Romans deprived Ephesos of its status as a 'free city' (which it did not get back until c. 47 BC), and imposed an enormous fine which, combined with the effects of the civil wars later, impoverished the city, until, under the regime of Augustus, peace was established and the administration and taxation of the provinces was put on a more regular basis. The result was that Ephesos and the other cities of Asia became very prosperous, and were able to undertake the lavish urban building programmes whose results we can still see (Rogers 1991: 2–16).

Ephesos is perhaps the best preserved of the great cities of Asia, and the site has recently been extensively restored; there is probably nowhere else where the visitor can get such a clear impression of how the ancient city was used to display the 'good works' of the leading citizens, and the recognition and fulsome praise of their fellow-citizens in the form of inscriptions to and statues of their benefactors (see pp. 106–7). The roads running through the city are lined with magnificent buildings, most of which were put up at the expense of private individuals, and the bases on which statues of these leading citizens once stood. Although most of what can now be seen is of the second century AD or later, there is no reason to doubt that in Paul's day the streets of Ephesos were similarly used to advertise the generosity of local wealthy families (though no doubt on a less lavish scale). Especially important buildings were placed at the point where the main road bends, making them more prominent. One example is the Library of Celsus (see pp. 106–7). Adjacent to it is a ceremonial gateway to the commercial *agora*, put up in 3 BC in honour of Augustus and Agrippa by two freedmen, Mithridates and Mazaeus, striking evidence of the wealth and social position which could be achieved by ex-slaves (see p. 83).

The theatre (Fig. 11.1) in which the riot took place during one of Paul's visits to Ephesos (Acts 19, 23–41) is placed in a similarly prominent position, at the head of the road which led to the harbour, which in its present form is of the late fourth century AD; the harbour is long gone, due to silting, and the place where it was is now swampy ground. The original hellenistic theatre may have been erected by Lysimachos, but it was later altered to adapt it to changing tastes in entertainment, and substantially enlarged. One phase of this work began in the middle of the first century AD, and so was probably still in progress when Paul's riot was taking place (Bean 1979b: 128–46; for a discussion of the riot see Wallace and Williams 1993: 103–10). The occasion of this riot is reported (in Acts 20, 24–7) as being the indignation of one Demetrius, a silver-smith, who made silver 'shrines' (presumably miniature shrines containing the cult-image) of Artemis of Ephesos, that Paul's preaching was a threat to the worship of the goddess (and that trade might thereby be affected). Though the author of Acts may be being unduly cynical in attributing financial motives to Demetrius, it is certainly true that at Ephesos the worship of Artemis was central to the identity of the city, and Demetrius' claim (Acts 20, 27) that the goddess is one 'whom all Asia and the world worship' is borne out by the wide distribution of copies of her cult image (for a comprehensive catalogue, see Fleischer 1973: 1–46).

Figure 11.1 The theatre at Ephesos

The temple of Artemis, famous in antiquity for its size and magnificence (its base was 255 feet wide and 425 feet long; it had 127 columns, highly decorated with sculpture, and 60 feet high), was on flat ground just outside the city. It had been built after an earlier temple had been destroyed in 356 BC by fire, allegedly started by one Herostratos, who hoped that as a result he would be remembered forever. In late antiquity it was used as a marble quarry, and eventually the site was lost completely, until in 1867 the British engineer John Turtle Wood rediscovered it after finding in the theatre an inscription put up by C. Vibius Salutaris (see p. 101), describing a sacred procession endowed by him which was to proceed to the temple from the Magnesian Gate. Having identified this gate, Wood followed the road leading from it which brought him eventually to the temple (for a full account see Stoneman 1987: 225–36). The temple has recently been excavated, and a single column has been reconstructed, but there is little else to see on the site today.

The cult of Artemis at Ephesos had a number of peculiar features. According to Strabo:

> They have eunuchs as priests, and they call them *Megabyzoi* [the word is apparently Persian and means 'set free by the god']; they seek out people from abroad who are worthy of this honour, and hold them in the highest respect. Unmarried women must help them in their priestly duties.
>
> (Strabo, *Geography* 14, 1, 23)

Strabo does add that not all of these ancient practices were still observed in his own day. The cult, then, was not a typically Greek one, and undoubtedly there were local Anatolian influences at work. Ephesian Artemis is, however, best thought of as a Greek goddess influenced by foreign practices, rather than an imported goddess who had been hellenised (Oster 1990: 1728). The power and influence of the goddess was not just spiritual: she was a major landowner and her temple acted as a bank and would give loans (Oster 1990: 1717–19). It also had the right of asylum (Oster 1990: 1716). A rare privilege which the temple enjoyed was the right to be an heir in a will; Roman law in general did not allow organisations or 'corporations' to be heirs, but a very few temples could be; the list included, apart from Ephesian Artemis, Apollo of Didyma, Nemesis of Smyrna and Athena of Ilium (see *Tituli ex corpore Ulpiani* 22.6 and Crook 1967: 121).

The cult image of Ephesian Artemis was quite distinctive, and had some unusual features. She was depicted covered in representations of exotic animals and the signs of the zodiac, with a series of odd protuberances in the chest area. These were first identified as breasts by the third-century Christian writer Minucius Felix (*Octavius* 22, 5). Recently this has been doubted, partly because polemical motives on the part of Minucius Felix have been suspected, though in fact he does not seem to make a great deal of the fact that Ephesian Artemis is many-breasted (LiDonnici 1992: 392, n. 11), and partly because Pliny the Elder tells us (*Natural History* 16, 213–14) that the cult-image was of wood, and was made by Endoios (a sculptor of the sixth century BC), so that, since copies of the image do not have the protuberances in the chest area before the second century BC, they must be on some sort of adornment of the goddess, rather than a part of her body (for a full discussion see Fleischer 1973: 74–88). The protuberances are not generally represented as having nipples (for exceptions see LiDonnici 1992: 392, n. 9), and so a number of alternative suggestions have been put forward, including the genitals of sacrificial bulls. It is, however, worth observing that Pliny himself is sceptical about the report that the image was an ancient wooden one, and that the protuberances become more, rather than less, breast-like as time goes on (LiDonnici 1992: 396). It has therefore recently been argued that, whatever the origins of the form, by Paul's day the protuberances were indeed being interpreted as breasts (or even udders) as part of the goddess's image as protector of the city, symbolised by the rôle of legitimate wife (LiDonnici 1992: 408–11).

In the event, Demetrius' apprehensions were misplaced. When Christianity triumphed in the fourth century, Ephesos was able to exploit its experience as a centre for religious tourism to build a flourishing trade based on its Christian connections. John (both the author of Revelation and the companion of Jesus) and one of the daughters of Philip were supposed to have lived and died there (Eusebius, *Ecclesiastical History* 3, 24, 4 and 31, 2–4), and the tomb of John in particular was greatly venerated. Even when in the seventh century a combination of the silting of the harbour, a serious earthquake and Arab raids led to the abandonment of the old city, a new community on a more defensible site on the hill now called Ayasuluk (derived from the Greek *Agios Theologos* = holy theologian, i.e. John) continued to flourish well beyond the fourteenth century until a long decline reduced it to a small village in the nineteenth century. The town presently on the site, Selçuk, dates only from the coming of the railway. Near Ephesos visitors are shown a house in which it is claimed that Mary the mother of Jesus lived and died. This rests on no ancient tradition, but on a vision experienced by a Bavarian nun, Catherine Emmerich, in the late nineteenth century. Though some of the foundations of the house may be very old, it is unlikely that the sort of archaeological investigation necessary to establish their date firmly will ever be undertaken. The more usual tradition is that Mary died and was buried in Jerusalem, where the Dormition Church on Mount Sion marks the supposed place of her death.

TROAS

In Acts, Troas usually appears as the normal port for journeys to and from Macedonia (16, 8; 16, 11; 20, 5–6), though Paul took the opportunity to preach there as well (Acts 20, 6–12; 2 Corinthians 2, 12). More properly called Alexandria Troas, the city was originally founded by Alexander's general Antigonos by the forced amalgamation of a number of small Greek communities in the area, and was to be called Antigoneia; after the death of Antigonos in 301 BC his rival Lysimachos renamed it Alexandria in honour of Alexander 'the Great', with the addition of Troas ('Trojan') to distinguish it from numerous other Alexandrias. The whole area was known as 'the Trojan land' (the Troad, in English). However, the actual site of Homer's Troy was believed to lie beneath that of Ilium, a *polis* wholly independent of Alexandria Troas, and one highly favoured by the Romans because of the legend that the Romans were descended from the followers of Aeneas, who had fled to Italy from the sack of Troy which they identified with Ilium. The harbour of Troas was an artificial one, but the city's site, near the mouth of the straits between the Mediterranean and the Black Sea, and on the shortest convenient sea-crossing from Asia to Europe, helped to make it the most important city in the region; Augustus refounded it as a Roman colony. Apart from a bath-house of the second century AD there are no significant remains on the site today.

ASSOS

The most important remains on the site at Assos, the fortification walls, were built in the great days of the city, in the fourth century

BC, when it was the centre of a small principality detached from the Persian empire and ruled by Hermeias, who was according to Strabo (13, 57) a eunuch and an ex-slave. He was apparently a pupil of the philosopher Plato, and invited a number of philosophers to stay with him in Assos (including Plato's greatest pupil, Aristotle, who also married his niece) until the area was reoccupied by the Persians in 341 BC; Hermeias was captured by the Persians, tortured and put to death; Aristotle wrote a moving *Ode to Virtue* (which still survives) in his honour. Later Assos was eclipsed by Alexandria Troas, and went into decline. As a result, there was not a great deal of building in the Roman period and remains of much of the hellenistic city survive, including the *agora* and the buildings associated with it. There are also ruins of a temple of Athena of the sixth century BC. We are given no clue as to why Paul chose to travel overland to Assos, rather than taking ship from Troas, like his companions (Acts 20, 13–14).

MITYLENE

From Assos it is possible to see the island of Lesbos, of which Mitylene was the biggest city, so that it was a short trip there for Paul's ship (Acts 20, 14). Mitylene was an ancient Greek *polis*, which for centuries had been in the mainstream of Greek history and culture. Despite the complaints of the Roman architect Vitruvius (1, 6, 1) that the layout of the town exposed the inhabitants to the deleterious effects of the winds, it seems to have been popular with the Romans, and the signs are that under their rule Mitylene did well: Vitruvius describes it as a 'splendidly and elegantly constructed city' (1, 6, 1), and Strabo says that it was 'well provided with everything' (13, 2, 2). Few ancient remains survive, apart from a theatre just to the north-west of the modern town.

CHIOS

Chios had been one of the richest and most prominent states of Greece, and had maintained its independence as a self-governing *polis* through most of the hellenistic period, until it came into the Roman Empire in the first century BC as a 'free city' (see p. 113), a status which it seems to have maintained until the second half of the first century AD. Strabo (14, 1, 35) mentions several good harbours on the island, including one which would hold eighty ships, so it was a natural stopping place for Paul's ship (Acts 20, 15). We know very little about what went on there in the Roman period, but traces of numerous buildings seem to indicate that the city was flourishing. The modern city is on the site of the ancient *polis*, but few traces from antiquity can now be seen.

SAMOS

At times, and especially in the sixth century BC, Samos, a large and strategically placed island, had approached the status of a substantial regional power. It became part of the Roman province of Asia in 129 BC. Samos suffered badly in the turmoil which preceded the rule of Augustus, who favoured it and gave it the status of 'free city' (see p. 113); the privilege was removed by Vespasian in AD 70. The site of the ancient *polis* is now occupied by the principal town on the island, Pithagorio (named after Pythagoras, the most famous of the Samians), and nearby there are a number of remains, the most remarkable of which is a tunnel driven through a hill in the sixth century BC. There are also a few traces of the ancient theatre, and a well-preserved section of the city wall. The excavations at the sanctuary of Hera, along the coast to the west, have revealed buildings from all periods of Samos's ancient history.

MILETOS

Today, because of silting, Miletos is about five miles from the sea, but in ancient times it was one of the most famous ports and trading cities in the Mediterranean. Early in the fifth century BC it was captured and completely destroyed by the Persians; the men were killed, and the women and children enslaved. After the Persian defeat in their wars with the Greeks the city was rebuilt, but never regained its earlier prosperity. Under the Romans it was a 'free city', but, although evidence of extensive new building in the city suggests that it did well under Roman rule, the problem of silting was already developing, and it had ceased to be a port by the fourth century AD, following which the city declined to a small village. The most prominent remains at Miletos are a Roman bath-house of the second century AD, and a theatre built probably around 100 AD (on the site of a smaller hellenistic theatre). This theatre offers striking evidence of the presence of Jews in Miletos. There are inscriptions on some of the seats allocating them to certain groups, among whom are 'the Jews who are also God-worshippers' (the precise translation is controversial, see Trebilco 1991: 159–62), suggesting a Jewish community here well integrated in the life of the city. Josephus (*Ant.* 14, 244–6) reproduces a letter from a proconsul to the archons, *boulē* and *dēmos* of Miletos insisting that the Jews be allowed to observe their customs. There is, however, nothing about the city to explain why Paul chose to land there rather than at Ephesos on his way to Jerusalem, and to summon the Ephesian elders to Miletos to meet him (Acts 20, 15–17). The reason for his visit to Miletos must be problems in Ephesos (not fully stated in Acts) rather than any advantage which Miletos possessed (Bean 1979b: 181–91).

KOS

Kos was one of the ancient centres of Greek culture, and flourished in the hellenistic period, maintaining its independence while remaining a close ally of the Ptolemies – it was the birthplace of Ptolemy II. Hence the links between Kos and the poetry composed in third-century BC Alexandria: Philetas (tutor of Ptolemy II) was a native of Kos; Theokritos' programmatic seventh Idyll is set in Kos; and Herodas' second and fourth (probably) mimiambs are also set there. It came into the Roman Empire as a 'free city', but under Augustus lost its status, perhaps as a result of its support for his rival, Marcus Antonius, in the civil war (S. M. Sherwin-White 1978: 145–9). It was a fertile island, famous for its production of perfume (S. M. Sherwin-White 1978: 242–3) and wine, one variety of which was flavoured by the addition of sea-water (S. M. Sherwin-White 1978: 236–41). It also produced a kind of silk from the cocoons of a native wild silk-moth, from which a very fine diaphanous fabric was made, much valued by rich Roman ladies and deplored by Roman moralists (Pliny, *Natural History* 11, 77); by Paul's day it was losing ground to the superior Chinese product imported from the East, and production ceased in the second century AD (S. M. Sherwin-White 1978: 379–83). Kos was the traditional home of Hippokrates, the father of medicine, and the Koan medical school which traced its origins back to him was celebrated even in Roman times. Through the intervention of one of these Koan doctors, Gaius Stertinius Xenophon, who was the personal physician of the emperor Claudius, the island was granted exemption from taxation (Tacitus, *Annals* 12, 61); it was rumoured that this doctor was also implicated in the emperor's murder (Tacitus, *Annals* 12, 67). There are a good number of archaeological remains on the island, from all periods of its history. The most spectacular (fittingly for an island famous for its doctors) is the shrine of Asklepios, the god of healing, situated on a series of terraces with a splendid view of the harbour. It is basically hellenistic, with later refurbishments.

RHODES

There were originally three independent self-governing cities on the island of Rhodes, none of them of any particular distinction, but in 408/7 BC they joined together to form a single state, and thereafter were able effectively to exploit their position off the south-west tip of Asia Minor, a natural stopping place for ships travelling to and from Egypt and Syria, which is why Paul calls there (Acts 21, 1). The beginning of the greatness of Rhodes was marked by its resistance to an attack in 305/4 BC by Demetrios Poliorketes, in a famous siege in which the attacker used all the latest technology for siege warfare. After Demetrios had admitted defeat and withdrawn, the sale of the scrap from his siege engines raised so much money that the Rhodians were able to erect, in thanksgiving for their victory, an enormous statue of Helios the sun, their patron god, which was later known as the Colossus of Rhodes and was reckoned to be one of the Seven Wonders of the World; the idea that this statue straddled the harbour mouth is a much later invention, and in fact it was probably up a hill overlooking the harbour. It fell down in an earthquake in 226 BC, but in Paul's day its monstrous remains were still visited as a tourist attraction. By the third century BC, Rhodes effectively controlled the seas in the eastern Mediterranean, and was responsible for the suppression of piracy. When Rome became active in the East, Rhodes became her ally, and was considerably strengthened by Rome's favour. In the Third Macedonian War, however, she offered her services as mediator, and so fell out with the Romans: Rome expected of her free allies not that they should act on their own initiative, but that, freely and entirely of their own accord, they should give total and unconditional support to Rome in all circumstances. Rhodes was stripped of her mainland possessions, and her commerce was ruined when the Romans gave considerable trading privileges to Delos. Thereafter Rhodes was very much a subordinate ally. Ironically, the weakening of Rhodes was one of the factors which led to the rapid growth of piracy, which ultimately forced the Romans to move into the East on a permanent basis (see p. 28). Rhodes remained famous as an intellectual centre, and especially for its philosophical schools; it was chosen as his residence by the future emperor Tiberius during a long period of enforced retirement from public life. Today there are few traces of Roman Rhodes to be seen (though a small theatre or odeum, a stadium and a couple of temples have been identified), and the city is dominated by the work of the Knights of St John, who occupied the island from 1309 to 1523. The pattern of streets, however, preserves that of the ancient city.

PATARA

Patara was the principal port of Lycia (a region with its own distinctive language, culture and institutions), and in Paul's day was one of the chief cities in the Lycian League; his ship calls there on his final journey to Jerusalem (Acts 21, 1). Though it existed at least as early as the fifth century BC, it made no mark in history until the hellenistic period. Its name in the Lycian language was Pttara, though later it was claimed that the city was named after Patarus, a son of the god Apollo (Strabo 14, 666). Patara was famous for a temple and oracle of Apollo, whose site has not yet been identified – the small Corinthian temple on the east side of the harbour walls which is sometimes called the temple of Apollo dates from the second century AD, and is certainly too small to be the famous temple. Like many cities in the region, it was badly affected by the civil wars which led up to the establishment of the regime of Augustus, but by Paul's time the city had recovered its earlier prosperity, which continued until silting of the harbour led to its abandonment in medieval times; today the site, now called Kelemiş, is completely deserted (though the fine beaches attract holiday-makers). The prominent Roman arch on the site was put up in about AD 100 in honour of the governor of Lycia-Pamphylia, Mettius Modestus. The theatre, now largely covered by sand-drifts, was put into the form in which it now survives in the mid-second century, but an inscription recording repairs to it in the reign of Tiberius show that a theatre must have existed on this spot much earlier. The baths at Patara were put up in Vespasian's reign (AD 69–79), and the well-preserved granary on the west side of the ancient harbour is Hadrianic (Bean 1989: 82–91).

12

GREECE AND MACEDONIA

SAMOTHRACE

This small rocky island was the natural stopping place for those who, like Paul (Acts 16, 11), were making the crossing from Troas to Neapolis. It was famous for its sanctuary of the mysterious (and perhaps non-Greek) gods, the Kabeiroi, which was in existence at least as early as the seventh century BC. The hellenistic kings were especially lavish in erecting buildings on the site, and most of the structures which can be seen there today are of the hellenistic or Roman periods. There were mysteries associated with the Kabeiroi into which visitors could be initiated, but we know only tantalising details of what they involved. For example, initiates were required to confess the worst thing they had ever done in their lives, which may make the cult of the Kabeiroi the only Greek mystery cult with a real moral content (Burkert 1985: 281–5). Under Roman rule Samothrace was a 'free city'. In 1893 one of the most striking surviving sculptures of the hellenistic period, the Nike of Samothrace, was discovered on the site of the sanctuary on the island. It represents winged Victory about to alight on the prow of a ship, and was probably set up to commemorate the naval victories of Rhodes over Antiochos III in 190 BC. It is on display in the Louvre in Paris.

NEAPOLIS

Like its modern counterpart Kavalla, Neapolis was the port for its immediate hinterland. No remains of the town in which Paul landed (Acts 16, 11) survive, though there are a number of interesting relics of the period of Turkish rule.

PHILIPPI

The Roman colony of Philippi owed its importance to a series of chances. Early Greek settlement in Thrace, the region around Philippi, had been restricted to the coast, because the local Thracian tribes were both warlike and aggressive. There were, however, in Thrace rich veins of silver and gold; the people of the island of Thasos planted a settlement called Krenides near one of these, thinking that the potential wealth was worth the risk. The mines were seized in 356 BC by Philip II of Macedon, ostensibly at the invitation of the inhabitants who wanted protection from the Thracians, but actually because he needed the money; he renamed the settlement Philippi after himself. The mines brought in the enormous income of 1,000 talents a year, which made it possible for him to finance his conquest of much of Greece, and his son Alexander III to begin the conquest of the Persian empire (so that one of the stories told in this book, the spread of Greek-style culture to the East, actually began here). Philippi, however, remained a simple mining town. In the middle of the second century BC, after Macedonia had been brought into the Roman Empire, one of the early governors, Gnaeus Egnatius, built a major road, the Via Egnatia, to link the Adriatic with the Aegean, and it passed through Philippi – Paul presumably followed this road from Neapolis (Acts 16, 12) – which thereby became a significant link in the communications of the Empire. In 42 BC, after the assassination of Julius Caesar, the armies of his assassins, Brutus and Cassius, and his avengers, Marcus Antonius and Octavian (the future emperor Augustus), both travelled along the Via Egnatia and met at Philippi. The victory of the partisans of Caesar guaranteed Philippi's place in history. Caesar's heir Octavian, probably shortly after the battle, created a Roman colony there, Colonia Julia Augusta Philippensis, thereby not only commemorating and advertising his piety in avenging the death of his adopted father, but also contributing to the solution of a perennial problem of Roman generals, how to find a place to settle retired soldiers. Paul's visit there gives us a valuable picture of how such a 'miniature Rome' functioned. When Paul and Silas were arrested for healing the girl possessed by a prophetic spirit (Acts 16, 16–22), they were taken to the forum and brought before the magistrates (Acts calls them *stratēgoi*, literally generals, but they will have been *duoviri iure dicundo* – see p. 88), charged with advocating 'customs which it is not lawful for us Romans to accept' (Acts 16, 21), a striking illustration of the way in which such colonies would cling to their Romanness, which marked them out from the Greeks among whom they lived. Later we are told that the magistrates had at their disposal officers called *rhabdouchoi* (= 'rod-holders', translated 'police' by the RSV: Acts 16, 35), who must have been the equivalent of the *lictores* who accompanied senior magistrates at Rome, and who carried bundles of rods symbolising the power of the magistrates to inflict punishment (for a full discussion, see Wallace and Williams 1993: 76–82).

Because of Paul's visit, Philippi could claim to be the home of the first Christian church in Europe, and became an important Christian centre in late antiquity. For this reason the most prominent remains on the site today are the ruins of two large churches of the fourth and fifth centuries. The forum in which Paul was tried and beaten, with the Via Egnatia running alongside it, can still be seen clearly (Fig. 12.1), though most of the visible masonry dates from a substantial remodelling in the second century. The theatre nearby is basically hellenistic, with Roman alterations in the second and third centuries AD. Visitors to the site may be shown the place by the riverside where Paul met Lydia (Acts 16, 13–14), but the identification rests on no old tradition. The city was abandoned in the tenth century because of unsettled conditions in the region.

AMPHIPOLIS

Paul's journey along the Via Egnatia brings him next to Amphipolis (Acts 17, 1), which had originally been another Greek settlement (founded by the Athenians in the fifth century BC) designed to exploit the wealth of Thrace – in this case, minerals and timber. Its strategic position on the route from Greece to Asia, and at the place where the Via Egnatia crosses the route north from the sea up the Strymon Valley, made it important both for the Macedonian kings and for the Romans, under whom it was a 'free city'. Excavation has revealed little of the city Paul would have known, but some hellenistic structures and sections of the early city wall have been found.

Figure 12.1 The forum at Philippi: the Via Egnatia runs along the further side

APOLLONIA

Apollonia was another stop on the Via Egnatia, roughly half-way between Amphipolis and Thessalonika. It was a place of no particular importance, and there is nothing of significance to be seen there today.

THESSALONIKA

When Alexander III of Macedon died in Babylon and his empire was divided up, the kingdom of Macedonia itself fell under the control of Cassander, who, in order to strengthen his position, married Alexander's half-sister Thessalonike, the daughter of Philip II by his Thessalian mistress Nikesipolis. When he decided to found a new port (to replace Pella where the harbour was silting up) at the head of the Thermaic Gulf (by destroying a number of existing towns in the area and concentrating their population at a single site) he called the new city after his wife. (Thessalonika thus has only an accidental connection with the region of Thessaly in northern Greece.) Being on the convergence of the routes from the Danube down the major river valleys and the coastal route which was eventually followed by the Via Egnatia, and equipped with excellent harbour facilities, the city grew rapidly and remained the most important city of Macedonia under Roman rule (Strabo 7, 21), when it was a 'free city'. As a new town, Thessalonika attracted a cosmopolitan population, and inscriptions reveal the presence in the city not only of a Jewish community, but also of Samaritans (Schürer 1973–87: III (1), 66–7). Indeed, the city continued to have a very large Jewish community until it was destroyed during the Second World War.

Though little remains of the Roman city today, the modern city preserves the pattern of streets of its ancient predecessor, and the Roman forum has been excavated and can be seen. Otherwise the only significant Roman remains are of the late third century AD – the arch of Galerius, and a monumental cylindrical tomb usually associated with Galerius. The most spectacular monuments in the city, however, date from the greatest period in Thessalonika's history, the Middle Ages, when it was the second city of the Byzantine Empire, and was adorned with a number of splendid churches. It may seem strange that, despite Paul's visit to the city and his surviving correspondence with the church there, no major church in Thessalonika is dedicated to him, and he is not the patron saint of the city. During the Middle Ages, however, Thessalonika was often under attack by the enemies of the Byzantine Empire, and it probably seemed more appropriate to have as their protector a soldier-saint, Demetrios, allegedly a Roman officer martyred in the early fourth century by the emperor Galerius.

BEROEA

Fleeing from Thessalonika Paul and Silas travelled south-west to Beroea, the most important city in its region. After the reduction of Macedonia to a Roman province there is evidence of substantial Roman settlement in the area, perhaps on land confiscated from the displaced Macedonian nobility (Tataki 1988: 438–47). In Paul's day Beroea was the meeting place of the Macedonian *koinon* ('league'), an organisation which existed already in the hellenistic period, but whose function (like that of similar organisations in other provinces) under Roman rule was to organise the imperial cult (Tataki 1988: 447–8). Today, only a few fortifications of the third century AD survive from the Roman period. The structure identified with the place from which Paul preached in Beroea is actually very recent.

ATHENS

In the fifth and fourth centuries BC Athens had been one of the leading Greek cities. After Philip II established Macedonian hegemony over Greece, Athens ceased to be important militarily and politically (though the Athenians failed to notice this for some time), but her cultural predominance remained, and indeed grew. Athens had produced an impressive body of literature, historiography and philosophy, which subsequently became the mainstay of a literary education throughout the hellenistic world; her dialect became the basis for *koinē* Greek, and a small selection of Athenian authors were regarded as the only proper models for a pure Greek style (see pp. 52, 54). As a consequence, non-Athenian authors tended to be forgotten, and Greek literature came to be disproportionately Athenian. So while Athens was no longer a significant power in the world, she came to be regarded as something like the cultural capital of the hellenistic world, the heart of everything that was Greek. This is perhaps why the Acts of the Apostles gives such prominence to Paul's visit there, though few converts were made, and no community seems to have been established (Acts 17, 16–34). Athens became an important stopping place for 'cultural tourists', and appears in a guide-book to Greece as early as the second (or perhaps third) century BC:

> There is a remarkable theatre, big and excellent, a lavish temple of Athena called the Parthenon, out of this world, worth looking at, just above the theatre; it makes a great impression on visitors. The half-finished temple of Olympian Zeus is impressive because of its plan, and would be superb if it were finished. There are three gymnasia: the Academy; the Lyceum; and the Kynosarges. They are all planted with trees and lawns. There are all kinds of festivals. Philosophers of every kind charm and refresh the mind. There are many things to do and sights to see.
>
> (Heraclides Creticus, *On the Cities in Greece* 1, 1)

Hellenistic kings who wished to assert their devotion to Greek culture could do so by erecting buildings in Athens. So Antiochos IV Epiphanes in the second century BC undertook the completion of the temple of Olympian Zeus (started in the sixth century but still unfinished); he too, however, failed to finish it (Wycherley 1978: 155–62). The kings of Pergamon erected several buildings, including a monumental stoa on the east side of the *agora*, put up by Attalos II, which has now been completely reconstructed and houses a museum (Camp 1986: 172–5). Later, Josephus tells us that Herod the Great himself was a benefactor of Athens (*War* 1, 425); though no trace of his benefactions can now be identified, inscriptions in Athens honouring him and his family have been discovered (Schürer 1973–87: I, 308, n. 70; Geagan 1979: 302). Today, one of the most prominent antiquities in Athens is a monument on the Hill of the Muses erected in the early second century AD by one C. Julius Antiochos Philopappos, a prince from Commagene, who was both an Athenian citizen and a Roman senator and consul.

As might be expected, educated Romans also visited and wished to show their attachment to what Athens represented (see p. 86). The city's relationship to Rome, however, was somewhat complex. Initially, good relations had been established and Athens had the status of 'free city', but when in 88 BC the king of Pontus, Mithridates VI, invaded the Roman East, ostensibly to free it from Roman tyranny, he was enthusiastically received by the Athenians. In 86 BC the Roman general Sulla besieged the city, captured it and sacked it brutally. Thereafter, in the civil wars, Athens seems to have had the unerring knack of choosing the losing side (Pompeius against Caesar; Caesar's assassins against his avengers; Marcus Antonius against the future Augustus). However, such was the city's cultural prestige that even so she continued to receive Roman bene- factions and Roman visitors. In the first century BC virtually every Roman of importance seems to have visited Athens at some time (Geagan 1979: 376–7). Under Augustus, who actually seems to have been rather unpopular in Athens (Hoff 1989: 4–5), an ambi- tious building programme substantially changed the character of the city, and especially its main open space, the *agora*, which had been the centre of the city's political, commercial and social life (Fig. 12.2). Augustus' right-hand man, M. Vipsanius Agrippa, built a large Odeum (an enclosed hall for recitals) right in the middle of the open space, and at about the same time a fifth-century BC temple of Ares from elsewhere in Attika was dismantled and re- erected there (Camp 1986: 181–7). Whether or not this, and other new structures, were really intended to mark symbolically the closing down of the political life of Athens, the effect was that it became necessary to create a new centre for Athenian commerce. Competitive benefactions had been tending to clutter up the *agora* for some time, and a new market area had developed to the east of it; this was put on a regular basis and permanent buildings were established, using funds supplied by Augustus (Hoff 1989: 1–7); today it is usually referred to as the Roman Agora. The *agora* continued to be a meeting place for philosophers and students, as well as for other less intellectual pursuits: one of the characters in Apuleius' novel reports that he saw a sword-swallower performing there (*Metamorphoses* 1, 4). It is, of course, the place where Paul preached and encountered the philosophers (Acts 17, 17–18). All the great philosophical schools which still survived in Paul's day (Stoics, Epicureans, Platonists and Peripatetics) had started up in Athens, and the city had become something like the ancient equiva- lent of a university town, where young men came to spend some time to finish their education (Wallace and Williams 1993: 85–90). It was therefore an appropriate setting for Paul's encounter with Greek philosophers.

Though Athens had retained her status as 'free city' after Sulla captured the city, he reformed its constitution to bring it into line with Rome's preference for upper-class rule, except that the place of the archons (see p. 112) was taken by the venerable Areopagus

Figure 12.2 The *agora* at Athens: a view from near the Areopagus

Council, a very unusual arrangement (Wallace and Williams 1993: 92). Whether it was to this Council that Paul was taken to explain himself (Acts 17, 19), or to the hill of the same name, which is a little distance from the *agora* and not a convenient place for a meeting, is a matter of some controversy. If, as some believe, the Areopagus Council met in the *agora* at this period, then a hearing before the Council would seem to be the most natural interpretation of the events (for a full discussion, see Wallace and Williams 1993: 91–4). In the second century AD, Athens received extravagant benefactions from the philhellenic emperor Hadrian. It was he who finally completed the temple of Olympian Zeus, whose precinct became the headquarters of the Panhellenion, an association of Greek cities founded by Hadrian; it contained a forest of statues of the emperor, one of which was dedicated by each member city. Before becoming emperor, Hadrian had held the office of archon at Athens, and acted as lawgiver afterwards; as emperor he visited the city frequently.

CORINTH

The importance of Corinth was guaranteed by two geographical factors. First, its position on a narrow isthmus not only allowed it to control land traffic between the Peloponnese and the rest of Greece, but also made possible a lucrative business in transporting goods by land across the isthmus from sea to sea, a distance so short that in antiquity serious consideration was given to cutting a canal through it (Wiseman 1979: 441–4), and the emperor Nero actually began work on such a project, the remains of which were almost completely obliterated when a canal was cut on the same route in 1893. Corinth had two ports on opposite sides of the isthmus, Lechaion and Cenchreae, and a paved way, the *diolkos*, over which cargoes and ships could be dragged across the isthmus (a section of it can still be seen beside the north end of the present canal). Second, it possessed a superb natural fortress, Acrocorinth. The combination of these factors made it of great strategic importance but ultimately led to its ruin. Throughout history, no one wishing to control Greece has been willing to leave Acrocorinth unoccupied. In the hellenistic period it had a Macedonian garrison; in the Middle Ages it was an important Byzantine fortress; after the occupation of Greece by the Fourth Crusade in 1204 it was held first by the Franks and then by the Venetians; it remained a Turkish stronghold until the nineteenth century (and the fortifications and buildings visible there now are a muddle from all those periods). It was, therefore, almost inevitable that the Romans, exasperated by what they saw as the Greeks' abuse of their freedom – freedom which the general Titus Quinctius Flamininus had announced with a flourish at the Isthmian sanctuary in 196 BC, though he took the precaution of keeping a Roman garrison in Acrocorinth for another two years – and looking for a city of which to make an example which the Greeks would never forget after the defeat of the Achaean League (of which Corinth was a leading member), should choose Corinth. In 146 BC the army of Lucius Mummius entered the unde-fended city; all the men were killed, the women and children were enslaved, and the entire city (with the exception of the ancient temple of Apollo, of which seven columns are still standing) was utterly destroyed (Wiseman 1979: 450–62). Though the evidence of recent excavations suggests that the destruction was not as complete as the literary sources seem to say, and certainly people continued to live there (Wiseman 1979: 491–6), Corinth as a city simply ceased to exist until a Roman colony, *Colonia Laus Iulia Corinthus*, was established on the site by Julius Caesar in 46 BC.

The land around Corinth was, and still is, extremely fertile. This, combined with its commercial importance, had made pre-Roman Corinth extremely wealthy (Salmon 1984: 23) and so proverbial for luxurious living. It is also possible that the famous temple of Aphrodite was served by sacred prostitutes (Salmon 1984: 398–9), a practice common in the worship of Aphrodite's Phoenician counter-part Astarte but unusual (though not unknown) elsewhere in Greece (Burkert 1985: 153). The city had, therefore, something of a repu-tation for dubious morality. There is, however, no continuity between this Corinth and the Roman Corinth which Paul knew, and attempts to make links between the alleged immorality of Corinth and the turbulent Christian community there revealed to us through Paul's two letters to the Corinthians are completely without foundation. The Corinth Paul knew was neither more nor less immoral than any other large city of the time. The first colonists included not only discharged soldiers, but also freed slaves and other members of the lower classes of Rome, many of whom might have been of Greek or eastern origin themselves (Wiseman 1979: 497). Its prosperity will also have attracted other non-Roman settlers, including perhaps the substantial Jewish community Paul found there. The central area of Corinth has been extensively excavated, and reveals a city generously equipped with splendid public buildings. It is perhaps the place where we can get closest to the events described in the Acts of the Apostles. Within the forum, near the centre of one of its long sides, is a large rectangular platform, probably erected about AD 44 (Fig. 12.3). This is certainly the platform, officially called the *tribunal*, where the governor would take his seat when giving justice, and on which Gallio sat when Paul was brought before him (Acts 18, 12). Corinth remained, despite various vicissitudes, an important town right down to the twelfth century, when it succumbed to the constant warfare in the area.

CENCHREAE

Of the two ports of Corinth, Cenchreae was the one to the south on the Saronic Gulf, and the natural place for Paul to take ship to Ephesos (Acts 18, 18). Though the site had been occupied since at least the early fifth century BC, the harbour installations and warehouses so far discovered are mostly of the first century AD, when a major redevelopment took place (and was perhaps going on while Paul passed through). The level of the land has fallen since antiquity, with the result that many of the ancient harbour buildings can now be seen under water.

Figure 12.3 The *tribunal* in the forum of Corinth

13

ROME AND THE WEST

MALTA

The island on which Paul was shipwrecked is identified in Acts 28, 1 as *Melitē* (*Melitēnē* in some manuscripts), and is almost certainly Malta. Attempts to identify it with other islands having similar names are unconvincing and unnecessary. Malta came under Roman control in 218 BC, in the course of Rome's conflict with Carthage, and it was administered as part of the province of Sicily, with local affairs being dealt with by an imperial procurator. Before Roman rule it had, from the sixth century BC, been under the control first of the Phoenicians and then of Carthage, and the culture of the island seems to have remained essentially Punic. If the inhabitants (as seems likely) spoke a dialect of Phoenician, it would explain why they are described as *barbaroi* (= 'barbarians', though the RSV translates more correctly 'natives': Acts 28, 2), a word which means simply that they spoke neither Latin nor Greek. (The inhabitants of Malta today speak a Semitic language, but it is one most closely related to Arabic, and probably has more to do with the long Arab occupation of the island in the Middle Ages than with the earlier Phoenician culture of Malta.) The Romans have left few traces, apart from a couple of inscriptions and the remains of a substantial house near the town of Mdina (at present in the basement of the local museum).

SYRACUSE

Once the largest and most powerful Greek city in the West, Syracuse was captured by the Romans in 211 BC during the second war against Carthage, after a long siege during which the great

218

mathematician and engineer Archimedes is said to have organised the city's defences (he was killed in the sack of the city). Syracuse paid a tax known as a *decumana*, originally a tithe of the grain crop, but by the Augustan period it had been converted to a cash payment. Under Augustus it received a Roman colony. Though it retained a measure of prosperity and importance (in part at least because of its excellent harbour, in which the Alexandrian ship in which Paul completes his journey to Rome makes its first call: Acts 28, 12), it never really recovered its earlier position. Though there are a good number of spectacular monuments of the classical and hellenistic period still to be seen there, little survives of Roman Syracuse. The theatre (on the side of a hill overlooking the city, and one of the largest known) was substantially modified in the Roman period, and near it is a large and elaborate Roman amphitheatre and, not far away, the foundations of an arch, both probably of the first century AD. Elsewhere on the outskirts of the city there is a complex of buildings including a temple and a small theatre, probably of the second century AD.

RHEGIUM

This ancient Greek city at the southernmost tip of Italy was an ally of Rome from the earliest period of Rome's involvement in the south of the peninsula, and remained loyal throughout. When many of Rome's allies in Italy went to war with Rome in 91–89 BC, Rhegium was one of the loyal communities granted full Roman citizenship, so that it became a *municipium* and in 33 BC was allowed to add the epithet Iulium to its name. It lies at one end of the Straits of Messina, between Italy and Sicily, which were regarded as notoriously treacherous waters in antiquity, so it is a natural place for a ship bound from Syracuse to Puteoli to wait until the weather conditions were right for the passage (Acts 28, 13). In fact the waters of the straits are not particularly hazardous, and the large number of shipwrecks there (evidence of which can be seen in the archaeological museums of Reggio di Calabria and Palermo) is attributable rather to the heavy traffic in antiquity. Rhegium is in a region prone to severe earthquakes, which have devastated the city on many occasions (most recently in 1908), with the result that few structures of any age survive there.

PUTEOLI

Until adequate port facilities close to Rome were built at Ostia at the mouth of the Tiber under Claudius and Nero, Puteoli (modern Pozzuoli) at the north end of the Bay of Naples was the principal port for Rome, and the place at which the Alexandrian grain fleet would put in (Acts 28, 13). Indeed, Seneca (roughly contemporary with Paul) describes how 'the whole population of Puteoli stood on the piers' to catch sight of the first Alexandrian ships of the season arriving (*Moral Epistles* 77, 1). It was originally a Greek foundation, settled in the sixth century BC, but its strategic importance became obvious during Rome's wars with Carthage, and it became a Roman colony in 194 BC. By Paul's day it was a large, cosmopolitan commercial town, and it is no surprise at all, in view of the frequent traffic from the east of the Empire, that Paul found Christians there already when he arrived (Acts 28, 14).

The area round Puteoli was heavily settled by the Roman period, and many very grand Roman families had villas there, to which they could retire during the summer months when Rome was intolerable, and the pleasant climate of the Bay of Naples very attractive. The whole region is littered with remains from the Roman period, in various states of preservation. In Puteoli itself, some traces of the ancient harbour can be seen under water (the level of the land has sunk since antiquity). Perhaps the most striking monument in the town is a complex of buildings of the first century AD, often referred to as the Serapeum, but actually a market. Columns in this complex bear the traces of being eaten away by shellfish, showing that since Roman times it has been submerged in the sea and then raised up again. Indeed, volcanic activity in this area makes the whole of the town very unstable, a factor perhaps contributing to the decline of the port in the Middle Ages. Later a legend grew up that while Paul was at Puteoli he went to Naples to visit the tomb of the Roman poet Virgil, whose fourth Eclogue, celebrating the birth of a child who was to bring in a new Golden Age, was regarded as a prophecy of the coming of Christ. The event was commemorated in verses sung as late as the fifteenth century in the Mass of St Paul at Mantua (Virgil's home town): 'Brought to Virgil's tomb he shed pious tears over it; "Greatest of poets", he said, "What might I have made of you if I had found you alive"' (Comparetti 1966: 98). Today, a Roman tomb in a park in the Mergellina district of Naples is shown as Virgil's tomb (though there is no reason to connect it with him).

ROME

The author of Acts is remarkably uninformative about Paul's stay in Rome. We are not told where he stayed, under what conditions (except that it was in lodgings paid for by himself, with a soldier as guard – Acts 28, 16) or, crucially, how the stay ended. The city Paul knew would have contained very few of the monumental structures whose remains we can see today. It must be admitted that the site of Rome is not a particularly attractive one. The climate was unhealthy and damp because of the marshy ground, and in summer was (and is) intolerable, so that throughout history wealthy Romans have escaped to villas in the hills or to resorts like those round the Bay of Naples. Compared to the great cities of the East, Rome must have seemed very modest. Though Augustus had boasted: 'I found Rome a city of brick, and left it a city of marble' (Suetonius, *Augustus* 28), and had undertaken a building programme which extended the built-up area into the Campus Martius, the really spectacular buildings which we associate with ancient Rome today were constructed by later emperors. Most of the city will have been occupied by sprawling, uncontrolled development caused by the burgeoning population of the city, who were largely housed in badly planned and shoddily built blocks of flats. Fires were frequent, and a constant preoccupation of emperors. The great fire of AD 64, in the reign of Nero, was only the most severe of many. Nero responded with very sensible building regulations designed to minimise danger from fire in the future; even so, some complained that the old city had been more healthy, because the high buildings and narrow streets gave protection from the sun (Tacitus, *Annals* 15, 43).

Rome held a very large non-Italian population, some of them freed slaves, and some immigrants, so Paul would have found no problems in finding a Greek-speaking community within which to live (see p. 66). There was a large Jewish community (Acts 28, 17–24), and Christianity had got there before him (Acts 28, 15). If we had to make a guess, it is at least possible that he stayed in the region on the other side of the Tiber to the main city, now known as Trastevere, which appears to have been a place where immigrants tended to gather. According to Eusebius (*Ecclesiastical History* 2, 25)

Paul was put to death by beheading in Rome, at the same time that Peter was crucified there (as a Roman citizen Paul, unlike Peter, would have escaped the more humiliating form of execution); Eusebius quotes as his authority for this one Caius, who lived when Zephyrinus was bishop of Rome, in the reign of Septimius Severus at the beginning of the third century. The traditional place of his martyrdom, at Tre Fontane on the Via Ostiensis, was marked in the reign of Constantine by a small shrine, which was replaced in 384 by the great basilica of S. Paolo fuori le mura; the church on the site today is a reconstruction of the old basilica, built following the destruction of the original building by fire in 1823.

BIBLIOGRAPHY

Alcock, S. E. (1993) *Graecia Capta: The Landscapes of Roman Greece*, Cambridge: Cambridge University Press.

André, J.-M. and Baslez, M.-F. (1993) *Voyager dans l'Antiquité*, Paris: Fayard.

Applebaum, S. (1979) *Jews and Greeks in Ancient Cyrene*, Leiden: E. J. Brill.

Bammer, A. (1988) *Ephesos, Stadt an Fluss und Meer*, Graz: Akademische Druck- und Verlaganstalt.

Barnes, T. D. (1971) *Tertullian. A Historical and Literary Study*, Oxford: Clarendon Press.

Bean, G. E. (1979a) *Turkey's Southern Shore*, London: John Murray.

——(1979b) *Aegean Turkey*, London: John Murray.

——(1989) *Lycian Turkey*, London: John Murray.

Bickerman, E. (1976) *Studies in Jewish and Christian History* (3 vols), Leiden: E. J. Brill.

——(1979) *The God of the Maccabees: Studies in the Meaning and Origin of the Maccabaean Revolt*, trans. H. R. Moering, Leiden: E. J. Brill.

——(1988) *The Jews in the Greek Age*, Cambridge, MA and London: Harvard University Press.

Billerbeck, M. (1991) 'Greek Cynicism in imperial Rome', in M. Billerbeck (ed.) *Die Kyniker in der moderne Forschung*, Amsterdam: B. R. Grüner.

Blass, F. and Debrunner, A. (1961) *A Greek Grammar of the New Testament*, trans. R. W. Funk, Cambridge: Cambridge University Press.

Boardman, J. (1994) *The Diffusion of Classical Art in Antiquity*, London: Thames and Hudson.

Boatwright, M. T. (1993) 'The city gate of Plancia Magna in Perge', in E. D'Ambra (ed.) *Roman Art in Context: An Anthology*, Englewood Cliffs, NJ: Prentice Hall.

Boswell, J. (1988) *The Kindness of Strangers: The Abandonment of Children in Western Europe from Late Antiquity*, London: Allen Lane.

Bowersock, G. W. (1983) *Roman Arabia*, Cambridge, MA: Harvard University Press.

Bowie, E. L. (1974) 'Greeks and their past in the Second Sophistic', in M. I. Finley (ed.) *Studies in Ancient Society*, London: Routledge and Kegan Paul.

Braudel, F. (1972) *The Mediterranean and the Mediterranean World in the Age of Philip II*, trans. S. Reynolds, London: Collins.

Braund, D. C. (1984) *Rome and the Friendly King*, London: Croom Helm.

Browning, R. (1969) *Medieval and Modern Greek*, London: Hutchinson.

Burkert, W. (1985) *Greek Religion*, trans. J. Raffan, Oxford: Basil Blackwell.

Burstein, S. M. (1985) *Translated Documents of Greece and Rome, 3: The Hellenistic Age From the Battle of Ipsos to the Death of Kleopatra VII*, Cambridge: Cambridge University Press.

Camp, J. M. (1986) *The Athenian Agora: Excavations in the Heart of Classical Athens*, London: Thames and Hudson.

Cartledge, P. A. and Spawforth, A. J. S. (1989) *Hellenistic and Roman Sparta*, London: Routledge.

Casson, L. (1974) *Travel in the Ancient World*, London: George Allen & Unwin.

——(1986) *Ships and Seamanship in the Ancient World*, Princeton: Princeton University Press.

——(1991) *The Ancient Mariners*, Princeton: Princeton University Press.

Chevallier, R. (1988) *Voyage et Déplacement dans l'Empire Romain*, Paris: Armand Colin.

Clay, D. (1990) 'The philosophical inscription of Diogenes of Oenoanda: new discoveries 1969–83', in W. Haase (ed.) *Aufstieg und Niedergang der Römischen Welt* 2, 36, 4, Berlin and New York: Walter de Gruyter.

Colish, M. L. (1992) 'Stoicism and the New Testament: an essay in historiography' in W. Haase (ed.) *Aufstieg und Niedergang der Römischen Welt* 2, 26, 1, Berlin and New York: Walter de Gruyter.

Comparetti, D. (1966) *Vergil in the Middle Ages*, trans. E. F. M. Beneke, London: George Allen & Unwin.

Crook, J. A. (1967) *Law and Life of Rome*, London: Thames and Hudson.

Delcor, M. (1989) 'Jewish literature in Hebrew and Aramaic in the Greek era', in W. D. Davies and L. Finkelstein (eds) *The Cambridge History of Judaism* 2, Cambridge: Cambridge University Press.

De Sainte Croix, G. E. M. (1975) 'Early Christian attitudes to property and slavery', in D. Baker (ed.) *Studies in Church History, 12: Church, Society and Politics*, Oxford: Basil Blackwell.

——(1981) *The Class Struggle in the Ancient Greek World*, London: Duckworth.

Dillon, J. (1977) *The Middle Platonists*, London: Duckworth.

Dodds, E. R. (1965) *Pagan and Christian in an Age of Anxiety*, Cambridge: Cambridge University Press.

Downey, G. (1961) *A History of Antioch in Syria*, Oxford: Clarendon Press.

Downing, F. G. (1993) 'Cynics and early Christianity', in M.-O. Goulet-Cazé and R. Goulet (eds) *Le Cynisme Ancien et ses Prolongements*, Paris: Presses Universitaires de France.

Dudley, D. R. (1937) *A History of Cynicism*, London: Methuen.

Easterling, P. E. (1985) 'Books and readers in the Greek world: the Hellenistic and Imperial periods', in P. E. Easterling and B. M. W. Knox (eds) *The Cambridge History of Classical Literature*, 1: *Greek Literature*, Cambridge: Cambridge University Press.

Eddy, S. K. (1961) *The King is Dead: Studies in Near Eastern Resistance to Hellenism*, Lincoln, NB: Nebraska University Press.

Eissfeldt, O. (1965) *The Old Testament. An Introduction*, trans. P. R. Ackroyd, Oxford: Basil Blackwell.

Farrington, A. (1987) 'Imperial bath buildings in south-west Asia Minor', in S. Macready and F. H. Thompson (eds) *Roman Architecture in the Greek World*, London: Society of Antiquaries.

Ferguson, J. (1990) 'Epicureanism under the Roman Empire', in W. Haase (ed.) *Aufstieg und Niedergang der Römischen Welt* 2, 36, 4, Berlin and New York: Walter de Gruyter.

Finley, M. I. (1973) *The Ancient Economy*, London: Chatto and Windus.

Fleischer, R. (1973) *Artemis von Ephesos und verwandte Kultstatuen aus Anatolien und Syrien*, Leiden: E. J. Brill.

Fraade, S. D. (1992) 'Rabbinic views on the practice of Targum, and multilingualism in the Jewish Galilee in the third–sixth centuries', in L. I. Levine (ed.) *The Galilee in Late Antiquity*, Cambridge, MA and London: Harvard University Press.

Fraser, P. M. (1972) *Ptolemaic Alexandria* (3 vols), Oxford: Clarendon Press.

Gardner, J. F. (1993) *Being a Roman Citizen*, London: Routledge.

Garnsey, P. (1966) 'The *Lex Iulia* and appeal under the empire', *Journal of Roman Studies* 56: 167–89.

——(1970) *Social Status and Legal Privilege in the Roman Empire*, Oxford: Clarendon Press.

——(1988) *Famine and Food Supply in the Graeco-Roman World*, Cambridge: Cambridge University Press.

Gawlikowski, M. (1990) 'Les dieux des Nabatéens', in W. Haase (ed.) *Aufstieg und Niedergang der Römischen Welt* 2, 18, 4, Berlin and New York: Walter de Gruyter.

Geagan, D. J. (1979) 'Roman Athens I', in H. Temporini (ed.) *Aufstieg und Niedergang der Römischen Welt* 2, 7, 1, Berlin and New York: Walter de Gruyter.

Ginsberg, H. L. (1989) 'The Book of Daniel', in W. D. Davies and L. Finkelstein (eds) *The Cambridge History of Judaism* 2, Cambridge: Cambridge University Press.

Goodman, M. (1987) *The Ruling Class of Judaea*, Cambridge: Cambridge University Press.

Goulet-Cazé, M.-O. (1990) 'Le cynisme à l'époque impériale', in W. Haase (ed.) *Aufstieg und Niedergang der Römischen Welt* 2, 36, 4, Berlin and New York: Walter de Gruyter.

Grainger, J. D. (1990) *The Cities of Seleucid Syria*, Oxford: Clarendon Press.

——(1991) *Hellenistic Phoenicia*, Oxford: Clarendon Press.

Green, P. (1990) *From Alexander to Actium*, London: Thames and Hudson.

Hajjar, Y. (1990) 'Baalbek, grand centre religieux sous l'Empire', in W. Haase (ed.) *Aufstieg und Niedergang der Römischen Welt* 2, 18, 4, Berlin and New York: Walter de Gruyter.

Hall, A. S. (1973) 'New light on the capture of Isaura Vetus by P. Servilius Vatia', in M. Wörrle (ed.) *Akten des VI. Internationalen Kongresses für Griechische und Lateinische Epigraphik München 1972*, Munich: Beck.

Hands, A. R. (1968) *Charities and Social Aid in Greece and Rome*, London: Thames and Hudson.

Harris, H. A. (1976) *Greek Athletics and the Jews*, Cardiff: University of Wales Press.

Harris, W. V. (1989) *Ancient Literacy*, Cambridge, MA: Harvard University Press.

Head, B. V. (1911) *Historia Numorum: A Manual of Greek Numismatics*, Oxford: Clarendon Press.

Hengel, M. (1989) 'The political and social history of Palestine from Alexander to Antiochus III (233–187 BCE)', in W. D. Davies and L. Finkelstein (eds) *The Cambridge History of Judaism* 2, Cambridge: Cambridge University Press.

Hoff, M. (1989) 'The early history of the Roman Agora at Athens', in S. Walker and A. Cameron (eds) *The Greek Renaissance in the Roman Empire: Bulletin Supplement 55*, London: Institute of Classical Studies.

Holum, K. G., Hohlfelder, R. L., Bull, R. J. and Raban, A. (1988) *King Herod's Dream: Caesarea on the Sea*, New York and London: W. W. Norton.

Hopkins, K. (1978) *Conquerors and Slaves*, Cambridge: Cambridge University Press.

——(1980) 'Taxes and trade in the Roman Empire (200 BC–AD 400)', *Journal of Roman Studies* 70: 101–25.

Hornblower, S. (1982) *Mausolus*, Oxford: Clarendon Press.

Hornblower, S. and Spawforth, A. (eds) (1996) *The Oxford Classical Dictionary* (third edn), Oxford: Oxford University Press.

Hornsby, H. M. (1991) 'The Cynicism of Peregrinus Proteus', in M. Billerbeck (ed.) *Die Kyniker in der moderne Forschung*, Amsterdam: B. R. Grüner.

Houston, G. W. (1987) 'Lucian's *Navigium* and the dimensions of the *Isis*', *American Journal of Philology* 108, 3: 444–50.

Hunt, A. S. and Edgar, C. C. (1932–4) *Select Papyri*, London: Heinemann.

Isaac, B. (1992) *The Limits of Empire*, Oxford: Clarendon Press.

Jacobson, H. (1983) *The* Exagoge *of Ezekiel*, Cambridge: Cambridge University Press.

Jones, A. H. M. (1940) *The Greek City from Alexander to Justinian*, Oxford: Clarendon Press.

——(1960) *Studies in Roman Government and Law*, Oxford: Basil Blackwell.

——(1973) *The Criminal Courts of the Roman Republic and Principate*, Oxford: Basil Blackwell.

——(1974) *The Ancient Economy*, Oxford: Basil Blackwell.

Jones, C. P. (1978) *The Roman World of Dio Chrysostom*, Cambridge, MA and London: Harvard University Press.

Kashtan, N. (1988) 'Akko-Ptolemais: a maritime metropolis in hellenistic and early Roman times, 332 BCE–70 CE, as seen through the literary sources', *Mediterranean Historical Review* 3, 1: 37–53.

Kearsley, R. (1986) 'The Archiereiai of Asia and the relationship of the Asiarch and the Archiereus of Asia', *Greek, Roman and Byzantine Studies* 27: 183–92.

——(1994) 'The Asiarchs', in D. W. G. Gill and C. Gempf (eds) *The Book of Acts in its First-Century Setting*, 2: *The Graeco-Roman Setting*, Carlisle: The Paternoster Press.

Kraemer, R. S. (1992) *Her Share of the Blessings*, Oxford: Oxford University Press.

Lane-Fox, R. (1986) *Pagans and Christians*, Harmondsworth: Viking.

Lassus, J. (1977) 'La ville d'Antioche à l'époque romaine d'après l'archéologie', in H. Temporini and W. Haase (eds) *Aufstieg und Niedergang der Römischen Welt* 2, 8, Berlin and New York: Walter de Gruyter.

Lentz, J. C. (1993) *Luke's Portrait of Paul*, Cambridge: Cambridge University Press.

Levick, B. (1967) *Roman Colonies in Southern Asia Minor*, Oxford: Clarendon Press.

Levine, L. I. (1975) *Caesarea under Roman Rule*, Leiden: E. J. Brill.

Lewis, N. (1983) *Life in Egypt under Roman Rule*, Oxford: Oxford University Press.

——(1986) *Greeks in Ptolemaic Egypt*, Oxford: Oxford University Press.

LiDonnici, L. R. (1992) 'The images of Artemis Ephesia and Greco-Roman worship: a reconsideration', *Harvard Theological Review* 85, 4: 389–415.

Liebescheutz, J. H. W. G. (1972) *Antioch: City and Imperial Administration in the Later Roman Empire*, Oxford: Clarendon Press.

Lieu, J., North, J. and Rajak, T. (eds) (1992) *The Jews among Pagans and Christians in the Roman Empire*, London: Routledge.

Lifshitz, B. (1977a) 'Jérusalem sous la domination romaine', in H. Temporini and W. Haase (eds) *Aufstieg und Niedergang der Römischen Welt* 2, 8, Berlin and New York: Walter de Gruyter.

——(1977b) 'Césarée de Palestine, son histoire et ses institutions', in H. Temporini and W. Haase (eds) *Aufstieg und Niedergang der Römischen Welt* 2, 8, Berlin and New York: Walter de Gruyter.

Long, A. A. (1974) *Hellenistic Philosophy*, London: Duckworth.

MacKay, T. S. (1990) 'The major sanctuaries of Pamphylia and Cilicia', in W. Haase (ed.) *Aufstieg und Niedergang der Römischen Welt* 2, 18, 3, Berlin and New York: Walter de Gruyter.

McKenzie, J. (1990) *The Architecture of Petra*, Oxford: Oxford University Press.

MacMullen, R. (1981) *Paganism in the Roman Empire*, New Haven and London: Yale University Press.

——(1982) *Enemies of the Roman Order*, London and New York: Routledge.

——(1986) 'What difference did Christianity make?', *Historia* 35, 3: 322–43.

McPherson, J. M. (1990) *Battle Cry of Freedom*, London: Penguin.

Malherbe, A. J. (1992) 'Hellenistic moralists and the New Testament', in W. Haase (ed.) *Aufstieg und Niedergang der Römischen Welt* 2, 26, 1, Berlin and New York: Walter de Gruyter.

Marrou, H. I. (1956) *A History of Education in Antiquity*, trans. G. Lamb, London: Sheed and Ward.

Meeks, W. A. (1983) *The First Urban Christians*, New Haven and London: Yale University Press.

Millar, F. G. B. (1981) 'The world of the *Golden Ass*', *Journal of Roman Studies* 72: 63–75.

——(1992) *The Emperor in the Roman World*, London: Duckworth.

——(1993) *The Roman Near East 31 BC–AD 337*, Cambridge, MA and London: Harvard University Press.

Mitchell, S. (1993) *Anatolia: Land, Men, and Gods in Asia Minor* (2 vols), Oxford: Clarendon Press.

Mitford, T. B. (1980) 'Roman Cyprus', in H. Temporini (ed.) *Aufstieg und Niedergang der Römischen Welt* 2, 7, 2, Berlin and New York: Walter de Gruyter.

Nock, A. D. (1972) *Essays on Religion and the Ancient World* (2 vols), Oxford: Clarendon Press.

Orlinsky, H. M. (1989) 'The Septuagint and its Hebrew text', in W. D. Davies and L. Finkelstein (eds) *The Cambridge History of Judaism*, 1: *The Hellenistic Age*, Cambridge: Cambridge University Press.

Osborne, R. (1987) *Classical Landscape with Figures*, London: George Philip.

Oster, R. E. (1990) 'Ephesus as a religious centre under the principate: I. Paganism before Constantine', in W. Haase (ed.) *Aufstieg und Niedergang der Römischen Welt* 2, 18, 3, Berlin and New York: Walter de Gruyter.

Pomeroy, S. B. (1975) *Goddesses, Whores, Wives, and Slaves*, New York: Shocken Books.

Price, S. R. F. (1984) *Rituals and Power: The Roman Imperial Cult in Asia Minor*, Cambridge: Cambridge University Press.

Raban, A. (1992) 'Sebastos: the royal harbour at Caesarea Maritima – a short-lived giant', *The International Journal of Nautical Archaeology* 21, 2: 111–24.

Rajak, T. (1983) *Josephus, the Historian and his Society*, London: Duckworth.

Rajak, T. and Noy, D. (1993) 'Archisynagogoi: office, title, and social status in the Greco-Roman synagogue', *Journal of Roman Studies* 83: 75–93.

Rawson, E. (1976) 'The Ciceronian aristocracy and its properties', in M. I. Finley (ed.) *Studies in Roman Property*, Cambridge: Cambridge University Press.

Reinhardt, W. (1995) 'The population size of Jerusalem and the numerical growth of the Jerusalem church', in R. Baukham (ed.) *The Book of Acts in its First-Century Setting*, 4: *The Palestinian Setting*, Carlisle: The Paternoster Press.

Reynolds, J. (1982) *Aphrodisias and Rome*, London: Society for the Promotion of Roman Studies.

Reynolds, J. and Tannenbaum, R. (1987) 'Jews and godfearers at Aphrodisias', *Proceedings of the Cambridge Philological Society*, supplementary volume 12.

Rickman, G. (1980) *The Corn Supply of Ancient Rome*, Oxford: Clarendon Press.

Robert, L. (1937) *Études Anatoliennes*, Paris: Boccard.

——(1971) *Les Gladiateurs dans l'Orient Grec*, Amsterdam: Adolf M. Hakkert.

——(1977) 'Documents d'Asie Mineure', *Bulletin de Correspondance Hellénique* 101: 43–132.

——(1981) 'Le serpent Glycon d'Abônouteichos à Athènes et Artémis d'Ephèse à Rome', *Comptes rendus de l'Académie des Inscriptions et Belles-Lettres*: 513–35.

Rogers, G. M. (1991) *The Sacred Identity of Ephesus*, London and New York: Routledge.

Rougé, J. (1960) 'Actes 27, 1–10', *Vigiliae Christianae* 14: 193–203.

——(1966) *Recherches sur l'Organisation du Commerce Maritime en Méditerranée sous l'Empire Romain*, Paris: S.E.V.P.E.N.

Russell, D. A. and Wilson, N. G. (eds and trans.) (1981) *Menander Rhetor*, Oxford: Clarendon Press.

Sáenz-Badillos, A. (1993) *A History of the Hebrew Language*, trans. J. Elwolde, Cambridge: Cambridge University Press.

Saller, R. P. (1982) *Personal Patronage under the Early Empire*, Cambridge: Cambridge University Press.

Salmon, J. B. (1984) *Wealthy Corinth: A History of the City to 338 BC*, Oxford: Oxford University Press.

Schürer, E. (1973–87) *The History of the Jewish People in the Age of Jesus Christ* (3 vols), revised and edited by G. Vermes and F. G. B. Millar, Edinburgh: T. & T. Clark.

Schwartz, S. (1995) 'Language, power and identity in ancient Palestine', *Past and Present* 148: 3–47.

Sedley, D. (1989) 'Philosophical allegiance in the Greco-Roman world', in M. T. Griffin and J. Barnes (eds) *Philosophia Togata*, Oxford: Clarendon Press.

Sharples, R. W. (1996) *Stoics, Epicureans and Sceptics*, London: Routledge.

Shaw, B. D. (1984) 'Bandits in the Roman Empire', *Past and Present* 105: 3–52.

Sherwin-White, A. N. (1963) *Roman Society and Roman Law in the New Testament*, Oxford: Clarendon Press.

——(1967) *Racial Prejudice in Imperial Rome*, Cambridge: Cambridge University Press.

——(1973) 'The *tabula* of Banasa and the *Constitutio Antoniniana*', *Journal of Roman Studies* 63: 86–98.

——(1984) *Roman Foreign Policy in the East*, London: Duckworth.

Sherwin-White, S. M. (1978) *Ancient Cos*, Göttingen: Vandenhoek & Ruprecht.

Smallwood, E. M. (1967) *Documents Illustrating the Principates of Gaius, Claudius, and Nero*, Cambridge: Cambridge University Press.

Smith, M. J. (1993) *Diogenes of Oenoanda: The Epicurean Inscription*, Naples: Bibliopolis.

Smith, R. R. R. (1991) *Hellenistic Sculpture*, London: Thames and Hudson.

Spivey, N. (1996) *Understanding Greek Sculpture: Ancient Meanings, Modern Readings*, London: Thames and Hudson.

Starr, R. J. (1987) 'The circulation of literary texts in the Roman world', *Classical Quarterly* 37, 1: 213–23.

Stern, M. (1974) *Greek and Latin Authors on Jews and Judaism* (3 vols), Jerusalem: Israel Academy of Sciences and Humanities.

Stoneman, R. (1987) *Land of Lost Gods: The Search for Classical Greece*, London: Hutchinson.

Swain, S. (1991) 'Arrian the epic poet', *Journal of Hellenic Studies* 111: 211–14.

——(1996) *Hellenism and Empire*, Oxford: Clarendon Press.

Tataki, A. B. (1988) *Ancient Beroea: Prosopography and Society*, Paris: Boccard.

Taylor, J. (1992) 'The ethnarch of King Aretas at Damascus', *Revue Biblique* 99: 719–28.

Tcherikover, V., Fuks, A. and Stern, M. (1957–64) *Corpus Papyrorum Judaicorum* (3 vols), Cambridge, MA and Jerusalem: Harvard University Press.

Thompson, D. J. (1988) *Memphis under the Ptolemies*, Princeton: Princeton University Press.

Trebilco, P. (1991) *Jewish Communities in Asia Minor*, Cambridge: Cambridge University Press.

Veyne, P. (1990) *Bread and Circuses*, trans. B. Pearce, London: Allen Lane.

Wallace, R. and Williams, W. (1993) *The Acts of the Apostles: A Companion*, London: Bristol Classical Press.

Ward-Perkins, J. B. (1981) *Roman Imperial Architecture*, Harmondsworth: Penguin.

Williams, W. (1975) 'Formal and historical aspects of two new documents of Marcus Aurelius', *Zeitschrift für Papyrologie und Epigraphik* 17, 1: 56–78.

——(1990) *Pliny the Younger: Correspondence with Trajan from Bithynia (Epistles X)*, Warminster: Aris and Phillips.

Wilson, S. G. (1983) *Luke and the Law*, Cambridge: Cambridge University Press.

Wiseman, J. (1979) 'Corinth and Rome I: 228 BC–AD 267', in H. Temporini (ed.) *Aufstieg und Niedergang der Römischen Welt* 2, 7, 1, Berlin and New York: Walter de Gruyter.

Wycherley, R. E. (1978) *The Stones of Athens*, Princeton: Princeton University Press.

INDEX

231

tax paid by adult male Jews
101, 108, 118
theatres, Greek 104; Miletos 64,
104, 201–2; uses other than for
classical drama 89, 105–6
Thessalonika 13, 14, 111, 113,
209–10
tourism 17–18, 86
travel: of early Christians,
unremarked 15; frequency of 16;
for health 17; by land slower
and more costly than by water
18–19; on official business 27,
114; by sea 20–5; *see also*
diplomata; requisition
Troas (Alexandria Troas) 199; cult
of Apollo Smintheus at 99
Tyre 11, 173–4

Vespasian, emperor (AD 69–79),

deathbed comment on
deification by 116
Via Egnatia 13, 14, 19, 206,
207, 208
Virgil, poet (70–19 BC): Paul's
alleged visit to tomb of 220–1

wills of client kings of Rome:
Attalos III 79; Herod I 77; king
of Bithynia 79; king of Cyrene
79; Ptolemy VIII when ruler of
Cyrene 75
women: educational opportunities
for 59–60; greater visibility of
in hellenistic age 61–2, 147; *see
also* Plancia Magna

Zeno of Kition (d. 263 BC):
founder of Stoicism 126;
possible Phoenician origin of 57